Santa Monica Pier

A history from 1875 to 1990

by Jeffrey Stanton

Jeffrey Stanton
3710 Pacific Avenue #16
Venice, California 90291
(213) 821-2425

Donahue Publishing
5716 W. Jefferson Blvd.
Los Angeles, Ca. 90016
(213) 938-4545

For those readers who like this book and would like to learn more about Venice and Ocean Park's amusement pier and communities, the author has written the book 'Venice of America - Coney Island of the Pacific'. It has the same page size and album style format as this book. The book is 196 pages, contains 251 historic photographs - forty of them in color, and sells for $15.95. If you have trouble finding the book, please feel free to contact the author.

Acknowledgements

This book completes the history of Santa Monica Bay's three great amusement piers. It is the companion volume to my 'Venice of America - Coney Island of the Pacific' that covers in detail each of Venice and Ocean Park's piers; (251 photos). While the Santa Monica Pier was the smallest and financially the least successful of the three, it is the only survivor of those bygone days of fun and frivolity. In a sense it is the last important link to our past.

Unfortunately amusement piers during the last half century were considered unimportant low class enterprises and consequently were ignored by the historians that followed. The few articles written for the Santa Monica Evening Outlook's various anniversary editions were poorly researched rehashes of earlier articles, each riddled with errors and misnomers. Worse yet, recent Santa Monica histories have used this material as their source without spending the necessary time and effort to verify it.

I'm sure that readers will consider this book revisionist for it tells a history that few but some of the oldtimers are familiar. I spent over eighteen months in the Santa Monica library reading microfilm from 1887 to the present of the Santa Monica Evening Outlook Newspaper. I also searched for clues in Billboard magazine at Long Beach library, in the minutes of the City Council meetings, and in boxes of old documents stored in the city hall vaults.

I would especially like to thank Ernest Marquez for not only reading an early draft of the book for historical accuracy, but for making his extensive photographic library available to me. Ernie constantly reminded me that Santa Monica's pier was a fishing pier, not just an amusement pier. Special thanks to Marc Wanamaker of Bison Archives who made my copy negatives from borrowed photographs and whose large photo archives was an immense help. Thanks goes to John Gilchrist at his staff at the Pier Restoration Corporation and Judith Meister, City Pier Manager for helping thread the bureaucratic city maze, providing me with architectural blueprints of the future pier, and also facts about the pier's operation and budget. Others that deserve recognition are David Pann, pier superintendent and Jack Bayer, city engineer for providing information about the pier's reconstruction; Barbara Williams for photos and information concerning the carousel's restoration; Lynn Hollingsworth for his knowledge about the pier's sports fishing industry; Elisabeth Gros and Mary Henderson for editing portions of the manuscript.

The success of any photographic history book requires finding fresh, exciting quality photographs that have never before been published. These photographs are difficult to find because public archives either have a poor selection of material related to the pier or had photographs that had been published numerous times. Since I knew that the book's photographic quality would be judged against Fred Basten's 'Santa Monica Bay - The First 100 Years' and my own book 'Venice of America - Coney Island of the Pacific', I put considerable pressure on individuals and organizations that claimed they were too busy or were reluctant to cooperate. All known collections were accessed except the extensive Bartlett Collection that was donated to UCLA many years ago. It is unfortunately inaccessible until it is cataloged and that depends on time and funding. I believe I found a representative selection of photographs that illustrate the pier's history. But if any reader has better photographs or more interesting ones in their own collection, feel free to contact me.

Photographic Credits

Ernest Marquez (4, 5, 6 all, 7, 8, 10, 12, 13 all, 14 top, 16, 17, 19 all, 20, 22 all, 23, 26, 27, 28 top, 29, 32 bottom, 34, 35, 36, 37 bottom, 38 top, 39, 41, 43, 51, 55, 69, 75 top, 79 top, 86, 95 left, 97 all, 99, 112, 113, 129, 130 left, 134); Bison Archives (11, 21, 24, 30, 37 top, 38 bottom, 48, 63, 64, 126 top, 137, 139); Emerson Gage courtesy of Bill Beebe (70 bottom, 76, 77, 78, 79 bottom, 82 bottom, 83, 87, 96 bottom, 98, 100, 102, 103 all, 104, 105, 106, 107, 108, 115 all, 117 left, 121, 122, 123, 124, 132); David Pann (70 top, 84 top, 89 left, 90, 126 bottom, 128, 131); Barbara Williams (Front Cover, 33, 80, 133, 146, 150 all, 151 all); USC Special Collections (58, 59, 61, 67, 68, 111, 114); Seaver Center @ Museum of Natural History (110); Evening Outlook Newspaper (62 top, 66, 136, 140 all); Heritage Museum (40, 57, 88, 89 rt, 109, 117 rt, 153, 154); Santa Monica Historical Society (28 left & bottom, 81); Mike Chew (33 top); Fred Basten (54 bottom); Lynn Hollingsworth (62 bottom, 95 top); Ken Strickfaden (47); Pier Restoration Corporation (75 bottom, 120, 125, 144, 155 all); L.A. Library (44); Speed Peterson (145, 147, 148, 149 all); Lynn Cunningham (92 all); Carousel Arts (26 bottom); Elliot Welsh (33 top, 42); Mary Bethel (127); Victor Plukas (14 bottom, 56, 60); Darnell Gadberry (176). All other photos are from the author's collection and all color photos were taken by the author for this book. The four 3-D perspective maps were also drawn by the author.

CONTENTS

CHAPTER 1

Santa Monica's North Beach (1875-1907)

In the decade following the American Civil War (1861-1865), when Los Angeles was little more than a hot, dusty pueblo with a population of less than 6000, those living inland were beckoned by the cool Pacific Ocean breezes along Santa Monica Bay. They came mostly by horse drawn wagons, some by stage. It was a journey across fourteen miles of parched ranch land on roads that were nothing more than rutted wagon tracks, a trip that took the better part of a day. Whole families, and some young couples sought a glimpse of the sea and a reprieve from the stifling heat that plagued the Los Angeles Basin each summer and fall. Their destination was the flat creek bed of Santa Monica Canyon where it met the Pacific, or the area further south beneath the towering bluffs that faced Santa Monica Bay.

These tourists were welcomed by Francisco Marquez and Ysidro Reyes, who in 1839, a decade before California became a state, were granted title to Rancho Boca de Santa Monica by the Mexican governor. Their property extended north to Topanga Canyon, south to what is now Montana Avenue and from the ocean to a line paralleling 26th street in Santa Monica.

Canvas tents were pitched, often for weeks at a time, amidst clusters of sycamore trees and bushes alongside the canyon's stream bed, or on the wide flat sandy beach at the canyon's outlet. The visitors enjoyed the sun and surf, lit bonfires at night and held Saturday night dances.

As the popularity of the area grew, various entrepreneurs began catering to the tourists' needs. First there was a general store, but then in 1870 a saloon opened, and a year later a small inn on the property flourished. While the ranchero families at first received little compensation from the tourist trade, Pascaul Marquez, Francisco's son eventually built the canyon's first bath house in the late 1870's.

One of the visitors to the Santa Monica area in 1872 was a wealthy San Francisco merchant named Colonel Robert S. Baker. He made his fortune in the sheep ranching business in Kern County's Tehachapi Mountains and had come south to investigate Southern California's booming wool industry. He arrived by steamer at the Shoo Fly Landing, a small pier several hundred yards south of the present pier, near what is now the foot of Pico Blvd. The pier was used for loading shipments of "asphaltum" that was brought overland by wagon from

The 1740 foot long Los Angeles & Independence Railroad Wharf near the present site of the Santa Monica Pier was built in 1875 to facilitate the unloading of passengers and cargo from steamers plying Pacific trade routes. Passengers and cargo destined for inland Los Angeles were transferred directly to trains for the ten mile trip. (above & opposite page).

View of North Beach at low tide in 1885 shows the beach facilities at the Santa Monica Bathhouse.

In 1886, a 99 step staircase was built along the bluffs to connect the Santa Monica Hotel with the beach facilities below.

Henry Hancock's Rancho La Brea tar pits. The tar was bound for San Francisco and its roofing and ship building trades.

Col. Baker found the nearby grassy mesa of the San Vincente Ranchero perfect for sheep raising. The 30,000 acre tract had been granted to Francisco Sepulveda by the Mexican governor in 1828. It was a large ranch that extended south from Marquez and Reyes property to the La Ballona Rancho marked by the stream bed at Pico Blvd, from the ocean east to Westwood Village, and into the mountains. Like most ranches at the time, it was virtually unused since the drought of 1862-1864 killed off most of the cattle.

Baker's business partner, General E. F. Beale arrived at the end of 1873. He had been an army surveyor who helped map out the 35th parallel route that pioneers bound for Los Angeles followed across the Mojave desert. He and Baker developed a scheme for a full blown port near the Shoo Fly Landing. In 1874 they bought the Sepulveda heir's entire San Vincente Ranchero for $55,000, and a one-half undivided interest in Boca de Santa Monica's 6,500 acre Ranchero from Maria Antonia Villa Reyes, Ysidro's widow.

Baker and Beale acquired a franchise for a fourteen mile narrow-gauge railroad designed to link their port with Los Angeles. They then tried but failed to convince Los Angeles merchants and officials to back the venture. They did manage to secure some financial backing from New York interests and christened their dream the "Los Angeles and Truxton Railroad."

Los Angeles, however, attempted to entice Southern Pacific to build a line into their city with an offer of $602,000. They even offered a twenty-one mile railroad to San Pedro harbor as an inducement. But soon they began to have second thoughts. They were afraid that once Southern Pacific established a railhead on the Tehachapi Pass, the lucrative Inyo County mining trade would be diverted away from Los Angeles to the San Joaquin Valley and hence to San Francisco.

In 1874 former California governor John C. Downey and the Workman Bank in Los Angeles decided to form their own railroad. The Los Angeles and Independence Railroad would keep the silver ore flowing over Cajon Pass and into Los Angeles. The new railroad wasn't a threat to Southern Pacific interests because they controlled the rail link from Los Angeles to the port at San Pedro.

Senator John P. Jones was looking for a way to stop high freight rates from cutting into the profits of his

Panamint City mines in Inyo. When he heard the Los Angeles & Independence Railroad's plans, he invested $220,000 and became its president. Baker realized that his Los Angeles and Truxton Railroad would be a natural extension to Jones' line so they sought a merger. His port would be seven miles closer to Los Angeles and several hours less sailing time from San Francisco.

Baker sold Jones a three-quarter interest in his Santa Monica property for $165,000. Together they decided to create the townsite of Santa Monica complete with railroad and pier.

The new railroad posed a threat to Southern Pacific interests because its Santa Monica terminus could kill their San Pedro facility. There was a rush to claim a route through the Cajon Pass since only one of the competing railroads could fit through the narrow pass. Los Angeles and Independence's general manager and chief engineer reached the pass first on January 7, 1885 and staked out a claim only one hour before Southern Pacific's surveying crew arrived. Southern Pacific owners then tried to stop them by obtaining an exclusive rail franchise from Congress, but Senator Jones quickly squashed their attempt.

By February 1875, road gangs of Chinese laborers were cutting through the soft palisades at the end of a Santa Monica arroyo to create rail access to a 1,740 foot long wharf. A freighter arrived at the Shoo Fly Landing on April 19th to unload a shipment of Oregon Fir logs. Three days later workers, using a steam driven pile driver, began pounding piles for the wharf into the bay's sandy bottom. Construction was also started on the Santa Monica Hotel located on the bluff north of the wharf. It served as lodgings for the railroad workers and latter became Santa Monica's first tourist hotel.

Senator Jones travelled to New York City to negotiate with Union Pacific president, Jay Gould for the purchase of rails and rolling stock. Despite pressure by Southern Pacific for Gould not to cooperate, they were too late. By June the pier was completed and the first ship landed. Rails were laid from Santa Monica to Los Angeles at a rapid pace.

Colis P. Huntington, who was the principal owner of the Southern Pacific, next began to pressure shipping companies to allow only half their ships to dock at Santa Monica. Jones counter attacked by purchasing the Panama Railroad to gain leverage on Atlantic-Pacific trade as it crossed the narrow isthmus. He insisted that the Pacific Mail Steamship Company schedule regular stops at Santa Monica.

The Santa Monica Bathhouse constructed in 1877 was located on the beach directly below the Santa Monica Hotel. It contained twenty-five rooms, each with hot fresh or salt water showers. Sea water for the showers was pumped into a 5000 gallon tank by the windmill on the hill. Its 52 x 15 foot, six foot deep swimming pool was located on its west side. The tent on the beach was E. G. Morrison's photographic studio.

This view looking north from the Arcadia Hotel in 1888 shows the tourist facilities at North Beach. At the far right on the bluff is the two-story Santa Monica Hotel at Ocean Avenue. The long structure in the center is Eckert & Hopf's Pavilion Restaurant and the large structure on the narrow beach is the Santa Monica Bathhouse. The tents for various businesses along the beach were supplied by William I. Hull who operated a tent manufacturing company there.

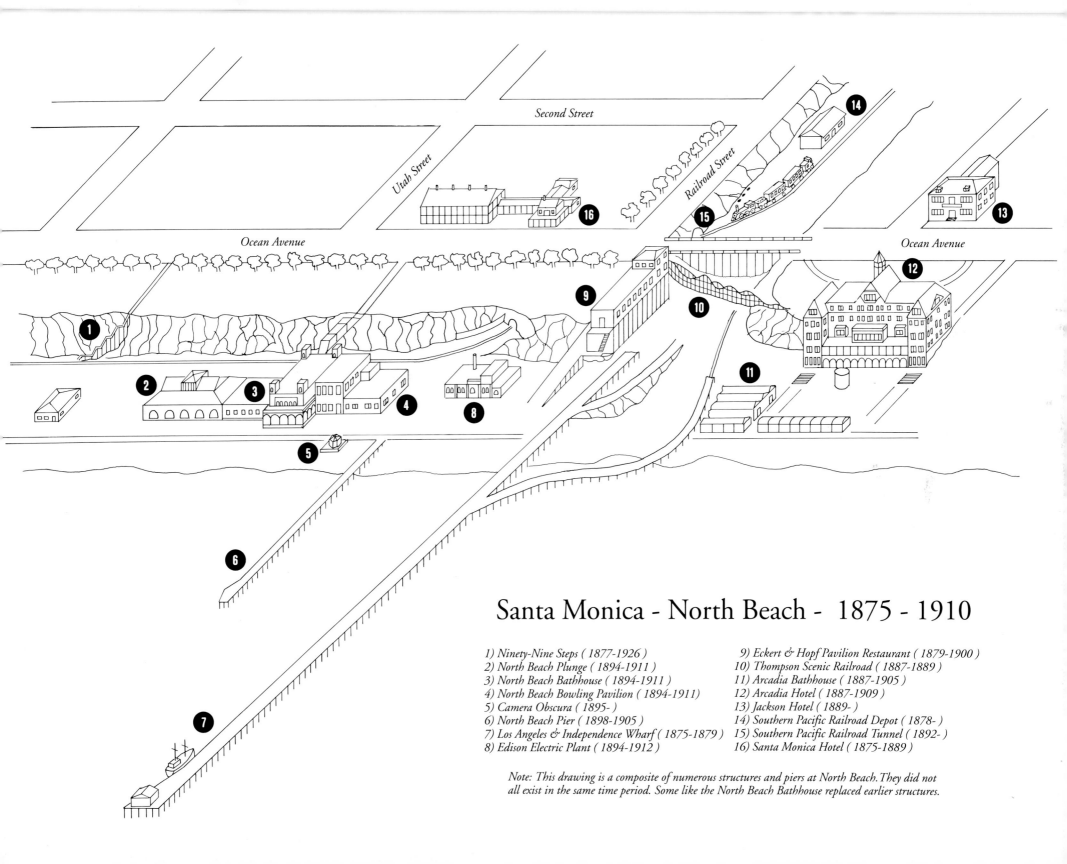

Santa Monica - North Beach - 1875 - 1910

1) Ninety-Nine Steps (1877-1926)
2) North Beach Plunge (1894-1911)
3) North Beach Bathhouse (1894-1911)
4) North Beach Bowling Pavilion (1894-1911)
5) Camera Obscura (1895-)
6) North Beach Pier (1898-1905)
7) Los Angeles & Independence Wharf (1875-1879)
8) Edison Electric Plant (1894-1912)

9) Eckert & Hopf Pavilion Restaurant (1879-1900)
10) Thompson Scenic Railroad (1887-1889)
11) Arcadia Bathhouse (1887-1905)
12) Arcadia Hotel (1887-1909)
13) Jackson Hotel (1889-)
14) Southern Pacific Railroad Depot (1878-)
15) Southern Pacific Railroad Tunnel (1892-)
16) Santa Monica Hotel (1875-1889)

Note: This drawing is a composite of numerous structures and piers at North Beach. They did not all exist in the same time period. Some like the North Beach Bathhouse replaced earlier structures.

Meanwhile the two partners hired J. E. Jackson, a civil engineer to survey their townsite. It was initially a modest town that stretched eight blocks along the shore atop the bluffs just north of their railroad terminal, and inland twenty five blocks. They filed a subdivision map for their city with the county recorder on July 10, 1875.

Advertisements announcing a land auction on Thursday July 15th were placed in Los Angeles and San Francisco newspapers. They boasted that Santa Monica was to be the site of two transcontinental railroads. Senator Jones hired Tom Fitch, a former Congressman and persuasive orator as auctioneer. Fitch stirred up enthusiasm in San Francisco and accompanied prospective buyers on one of two side-wheel steamers that left San Francisco in time to arrive at Santa Monica on the morning of the sale. Hundreds more eager investors traveled by carriage and stage over a crude road from Los Angeles to attend the sale.

The crowd of nearly two thousand bidders converged at the foot of Wilshire Boulevard, where Senator Jones had set up bleachers facing the bay. A makeshift tavern called "Grand Palace Saloon" was set up nearby and stocked with kegs of beer. After denying rumors that the Los Angeles and Independence Railroad was nothing more than a `paper' route and the city's title was in question, Senator Jones opened the bidding.

The first parcel, now at the corner of Broadway and Ocean Avenue, started at $250, and sold for $510. Others on that block went for $300, while those further inland sold for as little as $75. By the end of the day $40,000 in lots were sold, and another $43,000 were auctioned off the following day.

Work continued steadily on the railroad. A brass-trimmed locomotive accompanied by a string of flat cars and gondolas arrived by side-wheel steamer at the town's new pier in late September. It's maiden voyage on October 17, 1875 over ten miles of track took just 19 minutes. Travellers rode in open flat cars because of a shortage of passenger coaches, but the tremendous improvement over stagecoach times was worth the inconvenience. The train mostly hauled freight at a dollar per ton, but by December they had regular passenger service twice daily for a dollar fare.

At first, Santa Monica sought to capitalize on its seaside location and blossom into a commercial port. The new town experienced a building boom. By the end of the year there were more than one hundred buildings completed or under construction. The railroad brought quick prosperity, and weekend visitors spent freely on beach outings.

One of the first to capitalize on the tourist trade was Michael Duffy, who in April 1876, was the first to build a bathhouse on the beach about a block and a half north of the railroad pier. Shortly afterwards Senator John P. Jones and Robert S. Baker constructed a beach pavilion immediately south of Duffy's bathhouse. They built a 99 step staircase to the bluff above to connect it with their Santa Monica Hotel that they were enlarging.

A thousand lots had been sold by summer 1876 and the town contained more than two hundred buildings, mostly within six or seven blocks of the beach. The permanent population, excluding tourists and campers in Santa Monica Canyon, hovered around eight hundred.

In August 1876 financial panic hit the Comstock securities market when news revealed that the Inyo silver mines were failing. The Workman bank that was involved with the railroad went bankrupt and work stopped only eight miles east of Los Angeles. After the Southern Pacific Railroad completed its route to Northern California in late 1876, much of the freight between San Francisco and Los Angeles was shipped by rail rather than by sea. Passengers also choose the faster rail service rather than risk seasickness, although fares were twice the cost of an ocean passage.

Although Jones' Los Angeles and Independence Railroad soon began losing money for lack of freight, it was still doing well with its weekend excursion tourist business. The company completed its new Santa Monica Bathhouse at North Beach a short distance from the pier in January 1877. It was fully equipped with hot steam baths, a salt water plunge, and facilities for salt water bathing.

Senator Jones knew he was licked. He initially tried to sell the railroad to Los Angeles County. In March the presidents of the Central Pacific and Union Pacific Railroads visited Santa Monica to look over the property and begin negotiations. On June 4, 1877 Southern Pacific announced that they had purchased the Los Angeles and Independence Railroad for $195,000, less than one fourth the capital originally invested.

Southern Pacific had no intention of competing with itself in San Pedro harbor. The company immediately raised railroad and steamer rates, and when business in Santa Monica dwindled it announced that only two small steamers, Senator and Ancor would ply the coast. Soon the railroad concocted a story that teredo worms had infested the pier pilings and that it was no longer safe for train traffic unless at least three quarters of the pier pilings were replaced. The last ship, the Senator, landed in September 1877.

This was a crushing blow to the newly founded town. Naturally business dropped off and people began moving away. The Santa Monica Hotel closed and even the local newspaper, the Evening Outlook, folded Christmas Day, 1878. When the wharf was ordered removed in 1879, the remaining citizens protested and offered to purchase it. The offer was refused and soon efforts began to dismantle the pier and knock over the pilings. When the pilings failed to budge, company engineers went out in boats and chopped them off at low tide. Ironically the piles were only slightly worm eaten and the pier could have been saved.

By 1880, Santa Monica was experiencing a deep business depression. The population had bottomed out at 350 citizens, the hotel was closed and only a saloon, restaurant, and several grocery and dry goods stores remained. But Santa Monica's location as a beach area close to Los Angeles helped revive it. The number of excursionists and summer campers began to increase steadily. Santa Monica Hotel reopened in 1882, when J. W. Scott bought the hotel. He remodeled it and added a twenty room addition the following year.

Railroad rate wars soon played another part in Santa Monica's boom and bust cycle. In 1885 the Atchison, Topeka & Santa Fe Railroad managed to break Southern Pacific's monopolistic grip on Southern California when it completed a line to San Diego. The company laid rails north and secured the right-of-way to Ballona Creek, just three miles south of Santa Monica. The railroad in partnership with Ballona Harbor and Improvement Company, planned a massive seaport there. They built two piers and began digging a channel from the sea into the inland lagoon. Track was laid towards Palms and Los Angeles.

As real estate values surged in Santa Monica, people and businesses began moving back. J.W. Scott purchased a tract of land between Railroad and Front Street from the Southern Pacific for $3000. He subdivided this property in south Santa Monica into forty lots and sold thirty lots for $30,000. He then used the money in 1886 to begin construction of a first class hotel called the Arcadia.

His elegant 125 room hotel, which was named for Colonel Baker's beautiful wife Arcadia, became the finest seaside hotel in California when it opened on January 24, 1887. It was a huge, long rectangular, wooden structure located on the edge of the bluffs, just south of the railroad tracks that led to the old wharf. Its five stories rose from the beach on the ocean side, but it was only three stories high at its inland entrance that was topped by an observation tower. It had a dining room for two hundred guests, a sitting room, parlor, ladies billiard and reading

When the Arcadia Hotel opened in 1887, it was connected to the town across the old railroad gorge by a unique Thompson Switchback Gravity Railroad. It was the forerunner of the roller coaster and its gentle dips thrilled passengers. After passengers debarked, cars were pushed up an incline and placed on the other track for the return journey. The ride was removed two years later.

A primitive cable-driven steam powered Ferris Wheel was erected during the summer either on the beach or on the Santa Monica Hotel grounds.

Beach bathers in the 1890s wore heavy, cumbersome, woolen bath suits that covered nearly their entire body.

Thompson Switchback Gravity Railroad; 1887.

Senator Jones built the North Beach Bathhouse in 1894. The 450 x 150 foot structure contained a large plunge, hot salt-water baths, parlor, ballroom, roof garden, restaurant, and bowling pavilion. A trestle bridge connected the bathhouse roof garden with the top of Santa Monica's bluffs.

rooms on the first floor. There was a ballroom and conservatory on a lower level. The beach was accessible through the bottom floor where one could sit at the cafe or lounge on the sand. There were also therapeutic salt water baths available.

The Arcadia had a unique Thompson Switchback Gravity Railroad which carried passengers from the top of the bluff across the arroyo and back, on a short 500 foot undulating track that used natural gravity. La Marcus Thompson came to Santa Monica during the winter to supervise the ride's construction. One end of the gravity railroad terminated at the Arcadia Hotel and the other end at the Pavilion on the north side of the Southern Pacific track. This early style roller coaster, whose gentle dips thrilled passengers of the day, had a reverse track so visitors could ride both directions.

Legend has it that the town's early-day prostitutes and their pimps took it over one night for a joy-ride and frus-

This photograph of the beach looking south was taken from the North Beach Bathhouse in 1898. It shows a tented merry-go-round operated by the Davis Family in the foreground. The pier stub is the remains of the Los Angeles & Independence railroad wharf and the pier in the far distance is Kinney & Ryan's Ocean Park Pier.

The North Beach Bathhouse was remodeled in 1902. Its roof garden was enclosed and became the ceiling for an auditorium seating 1500. The new bowling pavilion on its south end had eight modern alleys.

trated the hotel patrons efforts to ride for an hour. Another account mentions a drunk who one night became trapped when the car he released began travelling back and forth between two of the larger dips.

In February Southern Pacific officials visited the Arcadia Hotel. They soon announced that they would build a new deep water wharf to compete with Santa Fe's nearby Port Ballona project. Santa Monica's merchants and realtors were ecstatic. This meant rebirth and prosperity

The Southern Pacific and Santa Fe railroads suddenly became locked in a deadly rate war. Fares from Kansas City to Los Angeles, normally about $100 began plunging. On the morning of March 6, 1887, the fare was down to $8. At noon, Southern Pacific lowered it to one dollar, a fare the Santa Fe found too ridiculous to match. Over the next few days, the fares rose steadily, but remained around $25 for the next few months.

Easterners and midwesterners, recognizing a bargain when they saw one, came to California by the thousands. Real estate agents eagerly awaited the newcomers, and offered them free transportation and meals in exchange for attending land auctions. Long Beach and Glendale were a few of the new towns that were instantly created and subdivided out of the remaining rancheros. Los Angeles's population mushroomed to 80,000 in 1887. By summer, 2000 to 3000 people a day were discovering the pleasures of Santa Monica's North Beach tourist facilities.

Nearly a million dollars in real estate changed hands from January to July that year. New businesses, many built of brick, filled in much of Santa Monica's unpaved downtown area along Second, Third and Fourth Streets. The Santa Monica Evening Outlook newspaper began publishing again, and W. D. Vawter, who opened the town's first general store in 1875, applied for a franchise to operate horse drawn trolleys on narrow-gauge tracks. His line, when it opened in June 1887, began at Ocean Avenue and Railroad Street (Colorado), weaved through the business district, and ran to 7th Street and Nevada (Wilshire).

But the boom was to be short lived, especially for Santa Monica. The Port Ballona developers suddenly discovered that a hard layer of clay lay under the marshes at the mouth of the creek. When their dredging machines couldn't dent it, they were forced to abandon the project. Once the threat of a competing port evaporated, the Southern Pacific, too, scrapped plans for its new wharf in Santa Monica.

Fortunately for Santa Monica, business was in recession rather than depression. The First National Bank that Vawter and others planned in 1887 finally opened in 1888. The trolley route was extended south along Ocean

Avenue to Pico and along Nevada to 17th street, then out to the Old Solider's Home in 1890.

Tourism remained the town's primary business. Southern Pacific brought 200,000 tourists to Santa Monica in 1889, and thousands more arrived by their own conveyance. On one warm Sunday 12,000 visitors arrived to watch a balloon ascension. Although the Santa Monica Hotel was destroyed by fire on January 15, 1889 because of a lack of water pressure, it had little effect on the tourist business. The owners, promptly rebuilt directly across the street from the Arcadia Hotel.

The influx of newcomer's and the growth of trade during the late 1880's led to the need for an improved deep-water harbor in Southern California. The Los Angeles Chamber of Commerce and the Southern Pacific preferred the San Pedro location. Senator Jones and Santa Monica civic leaders campaigned for a harbor nearby.

A congressional delegation headed by Senator William B. Frye of Maine was sent to inspect the two sites. The Senator was unimpressed with San Pedro but liked Santa Monica. His judgement, however, was overruled when the Army Corps. of Engineers's 1891 study favored San Pedro.

Congress was ready to give Los Angeles an initial $250,000 to begin the project when the Southern Pacific changed their mind. Company officials claimed that San Pedro's ocean floor was too rocky to build piers. They now preferred the Santa Monica site. But the real reason was the success of Santa Fe's Redondo Beach wharf which opened in 1889. Except for coal and lumber, 60% of all seaborne shipping in and out of the Los Angeles area was handled by that wharf. Its main appeal was that it was closer than San Pedro to San Francisco.

Southern Pacific acquired a fifty foot right-of-way along the beach beside the bluffs from Senator Jones and Colonel Baker after threatening condemnation proceedings. They dug a tunnel through the palisades in March 1892 and extended their rail line to a point one half mile beyond Santa Monica Canyon. They planned to connect it to a 4,750 foot curving pier called the Long Wharf. The project would be called 'Port Los Angeles.'

Despite a second Army Corp. of Engineer's report in 1892 favoring San Pedro as a port, the Southern Pacific on July 25, 1892 began driving piles for their wharf. 'Port Los Angeles' began operations on May 11, 1893 when the first coal freighter, the San Mateo docked amidst a crowd of one thousand cheering Santa Monicans.

Santa Monica experienced its third business boom in its short history. It is estimated that Southern Pacific spent more than $200,000 in the town during construc-

The North Beach Bathhouse cement plunge was 100 feet long by 50 feet wide. It was filled with clean salt water, heated to a temperature of 80 degrees. Bleachers along the sides allowed spectators to view the bathers.

tion of its wharf. The Arcadia Hotel, which had been closed for more than a year reopened in July under new management. Its new owners, the Pacific Improvement Company, a subsidiary of Southern Pacific spent $10,000 to remodel and expand the hotel. The hotel attracted so much business that cots had to be placed in some of the rooms instead of beds.

Senator Jones was determined to make North Beach's tourist facilities the best on the Pacific Coast. He formed the North Beach Bath House Company in December 1893, and with $50,000 began building the 450 x 150 foot structure north of the pier. When it opened in the spring, the bath house featured a large plunge where swimmers were watched by full-time attendants as well as spectators who filled the bleachers. Hot salt-water baths were advertised as "strengthening and refreshing for the weak and exhausted." The complex also featured an elegantly furnished parlor, ballroom, roof garden, bowling pavilion, and the Pavilion restaurant with two dining rooms.

The Edison Company's installation of an electric power plant on the bluff above the old railroad pier in 1894 gave the city the look of prosperity, especially at night. It was also the year that Senator Jones bought the town's bank from Vawter and renamed it the Santa Monica Bank.

North Beach's virtual monopoly on Santa Monica's tourist facilities began to weaken slightly in 1892 when Abbot Kinney and his partner Francis Ryan bought a strip of the old Rancho La Ballona property south of Strand Street. The terrain in what was to become Ocean Park was different from most of Santa Monica's. It was hilly rather than flat, and its beach was at the end of a gentle slope rather than at the bottom of steep cliffs.

It was Kinney and Ryan's intention to build a modest beach resort similar to Coney Island in New York. They persuaded the Santa Fe Railroad to extend its line from Ballona Creek up the coast, and donated the land for a depot at Hill Street in exchange for a promise that they would build a substantial pier and pavilion. A much larger tract was given to the Y.M.C.A. in hopes that construction of an auditorium and bathhouse would attract conventions and assemblies to Ocean Park. The remainder of the property was subdivided into small 25 x 100 foot, $45 lots that sold well. Unsold lots were rented for $15 per year with the understanding that `neat and substantial cottages' would be built on them.

Kinney and Ryan, who were both sports enthusiasts, built a golf course, race track, tennis club, and country clubhouse. The pier, which was completed by the railroad

in 1895, was a mere stub and offered nothing to attract visitors. Several years later the partners replaced it with a 1250 foot long pier built over the town's sewer outfall.

Competition encouraged North Beach developers to add attractions to make the area Santa Monica's premier tourist area, especially after Sherman and Clark extended electric trolley service to the city. The first Pasadena & Pacific Railroad trolleys from the depot at Hill and Temple in Los Angeles arrived on April 1, 1896. Two thousand residents and a band greeted the passengers as they embarked from the station located just above the North Beach Bathhouse at Santa Monica Boulevard and Ocean Avenue. By summer Sherman and Clark had extended service south to Ocean Park.

In January 1898 a businessman named J.C. Elliot proposed to build a sixteen foot wide $25,000 pleasure wharf at the foot of Railroad Avenue. He even talked about building a small rock breakwater to make boating possible near the wharf. Santa Monica's Trustees wanted him to widen his proposed pier to twenty four feet and deposit a thousand dollars to guarantee that he would start construction within sixty days. But just days prior to officially forming his company, the city denied the franchise. The city was worried about granting another wharf franchise only a few feet away from the one Southern Pacific's already held.

Two months later the Santa Monica Beach Improvement Company was organized with a capital stock of $100,000. It was a syndicate headed by F.A. Miller, proprietor of the Arcadia Hotel, Sherman and Clark of the Pasadena and Pacific Electric, and Robert Jones, president of the Santa Monica Bank. The company's goal was secure a lease with as much beach frontage as possible, build a pleasure wharf, lay a plank boardwalk, and erect attractive cottages and suitable buildings for beach activities. They claimed that the Southern Pacific wouldn't oppose their project.

In May the company applied to the city for a wharf franchise to build a 1300 foot long pier at the foot of Railroad Avenue. They were planning to construct the $20,000 project in two stages. The initial 700 foot section would be completed in time for the summer season. Another 600 feet would be added in the fall. They even sold stock to local businessmen at $25 per share three weeks before the Southern Pacific dropped a bombshell and claimed an exclusive franchise at that location.

The company was determined to build their 700 foot long pleasure wharf. It choose a location further north midway between the old railroad wharf pilings and the North Beach Bath House. This was a sufficient distance

to escape any conflict with Southern Pacific's claim that covered a set distance on either side of their old wharf. On July 11, 1898 the steamer Bonita arrived with building materials. The timber was sent ashore by raft from the anchored ship. Construction was rushed and the piles were hastily driven without even coating them for protection from sea barnacles. The narrow pier opened for fishing one a month later.

The company only built part of their planked boardwalk and none of the planned structures. Others, however, built an auditorium four years later to attract some of the numerous conventions that met frequently in Southern California.

Sherman and Clark's trolley lines eventually led to the Arcadia Hotel's closure in 1899. The hotel was a holding company for the Southern Pacific. When their railroad was the only road into Santa Monica, it was to their advantage to maintain a first class hotel. After the trolley lines came to Santa Monica, their interests turned elsewhere.

While North Beach was much more straight-laced than Ocean Park, each summer a few carnival ride operators set up their attractions on the beach near the pleasure pier. At various times there was steam powered cable driven wooden Ferris wheel, a haunted swing inside a tent and a shooting gallery. A portable Armitage Hershel merry-go-round operated by the Davis family was a frequent attraction.

Santa Monica's citizens and city government were becoming more and more puritanical as the turn of the century neared. In 1900, the town voted 305 to 218 to ban saloons, but allowed restaurants and hotels to continue to serve alcoholic beverages. That year Ocean Park's citizens became paranoid and circulated petitions advocating secession from Santa Monica. An election was finally held in the fall, but separatist's efforts failed; 341-59.

In 1902, Fredrick Ringe's Good Government League swept into power. A total prohibition ordinance, at the urging of the Anti-Saloon League, was placed on the June 1903 ballot. It lost 543 to 286.

Fredrick Ringe was a very stubborn but fair man with extremely strong beliefs. He was also very wealthy businessman who had investments in several successful companies. He knew that when he sponsored the successful anti-saloon issue in the 1900 elections that the town would suffer a loss of $2500 in saloon license fees. He reimbursed the city for its loss from his own funds.

He had purchased the Malibu Rancho in 1891, expanded it to 17,000 acres, and was determined to preserve and enhance its natural beauty at all costs. The Southern Pacific Railroad, which had effectively lost its bid to make the Long Wharf by 1899 into Los Angeles' only port, decided that it needed to link its Santa Monica tracks with those in Santa Barbara. It was important economically to Santa Monica that the town be located on the main rail line between Los Angeles and San Francisco.

In 1904, the railroad began condemnation proceedings to obtain a right-of-way through Ringe's ranch. Ringe, however, discovered an obscure California law prohibiting one railroad from condemning the right-of-way parallel to an existing operating railroad. He effectively thwarted Southern Pacific's plans by building his own twenty mile long standard gauge railroad from Las Flores Canyon to the Ventura County line at a cost of nearly one million dollars. He constructed the Malibu Pier for unloading material and rolling stock. The Hueneme, Malibu and Port Los Angeles Railroad was a scenic line that leaped canyons and spanned creeks along the coast. But its prime use was to bring in supplies for the ranch and ship hides and grain to market. His railroad did as much to stall Santa Monica's industrial growth as Abbot Kinney's new Venice of America resort did to its tourist business just one year later.

Abbot Kinney was a dreamer who had the knack of making his dreams come true. After he and his partners split up their Ocean Park property in 1904, Kinney looked at his seemingly worthless salt marsh acreage and saw the similarity to that of Venice, Italy. He envisioned a cultural resort and beach community called Venice of America.

He used his share of the profits of his family's tobacco business to create a planned community complete with a network of canals around a central lagoon. Venice of America also had a bathhouse with plunge, hotels, saloons, and restaurants along an arcaded Venetian styled business street, a miniature railroad for internal transportation, and a 1700 foot long pleasure pier complete with a huge auditorium, ship cafe, and bandstand pavilion. Three trolley lines provided transportation for thousands of visitors from Los Angeles and Santa Monica.

Venice of America, from its opening day on July 4, 1905, captured the public's fancy and imagination. It became Southern California's most popular beach resort. Kinney expanded its attractions and built larger facilities to accommodate the crowds. His former partners in Ocean Park were forced to compete and they too built a beautiful new plunge and expanded their pier facilities. Santa Monica's more conservative business community sat back and watched.

The North Beach Bathhouse Pier was built in 1898 by the Santa Monica Beach Improvement Company. It served as both a promenade for tourists and as a fishing pier.

A spring 1905 storm did considerable damage to North Beach's pier and promenade.

CHAPTER 2

Construction of Municipal & Looff Piers (1908-1918)

The growth of Santa Monica and the need to dispose of the city sewage became the primary impetus in building its first Municipal Pier. The city had been dumping its sewage at the Pier Street outfall beneath Ocean Park's Pier, but by 1907, its capacity was becoming overloaded and its agreement with Ocean Park ended. In those days it was necessary for health reasons to build a long pier or wharf to carry the outfall pipe far enough so that the tides would carry the untreated sewage out to sea.

Since the city wasn't able to make alternate arrangements, they had no choice but to hold a sewer bond election on September 27, 1907. The populace, aware of the health hazards, approved the $160,000 measure; 591 to 80. The funds were to be used both to construct a Municipal Pier whose concrete construction specifications were outlined on the ballot, and a sewage pumping plant near the foot of the pier.

The city engineer advertised for designers to submit plans after the War Department approved the project in November. Eleven plans were submitted. But controversy developed immediately after Erwin Warner's winning design for the $90,000 pier was chosen, modified and approved by the City Council in February.

Although concrete piers were considered stronger and longer lasting than traditional wooden piers, concrete engineering was in its infancy at the turn of the century. It was the most experimental of the building arts. There were some notable successes, particularly on the east coast where Atlantic City's pier was still as strong a year later as when it was first built in 1906. But there were problems with the concrete used in the Long Beach, California pier that caused it to crack. One contractor, who declined to bid, called the pier's concrete design "uncertain."

Five contractors bid on the job. Stutzer Cement Company of Venice won the contract with a low bid of $82,890. The contract called for a 1600 foot long, 35 foot wide reinforced concrete pier, 21 feet above the mean high tide. The design included three 40 x 90 foot 'T' shaped platforms; one at the pier's end and the others at 500 foot intervals from shore. Specifications called for a wood deck covered by asphalt. Work was expected to take six to seven months.

Stutzer set up a concrete casting plant alongside the bluffs near the site of the new pier. Wooden molds for the 14 to 72 foot long piles were set on an incline. Each con-

Construction started on the concrete Santa Monica Municipal Pier in May 1908. It was located at the foot of Colorado Avenue between the stub of the old railroad wharf and the North Beach Pier. The contractor first built a temporary wooden pier as a platform to work from during construction of the concrete pier.

A series of derricks were erected on the temporary wooden pier to support the pile driver and guide the jetting of each concrete pier pile for the Municipal Pier. About half of the pier's length had been constructed at the time of this photo.

21

Concrete piles 14-72 feet long were cast in wooden molds set at an angle on the beach.

View of the finished concrete piles beneath the completed pier.

crete pile was reinforced by coated steel rods arranged symmetrically. There was a hollow iron tube running down the center of each pile and a large bulb at the end to help anchor it in the sand. The cast piles were then seasoned for several weeks before they were used in construction.

Once logs arrived from the northwest in early May, the contractor also began building a wooden false pier to aid in construction. The false pier resembled a real pier except for numerous derricks that were used to lower the concrete piles through the deck and into place. They used a clever pile driving technique called jetting. Normally a steam- driven pile driver was used to pound wooden piles into place, but it tended to crack concrete piles. Instead, water was forced down through the iron pipe in the piling's center. The water jet forced the sand out from beneath the piling until it was sunk and anchored 16-20 feet beneath the surface. Then the pipe was removed and the hole was filled with concrete.

Work naturally took much longer than expected. In August 1908 Mr. Stutzer's crane at the concrete pile works fell and knocked down the power lines at the nearby Edison plant. Later that month heavy seas damaged both his false pier and the nearby North Beach Pier that was later declared unsafe.

Progress was maddeningly slow. The pace didn't pick up until mid-December when the steam schooner Commerce arrived carrying twenty one additional wooden piles. Fifty more arrived two days later on Wednesday December 16th.

But on Friday, February 12, 1909, a severe winter storm struck and carried much of the pier's temporary scaffolding (false work) out to sea. Many wooden pilings snapped and the pile driver rested on the bottom of the ocean. The concrete piles, which were out to the 1060 foot mark, held like a rock.

They expected to wait a week for the arrival of a ship carrying more piles to help raise the pile driver, but Stutzer used a grapple to recover both the engine and boiler several days before the ship arrived. The contractor finished the pier's false work by mid-April and city officials expected the pier to open by July 4th. But then the City Council's May 8th decision to change the pier's deck from asphalt to concrete delayed the pier's opening until Admission's Day.

North Beach property owners were enthusiastic about the city's new pier. They hoped to rehabilitate the area as an amusement center. They envisioned a first class cafe overlooking the ocean on one side of the pier and a pavilion on the other side which could be used for picnic par-

PIER DAY AT SANTA MONICA, CAL
SEPT. 9. 1909.
H. F. RILE, PHOTO.

The new 1600 foot long Municipal Pier was dedicated on Admission's Day, September 9, 1909. Five thousand people attended the festivities.

ties. The plaza, which the city was pouring at the foot of Colorado in front of the pier, would feature a bandstand.

Meanwhile Santa Monica officials were planning a big celebration to dedicate their Municipal Pier on September 9, 1909. The contractor was adding the finishing touches. There were pipes for drinking water, toilets, and a two inch thick galvanized railing. The pier's `T's would be fitted with a sun parlor, cafe, and concessions catering to the fishermen. The $10,000 electrolytic plant, established on shore for purifying the sewage, was tested and ready to discharge its sludge at the end of the pier.

A flotilla of Navy warships, two cruisers and four torpedo boats arrived in time for Admission's Day. The festivities began with a parade led by Gregory's Band and a contingent of marines from the cruisers St Louis and Albany. Five thousand people listened to the dedication speeches by Santa Monica's Mayor, T. H. Dudley, then adjourned to watch the afternoon swimming and surf boat races. A diving board was set up on the pier for the high diving contest.

The evening's entertainment included a band concert followed by a `Tableau vivant' (allegorical pageant) "Surrender of the Rex Neptune" that began after dark. The play was a modern day equivalent of a pagan ritual where King Neptune, god of the sea was asked to spare the new pier.

The show began when a monster with fiery eyes was seen approaching the outer end of the pier. A bugler on watch sounded the alarm. A fairy and a queen representing Santa Monica advanced to meet the monster at the pier's first `T'. The monster was commanded to halt and when the fairy waved her magic wand, it disappeared. A beautiful shell stood in its place.

The pier's lights, which were then turned on, revealed a shell bordered with a row of lights. King Neptune sat on the throne beside a reclining mermaid. The Queen asked why Neptune had destroyed so many bay piers. He jested that he did it for the fun of it. She informed him that his fun was now at an end as the cement age had arrived. The new pier on which he stood was concrete and indestructible.

Neptune surveyed the pier in amazement, surrendered to the Queen and was ordered back to the depths. The crowned Queen, attired in a flowing white robe and carrying a scepter mounted the throne vacated by Neptune. The lights went out and a blaze of fire erupted atop a 65 foot high tower. Neptune covered by flames dove into the sea. Afterwards a climatic fireworks show thrilled the thousands who watched from the bluffs, pier and beach. It was spectacular.

A flotilla of Navy vessels anchored offshore for the dedication of the city's Municipal Pier. The large ship at the end of the pier is the St. Louis. Others are the cruisers Albany and Yorktown; torpedo boats Davis, Lawrence, and Goldsborough.

Once the Municipal pier was open, the city and others began improvements. The city committed themselves to building a twenty foot wide esplanade (walkway) along the beach, south from Colorado to the Bristol Pier at Hollister Street. It formed a continuous walkway to Venice when it was completed the following spring. A syndicate, headed by Carl Schader planned to build a new luxury hotel on the site of the demolished Arcadia. But the most ambitious project of them all was unveiled in October 1909.

T.J. Hampton and W.H. Bainbridge filed an application with the U.S. Engineer's office to build a breakwater 4000 feet in length extending north from the Municipal Pier. This concrete wall, which was 2000 feet from shore in 5 1/2 fathoms of water, would enclose a harbor for pleasure and fishing boats. They also planned to construct a bathhouse and hotel. The hotel would have an open court with a waterway where motor boats could come to a landing inside the hotel. Government permission to build was secured at the end of the year.

The Santa Monica Harbor and Improvement Company was capitalized for $1,000,000 at a dollar per share. The company claimed that most of its financial backing was from Eastern financiers but it planned to put 300,000 shares on the open market to solidify support from the local business community. Newspaper advertisements and expectations that each share would eventually be worth five dollars each helped sell the first 50,000 shares of stock at fifty cents each and the second 50,000 shares at sixty cents each. The third block of shares sold for seventy cents each at the end of January 1910.

Scant progress was made during the spring. Bainbridge claimed that the bidding process was causing the delay. Sympathetic city officials granted them a six months extension to start work. But by July the City Council began to question if the harbor company was ever going to start construction. When the Council discovered that the company had no record of being able to complete the work, they began checking on the bonding company. The company eventually closed its office and vanished with the stockholder's money.

In December the Southern Pacific dashed any lingering hopes that the city would retain any semblance of a harbor. They gave notice that they were abandoning the Long Wharf, because as business declined and was diverted to San Pedro's better facilities, the cost of maintaining the wharf was too expensive. Local builders, beginning in 1911 had to pay fifty cents more per hundred dollars to ship lumber through Redondo's wharf and deliver it by electric trolley.

Ocean Park's new 'Million-Dollar Pier', which opened on June 17, 1911 about a mile south of the Municipal Pier, immediately began luring away much of North Beach's tourist business. The amusement pier was huge with two roller coasters, a dance hall, two carousels, vaudeville theater, several large restaurants, and numerous other attractions.

Santa Monica's businessmen, while aware of the problem, were not interested in the honky-tonk atmosphere that accompanied the development of an amusement pier. Instead they looked at half-hearted inexpensive measures like rehabilitating North Beach. A syndicate headed by Stadelman bought the old dilapidated North Beach Bath House and planned to replace it with a large modern bathing pavilion withput a plunge.

Edwin P. Benjamin purchased beach property held by Edison Electric in April 1912. That, combined with the 85 feet that he already owned gave him 250 feet of beach frontage. He planned a two story high bathing pavilion on half of his frontage and an apartment hotel on the remainder.

In the meantime he teamed up with Stadelman's North Beach Syndicate and was awarded a contract for a 40 foot wide, 250 foot long plaza. The walk had an ornamental concrete railing on the ocean side and at intervals, stairs to the beach. He hired a band to entertain visitors and converted the old powerhouse into assembly rooms and a meeting hall.

In 1913 numerous projects, including the imminent construction of the new North Beach Bath House, reported by the press never gelled. One syndicate was supposed to build a large addition to Schrader's Seaside Hotel and erect a 125 x 300 ft amusement pier in front. Another with eastern financing took an option on two beach lots directly opposite Utah Avenue (Broadway) and planned to build a 150 room hotel and a pleasure pier. And Dana Burke bought land in Vicente Terrace south of the pier and planned to build a hundred room inn and cafe modeled after the Glendale Mission Inn in Riverside.

By 1914 Santa Monica officials felt a need for a $150,000 auditorium. The Evening Outlook advocated building it on the Municipal Pier's third set of 'T's. They thought it could be built on both sides and arched over the roadway. The large auditorium would be on the second floor.

Carl Schader offered the city a free site for the auditorium a few weeks before the July 28th election. He vowed that he would buy land south of the Municipal Pier if the city couldn't obtain free land, and that he would donate $10,000 to buy an organ and furnish the gymnasium.

Even Ocean Park offered the city a site at the foot of Pier Avenue opposite their amusement pier but the voters weren't interested in either offer. The bond issue went down in defeat 1043 to 1152.

The first test of the Municipal Pier's strength occurred on February 2, 1914. A huge storm damaged Venice's breakwater protected pier. Pilings torn loose from the Long Wharf and Malibu Piers hammered against the Municipal Pier. Potential damage was averted by workers who seized runaway piles as they washed ashore.

But by August 1915 some damage to the pilings appeared. The area that was alternatively wet and dry, between the high and low water marks, needed repair. Sea water combined with the aluminum in the cement mixture, caused crystallization. The pilings began to peel. Repairs were made by binding them with a steel caisson and filling the four inch gap with the highest grade concrete. Some struts and concrete cross beams were cracked. Repairs cost the city approximately $4000.

In September Edwin P. Benjamin bought the beachfront south of Colorado for $125,000 and announced that he was going to build an amusement center. This additional property, which was adjacent to his Edison property, gave him 347 feet of beach frontage that extended inland to Ocean Avenue.

Benjamin assured the community that his new recreation center would be constructed "upon broad, progressive and refined lines." He predicted that his new 700 foot long by 200 foot wide amusement pier would be built within a year. The Chamber of Commerce endorsed the project because of Benjamin's reputation as the founder of Allenhurst N.J.

Benjamin's project encouraged W.J. Stadelman to begin construction of his Santa Monica Bath House after nearly four years of indecision. Workers poured the foundation for the 100 x 100 foot three story building on February 16, 1916. The domed sun parlor in the center separated the women's sixteen hot tubs on the building's south side from the men's sixteen hot tubs on the building's north side. There was a manicure department and 120 private dressing rooms on the second floor, and 240 changing rooms on the third floor. Since the top of the bath house was almost level with Palisades Park, there was an entrance directly opposite the Windemere Hotel.

Santa Monica's business community was introduced to Charles I.D. Looff at their weekly Chamber of Commerce meeting on Feb 22, 1916. He was a well known Long Beach amusement operator who had just purchased the northern 200 feet of Benjamin's beach frontage adjacent to the Municipal Pier for $50,000. Looff announced plans for a 700 foot long by 200 foot wide amusement pier that would open May 31st. He said that his initial investment would be approximately $400,000 and that in several years he expected to extend his pier further seaward.

Charles Looff had a remarkable reputation for building quality amusement projects. He built Coney Island's first carousel in 1876. Success in hand carving two more carousels in the early 1880's encouraged him to open a carousel factory. By 1890, he employed four carvers in his Brooklyn, New York shop.

In 1895 Looff set up a showcase carousel at Crescent Park in Rhode Island. The four-abreast machine was housed in a domed building with stained glass windows. New models of the factory's horses and menagerie animals were adorned with glittering jewels, gold and silver leaf paint, and lavish ornamentation. Prospective customers visited the carousel to select figures that they wanted included on their carousels.

When Brooklyn city officials in 1895 condemned the land on which Looff's factory stood to build a park, Looff packed and moved his business to Riverside, Rhode Island. His carousel business boomed there and he soon expanded into the production of other amusement rides and fun houses. He soon became a self-made millionaire.

Charles Looff decided to expand his business in 1910 by moving his entire factory, wife Anna and his six chil-

The unused portions of the Looff Pier were utilized for pier parking. The 'What is It' fun house is in the background.

View of Santa Monica's Municipal and Looff Piers in July 1917 from Ocean Avenue atop the Palisades. The domed carousel building is the dominant structure on the pier. (opposite page)

Charles I.D. Looff and his son Arthur built the Looff Pier in Santa Monica in 1916.

The Billiards building contained eight bowling lanes and seven billiard tables.

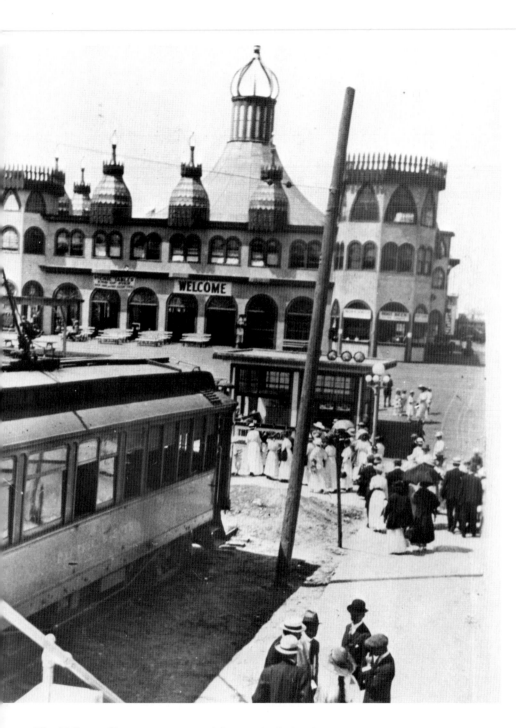

The Airline trolley route transported thousands of inland residents to the Looff Pier.

The Looff Pier hosted picnics nearly every summer day. These children and adults attended a Episcopal church picnic. (right)

dren to Long Beach, California. He set up his factory near the harbor and installed another showcase carousel at "The Pike," Long Beach's amusement zone. The family lived in a second floor apartment in the carousel's hippodrome building. He originally planned to erect a huge amusement pier nearby but was unsuccessful in 1914 in concluding negotiations with the city of Long Beach. An earlier carousel venture at Ocean Park's "Million Dollar Pier" ended with a disastrous pier fire in 1912.

Looff said he choose Santa Monica to build his amusement pier because, "the bathing beach at Santa Monica is well-known as one of the finest on the Pacific Coast, it attracts the highest class of people, and transportation facilities afforded are unequaled."

Charles Looff didn't waste time in starting the mammoth project. He began buying all the available creosoted wood pilings in Southern California including salvaged piles from the Long Beach Wharf that was being dismantled. The first load of 75 stout pilings arrived just three days after his announcement at the Chamber of Commerce meeting. He also contracted with the Hammond Lumber Company in Los Angeles for delivery within thirty days of forty-seven carloads or a half million feet of lumber for the pier platform. Additional piles were shipped from the northwest. He also increased his ocean frontage to 247 feet with an additional purchase from Benjamin at $250 / foot. By March 7th there was a sign at the corner of Ocean and Colorado Avenues that announced the development of a "Refined Amusement Center."

Edwin Benjamin and his partner B. N. Moss, who retained 350 feet of beach frontage north of the pier and the property east of Looff's ocean frontage, had filled and graded the entire east half of their property. They improved access to the Municipal Pier and Looff's construction site with a wide graded approach from Colorado Avenue.

They also built a roadbed for the extension of the Pacific Electric's 'Air Line' route from Sixth and Main Streets in downtown Los Angeles. The track, which passed under the extension of Appian Way, allowed passengers to arrive at Santa Monica's beach adjacent to the pier. The trolley route was the old Southern Pacific route used to haul freight from the Long Wharf to Los Angeles and the shortest route to the beach.

The trolley line also made it easy to transport pilings the length of two flat cars to the pier. Initially a single track was laid down the center of the roadbed so that cars carrying building materials could make the wide turn under the Appian Way viaduct. A two track roadbed

Looff's Aeroscope whirled passengers around at 35 MPH in six, six passenger flying boats.

replaced it by early summer. The first train on the `Air Line' extension arrived Saturday March 12th with a troop of one hundred Hollywood Boy Scouts. They were treated to lunch by Benjamin and Moss.

Looff and his two sons Arthur and William arrived on Monday March 13, 1916 to supervise construction. Arthur, who was born in 1889, was Charles's youngest son. Although he only had an eighth grade education, he took a correspondence course in engineering and drafting. When he was sixteen he built a roller coaster at Crescent Park in Rhode Island. His father recognized his talent and gave him full rein on numerous family amusement projects. He was given the job of civil engineer and superintendent of the Looff Pier project. William, an older son had managed the family's hippodrome in San Francisco before he was summoned south.

The material for starting the job had arrived. Pumps for filling in the shore bulkheads and timber for the pile driver were at the site and ready for assembly. The pilings for the pier's shore end were on the beach, and railroad cars of timber arrived daily.

The late arrival of the pile driver's electric transformers delayed driving the first pile until Saturday March 25th. Arthur Looff choose to use his own designed electric pile driver because it was less noisy and cheaper to run than a steam model. The power was derived from a thirty horsepower electric motor that lifted the hammer for a forty foot drop. He also used the `jet system' where a stream of water driven by a 75 horsepower centrifugal pump washed out the sand ahead of the pile enabling it to sink into the fourteen feet deep hole with only light blows of the hammer. The piles were much more firmly held than if driven in only by heavy blows of a traditional pile driver's hammer.

Charles Looff on March 27, 1916 made a formal written application to the City Council for a twenty year pier franchise. He said he was quite willing to abide by the decision of City Attorney Heney that all amusement piers must obtain a franchise and after the first five years of the franchise, he would pay the city 2% of gross receipts.

Work progressed rapidly. They drove rows of thirty piles along the pier's 247 foot width and reached the water line in eight days. Meanwhile several people applied for concessions on the pier. Arthur Looff said, "we want the best and if no one comes forward with what we consider the best in different lines of amusement, eating places, etc, we intend to install them ourselves. Amusements to get a place on this pier must be `different' and they must be backed by persons with records for good management and success."

Aerial photograph of the Looff and Municipal piers; 1918.

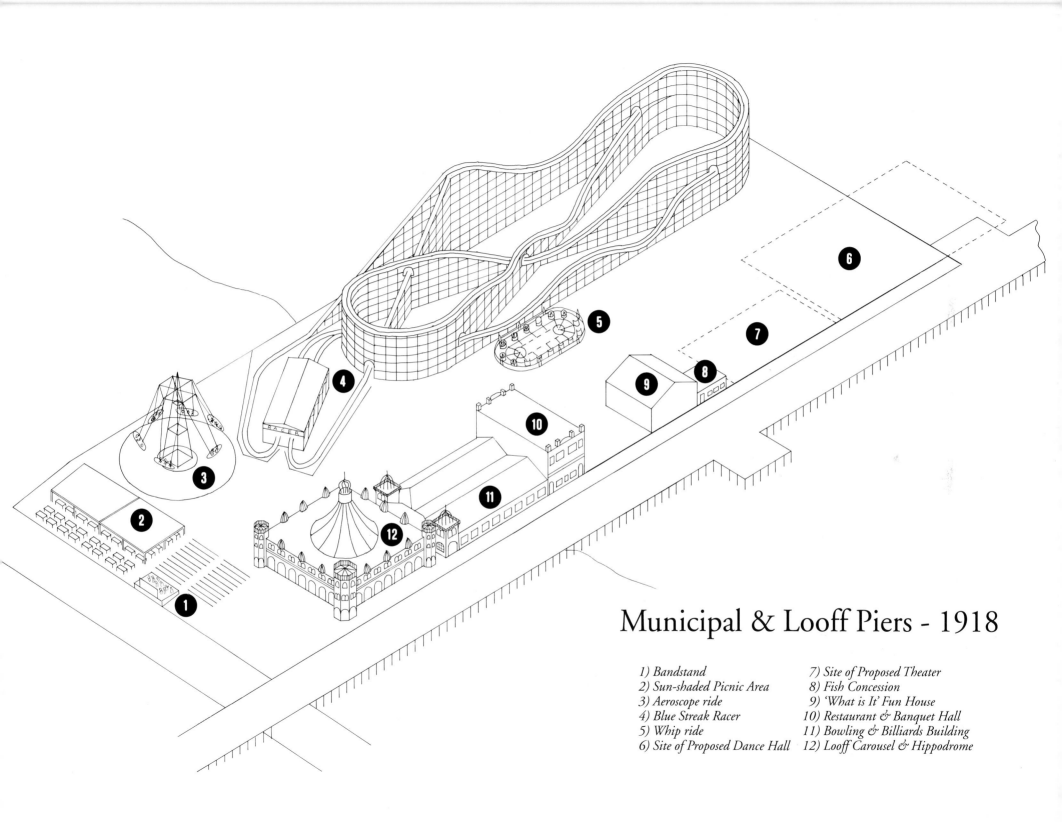

Municipal & Looff Piers - 1918

1) Bandstand
2) Sun-shaded Picnic Area
3) Aeroscope ride
4) Blue Streak Racer
5) Whip ride
6) Site of Proposed Dance Hall
7) Site of Proposed Theater
8) Fish Concession
9) 'What is It' Fun House
10) Restaurant & Banquet Hall
11) Bowling & Billiards Building
12) Looff Carousel & Hippodrome

The pier is still under construction in this panorama showing the just completed Blue Streak Racer roller coaster. The Whip ride is in the foreground. (above)

The Whip, which made a quick half circle turn at each end, was named for the sensation felt in the child's game 'Snap the Whip'. (left)

The four abreast menagerie carousel featuring goats, rabbits, giraffes and camels in addition to its horses, was built at Looff's factory at Long Beach. Its traditional ring dispenser gave outside row riders a chance to win a free ride. (opposite page)

Carl Schrader, a local businessman, tried to derail Looff's pier project on April 5th by offering the city $5000 for a franchise to build a pier west of the mean tide line and the right to connect with the Municipal Pier. He then protested at the City Council's next meeting that it didn't protect the public's interest if Looff were allowed to connect his pier to the Municipal Pier via a steel apron. He felt that the close proximity of Looff's wooden pier, in the event of fire, endangered the city's Municipal Pier, and that Looff shouldn't be allowed to build any closer than one hundred feet from the city's pier. He demanded that the city charge Looff $5000 per year for the use of 900 feet of prime frontage on the Municipal Pier. His calculation was based on the amount of yearly interest the public paid for the pier's bonds.

Several others opposed joining the two pier structures because it would make it difficult to repair the sewer pipe and electrical outlets on the Municipal Pier's south side. There was also the precedent of allowing Looff to build without a permit since the pier franchise had not been granted yet.

Mayor Berkley declared that he was in favor of Looff's pier project. Commissioner Carter added, "We have talked for twenty years about Santa Monica being a dead town and now we have the opportunity to establish an important project. I don't think we should let one or two men spoil it."

Neil Nettleship on behalf of the Santa Monica Chamber of Commerce went even further. He regretted that the beach had been permitted to lie idle for so many years without erecting a pier, and that the first effort to give the city its pier was met with opposition. "I believe that the majority of people are in favor of even going beyond strict legal limits to encourage the construction of this pier."

But opposition among a small minority of citizens continued to smolder. Schrader publicly challenged Looff's project with a large advertisements in the April 15th editions of the Evening Outlook and The Daily Sun newspapers. He claimed Looff didn't hold title to his beach property, that he was building his pier without a franchise, and that by connecting his pier to the city's Municipal Pier, he was turning it into a commercial pier at the taxpayer's expense.

First Looff had to dispel rumors that he didn't actually hold clear title to his property. On April 15th he stated that he purchased the first 200 feet of frontage for cash and received the deed, which was a matter of record. Further, he was currently taking title to the 47 feet balance of beach frontage that he paid Benjamin $250 per frontage foot.

The Blue Streak Racer was a 60 foot high twin track roller coaster. Passengers in two trains raced each other through dips and rises along 3500 feet of track. (above & opposite page)

Professor Caesare La Monica and his Royal Italian Band performed to enthusiastic audiences from the pier's bandstand adjacent to the Promenade in 1917.

Letters began arriving at city hall supporting Schrader and urging the city to get $5000 per year for the pier franchise. Local preachers, obviously riled up by Schrader, demanded that all gambling concessions and the sale of liquor be prohibited by the terms of the franchise. Schrader said that he only wanted a pier with proper amusements and no liquor.

Despite Looff's intention not to sell liquor or allow gambling on his pier, he initially opposed the insertion of a clause in the franchise prohibiting the sale of liquor on the pier during the life of the twenty year franchise. He felt that it discriminated against his pier and did not apply equally to others in the amusement business.

Eventually Looff conceded the point pressed by preachers and others and he consented to the insertion of a clause in the franchise forbidding the sale of intoxicating liquors on the pier. By appeasing his opponents, it enabled the City Council on April 28th to pass a resolution advertising the sale of the pier franchise. While it was unusual for an entrepreneur to build a pier before his franchise was granted, Looff had to proceed without it one he was to complete his pier for the 1916 summer season.

The auction for the pier franchise was held on May 31, 1916 at 10 A.M. Fortunately for Looff, he submitted the only written bid. Others were given an opportunity to make oral bids with an advance of 10% over the highest written bid. "Now's your chance," said Mayor Berkeley. "If you don't take it, forever after hold your peace." When none bid, Commissioner Carter moved that the franchise be given to Looff. Looff paid $200 cash for the right to erect a pier 900 feet into the Pacific and connect it to the Municipal Pier. He agreed to maintain a twenty foot wide public promenade belonging to the city between the two piers, install a large capacity pump for fire protection, and pay the city 2% of the pier's gross receipts after the first five years.

Additional details of the pier's new attractions were unveiled the day Looff secured his franchise. He announced that he purchased a racing roller coaster that had been erected at great expense the previous year for the San Diego Exposition. Fifty men were dismantling it and preparing it for shipment to Santa Monica in forty-eight railroad cars. Meanwhile his Long Beach factory was fabricating the world's largest circle swing for the new pier, and the large two story amusement building at the foot of the pier, which would house one of his carousels, would open by mid June. He also planned a gigantic dance hall 200 feet long by 130 feet wide that would be located 500 feet from the Promenade. Its entrance would face the Municipal Pier midway between the first and second 'T's.

Looff's Hippodrome was architecturally designed to be the most prominent building on his pier. The massive 100 foot square two story structure was a mix of California, Moorish and Byzantine styles. Four imposing octagon shaped towers, the largest 36 feet tall, were built at the buildings corners and an enormous domed cupola rose 65 feet high, far above the roof line. Rows of large high arched windows on each of the building's four sides served as doors and flooded the interior with light.

A beautiful brand new three row menagerie carousel, a virtual duplicate of the one at the Panama Pacific Exposition in San Francisco, operated on the ground floor when it opened Saturday June 10th. It had goats, giraffes and camels on it in addition to horses. A Wurlitzer Band organ provided the music. The ride featured a traditional brass ring dispenser that riders on the outside row stretched to reach as they whirled past. All the rings were steel but one, a winning brass ring that gave the holder a free ride. The ride was so popular that by fall Looff extended the platform and added an outer row of 24 horses to make it a four abreast merry-go-round.

On the Hippodrome's second floor, surrounding the center dome, were sixteen rooms that served as offices, storerooms and quarters for carousel employees. The office occupied the largest tower. Eventually many of the rooms would be rented as apartments.

The dismantlement of the Blue Streak roller coaster progressed rapidly, but there were only a handful of piles on hand for its foundation when the longshoreman's strike at San Pedro hit in mid June. Work abruptly stopped until July 3rd when a lumber schooner carrying piles arrived and anchored offshore on July 3rd. The piles were tossed overboard, then towed by launch towards shore. Chains were then attached and the timbers were pulled ashore by teams of horses.

Looff's workers made up for lost time and by July 31st they had driven piles 720 feet out from the Promenade. They were only weeks from completing the deck. The size of the completed pier would be over four acres (720 feet x 267 feet), about 20% smaller than the Abbot Kinney Pier in nearby Venice.

Meanwhile the Blue Streak Racer was methodically reassembled from blueprints and numbered beams and parts. It was a very compact coaster, 550 feet long by 110 feet wide and 60 feet tall. Yet its three tiers of parallel tracks, set one above the other, made the ride as long as any of the competing coasters in the Santa Monica Bay area with the exception of Prior and Church's enormous

Looff carousel inside the Hippodrome; 1916

An audience beneath shaded pergolas listens to a band concert.

Race Thru the Clouds racer in Venice. The 3500 feet of track for each train included six loops and twenty four dips, and each three car train held eighteen passengers.

Looff's crew tested the coaster in the evening on Aug 2nd, then let his fifty workers break it in on their noon lunch hour the next day. It was opened to the public that evening at ten cents per ride. Arthur Looff boasted that once the track was oiled, the Blue Streak Racer would be the fastest roller coaster in the world. But when a coaster's top speed is largely determined both by its height and its relative drop off the lift hill, the Blue Streak was no match for Venice's 90 foot tall 'Race Thru the Clouds'.

Both the Whip and the Aeroscope rides were installed on the pier in early August. The Whip was set immediately in front of the roller coaster. Its cars travelled in a straight line, then made a swift half circle turn at each end. Each car's passengers were thrown against each other and the far side of their car as it whipped around the turns. An organ furnished music for the ride.

The Aeroscope was a flying boat ride where six, six passenger boats hung by steel cables from the spinning arms

The Whip and 'What is It' attractions.

Twenty passenger electric tram service south of the pier ran along the Ocean Front Promenade between the Ocean Park and the Looff Piers.

`What is It´ was a multi-story walk-thru fun house where patrons encountered a crystal maze, drop floors, moving stairs, rotating turntables and various other fun devices.

Palisades Park overlooked the Santa Monica Pier. The circular building was a Camera Obscura that captured an outside image through a lens and mirrors and projected it on a flat table.

of a sixty foot tower. When the ride reached its 35 MPH top speed and the boats swung high into the air, the centrifugal force pasted passengers to their seats and made it impossible to fall out. The ride was illuminated at night by a thousand colored lights hung from the crown and down the cables. When it spun it created a whirling blaze of color that could be seen for miles.

Looff's pier was more successful than he hoped. It was crowded throughout the remainder of the summer, and on weekends throughout the fall. With the need for more space to accommodate the crowds, he announced plans to extend the pier to a length of 1055 feet from the Promenade. Even his Santa Monica Pier Tract directly across the promenade from the pier was selling well at from $75 to $325 a front foot. There were only a few choice lots left in which to develop businesses.

He continued to add attractions on the pier throughout the winter and spring. His single story bowling and billiards building immediately west of the Hippodrome opened as a concession on January 17, 1917. Eight Brunswick-Balke maple bowling alleys with patented pin-setting devices occupied the rear fifty foot width of the building. The front twenty five feet was devoted to billiards; one billiard and seven pocket billiard tables.

J.L. Ferris, the billiard hall's manager, scheduled as the opening event, a bowling tournament between the Los Angeles City All Stars and the Santa Monica Home Guard. Five hundred spectators watched the home team beat the All Stars, and Police Chief Ferguson out bowl Mayor Berkley two games out of three. The chief won a silver plated bowling pin, and the mayor a bottle of ketchup.

In May Looff opened a 50 x 50 foot multi-story walk-thru fun house called "What is It?" Patrons for an admission charge of ten cents wandered through 500 feet of passageways where they encountered various devices such as a swinging bridge, stepping stones, drop floors, a crystal maze, a rope walk, moving stairs, rotating turntables, and rolling floors. An operator controlled a gust of compressed air that torpedoed men's and woman's hats without warning. The attraction, which usually took a half an hour to get through, concluded on a seventy foot maple slide.

A larger picnic area, supplementing the one provided in the center of the roller coaster, was added along the pier's southeast corner. Rows of tables were shaded by a large 40 x 100 foot redwood lathed pergola. Picnickers could use its electric stoves free of charge.

The beginning of the pier's summer season featured Professor Caesare La Monica and his Royal Italian Band. They performed concerts to large enthusiastic crowds at

View shows the Blue Streak Racer, Aeroscope, picnic area, and Hippodrome at the Looff Pier; 1917.

Fishing on the Municipal Pier; 1920.

the new pier bandstand adjacent to the Promenade. The pier's 12% incline entrance opposite the bandstand enabled Looff to build rows of tiered seats that could accommodate 1600 people. The pier's buildings behind provided both shelter from the wind and afternoon shade. After the Royal Italian Band performed their last concert on June 29, 1917, the local businessmen demanded music everyday because it was good for business. They filed a petition with the city Commissioners asking that the city's municipal band be stationed on the Looff Pier half time and play alternate days at Ocean Park.

The city government as usual stalled on the issue of providing a municipal band for the Looff Pier. Two weeks latter the businessmen contributed $1600 to hire the Santa Monica Ladies Symphony Orchestra to play for the following eight weeks.

Fourth of July weekend brought the largest crowd ever to visit the Santa Monica Bay district; over 100,000 people. The Pacific Electric ran three car trains from Los Angeles at three minute intervals, while others arrived in a steady stream of 20,000 automobiles along Pico and Santa Monica Boulevards.

As far as the eye could see, the beach was black with people and the Ocean Front Walk was a mass of surging humanity. 60,000 bathers used the area's four bathhouses. The hotels were full and also every rooming houses and apartment in the area. Since many had no place to stay, Santa Monica and Venice permitted people to sleep on the beach under police protection.

On September 13, 1917, Charles Looff and his sons incorporated the 'Santa Monica Pleasure Pier' under the state laws of California. The corporation was capitalized at $600,000 with 6000 shares of stock divided equally between common and preferred. Technically the family transferred or sold their Looff Pier property to the new corporation in exchange for 2250 preferred and 1750 common shares of stock, thus retaining a 75% stake in the pier.

In mid January 1918 the corporation advertised the sale of 750 shares of preferred stock at $100 per share. The stock prospectus outlined numerous improvements on the pier. There would be a ballroom accommodating 500 people at the extreme seaward end of the pier. It would be a replica of the famous Atlantic City, N.J. resort palace Terpsichore, 110 foot wide x 170 foot long. A theater building with a seating capacity of 1000 would be built east of it that could be used for moving pictures, light operas and popular comedies or dramas. Its auditorium could also double as a convention hall. Plans also

The 'Red Car' trolley station near the Looff Pier. 1919

called for a restaurant building, a shooting gallery building, and a fresh water fire system to supplement the salt water system previously installed.

It was fitting, when Santa Monica voted in December 1918 for Prohibition of alcoholic beverages, that the pier required no changes since drinking and gambling were never allowed. In fact, it pleased the town that the Looff Pier was a resort of character and refinement lacking the 'honky-tonk' ribaldry that characterized many other seaside resorts. It gave crowds of pleasure seekers value for their dollar, and clean wholesome entertainment.

The initial $75,000 raised from the sale of stock was used to build a first class restaurant, 40 feet wide x 80 feet deep, on the seaward side of the bowling pavilion. It had a huge banquet room on the second floor suited for clubs, lodges and business organizations. Construction began in late February, time enough to finish for the Christian Endeavor Convention on March 15th.

The city, meanwhile, encountered some safety problems with their Municipal Pier. One of the concrete pilings broke off in March and the deck nearby sunk several inches. However, the pier was declared safe after a diver from San Pedro inspected each of the pilings.

The local businessmen met in May to hear a presentation of future Looff Pier plans. Arthur Looff, president and general manager of the Santa Monica Pleasure Pier Corporation, announced that they had already spent $300,000 and wanted to complete the pier's attractions by the end of the year.

The Beach Marine Band under the direction of Signor Chiaffarelli was hired for the summer. The $4000 raised by the Santa Monica Beach Association was matched by the City Council. The twenty five member band opened at the pier's bandstand on June 15th.

While everyone was optimistic in having a record summer season, things were not well within the Looff family. Charles Looff, who had been in failing health for several months, died at his home in Long Beach on Saturday July 1, 1918. He was 66 years old. All the attractions on the pier closed until after the funeral the following Wednesday. The pier's future plans were put on hold.

CHAPTER 3

Pier Expansion and Rebuilding (1919-1928)

The United States' triumph in World War I brought a spirit of infectious patriotism to the nation. Santa Monica was no exception. When the Pacific Fleet visited Santa Monica Bay on the weekend of August 16-17, 1919, thousands came to the area's three large amusement piers to board navy transports bound for tours of the fleet.

It was a large fleet that anchored in the bay. The key ships included the U.S.S. New Jersey, Virginia, Texas, North Carolina, Arkansas, Nebraska, and the flagship New Mexico. The battleship Texas, the supply ship Prairie, destroyers Wicks, Woosley, Anthony, and Sprotsum anchored directly off the Santa Monica Pier.

A large crowd, awaiting transport to the fleet, had gathered at the end of the Municipal Pier on Sunday afternoon when the north side at the end of the pier suddenly trembled, groaned and slowly slumped seaward. Within seconds it settled two feet lower than the main deck. Women screamed and scores began to panic. Mayor Berkley, who was on the pier at the time, tried to reassure those involved that there was no danger of the pier's collapse. The police moved quickly to evacuate the pier. Those already on the battleship were returned to Venice's Windward Pier.

W. H. Carter, commissioner of public works, made an immediate statement to the press that he thought the pier had been damaged several years earlier when wreckage from the Long Wharf battered the end of the pier. He also felt that the unusual weight of the spectators didn't help. Carter, declaring the pier unsafe and the city liable if anyone were hurt, ordered the pier closed on Sept 4, 1919 for at least sixty days while it was thoroughly examined by engineers.

In early November, the engineers condemned the Municipal Pier. They feared it could collapse at any time. Their report showed that sixty piles were rusted in their reinforcements, six were utterly gone, ninety one were cracked above the water line, and thirty cracked below the water line. The problem was that the contractor ten years previously mixed the concrete improperly. His mistake was that he used beach sand in the mix that proved to be too permeable. Salt water slowly seeped in and rusted the reinforcing rods that then swelled and cracked the piles. Also heavy ground swells during construction cracked several of the piles.

The Santa Monica Amusement Company bought the Looff Pier in late 1923 and constructed the Whirlwind Dipper roller coaster in March 1924. The sign on the coaster announced the La Monica Ballroom was under construction. It would replace the Palisades Dance Pavilion that appears in the distance in the center of this photo.

Engineers estimated that it would cost $200,000 to replace the damaged structure with a similar constructed concrete pier. However, it would only cost $72,000 if they salvaged the pier's deck and replaced the pier's pilings and struts with wood. They warned the city that a delay in replacing the pier was dangerous because a severe winter storm could cause the pier to collapse.

Mayor Berkley used scare tactics with the voting public who would have to approve $75,000 in bonds in the December election. He stressed that if disaster struck and the pier collapsed, the city's sewage would flow directly into the ocean and immediately ashore. Disease and possibly death might be a possibility. The worried voters overwhelmingly approved the bonds; 2042 to 599.

Contractors were asked to submit bids to rebuild the pier, but when they were opened on February 26, 1920, all exceeded the amount of the bonds. Bids ranged from $77,000 to $81,000. Worse yet, none of the banks elected to bid on buying the pier bonds. It wasn't because of Santa Monica's credit rating or even low interest rates. Bonds were just temporarily out of favor.

Commissioner Carter of the Department of Public Works suggested that the city engineers rebuild the Municipal Pier. That way they would save on the contractor's profit and come within their budget of $75,000. The City Council, after considerable discussion at their March 7th meeting, decided to allow the Department of Public Works to take charge of the pier's reconstruction. The work would be done under the supervision of Leeds and Barnard, an engineering firm.

By mid March Santa Monica's banks had bought the entire bond issue and the city was ready to begin construction. They ordered 477 creosated piles each 35 to 75 feet long to replace the concrete ones. Since they knew it would take thirty to fifty days to receive them, they borrowed piles from the Flood Control Commission.

The city started work on the pier when the borrowed piles arrived on March 30, 1920. The city's engineers used a pile driver rented from the Looff Pier company at a nominal fee. Their greatest difficulty was the removal of the existing concrete pilings. Many had to be blasted free.

Two loads of creosated pilings arrived by steamer from Washington on April 16, 1920. They were shipped by Pacific Electric rail from Redondo Beach. By May 21st all the material was on hand and eighty piles had been driven through holes cut into the concrete deck. Work was going much slower than expected. They had 320 piles to go.

Work proceeded through June and July at a rate of five piles per day. The concrete holes in the pier platform were cemented over as the work progressed. By mid August the pier was unofficially open to the first `L' to enable automobiles to park on the Looff side of the pier. The city predicted the pier would be completed within a month.

But as the engineers got further out on the pier into deeper water, it became more and more difficult to remove the old pilings. The last wood pile wasn't driven until November 16, 1920. The pile driver was then removed but there was still a considerable amount of work to complete. The pier officially opened without fanfare on January 19, 1921. The total cost of the project was $60,000, a considerable savings over the contractors' original bids.

The popularity of Santa Monica Bay's amusement piers began to wane at the beginning of 1920s. Radio, motion pictures and the widespread ownership of automobiles began to compete for the public's entertainment dollars. The need to revitalize the piers and offer the public new thrills and attractions offered both opportunity yet intense competition among Venice's, Ocean Park's and Santa Monica's amusement piers.

Cutthroat competition began in 1920 when Ernest Pickering doubled the size of his Ocean Park Pier, a 200,000 square foot expansion. He rebuilt and enlarged the pier's dance hall and added eight new amusement rides including a new racing roller coaster. The Kinney Company, in answer to the competition, upgraded their Venice Pier with a new roller coaster and several other attractions, but then faced disaster when their pier was destroyed by fire five days before Christmas.

The elimination of the Venice Pier from the competition, at least until it was rebuilt for the summer 1921 season, convinced several businessmen to try to negotiate a lease with the Looff family to build additional attractions. The Looff Pier at that time was a rather unexciting place because the family's dream of making their pier a modern amusement center failed with the death of Charles Looff in 1918.

The Looff family agreed that their pier needed a dance pavilion and entered into a lease agreement with Cramer and Reed. The men received a building permit in February 1921 for a $12,000 structure, 110 feet wide by 60 feet deep with a 40 x 80 foot maple dance floor. It was to be the first section of a $75,000 dance building on the site specified on Looff's original plans. The completed building's architectural style would be oriental with turrets and towers.

The Palisades Pavilion dance hall opened Saturday June 4, 1921. It was managed by P.A. Bishop who had operated Abbot Kinney's Venice Pier Dance Hall before the disastrous fire. Silvey's Orchestra featuring Frank Lewis, Harry Rowe, Bernard Saenz, and Chadwick Silvey entertained dancers Friday and Saturday evenings and on Sunday afternoons.

During the following year there was talk about extending the Municipal Pier another thousand feet to accommodate more fishermen, and the possibility of constructing a large harbor. Speakers at a dinner of the Greater Santa Monica Club at the Sunset Inn on June 9, 1922 discussed the proposed harbor. Five hundred diners, representing all the bay cities, listened to Jack Davis of Douglas Aircraft Company explain that his company was building torpedo sea planes for the government and they needed a protected harbor for practice. They hoped to interest the federal government in funding Santa Monica's harbor.

Commodore Soiland of the Southern California Yachting Association said,"a safe anchorage in the Santa Monica Bay will make it the haven of the yachting fleet on the Pacific, if not the world." The yachting clubs agreed. The harbor would draw yachtsmen and pleasure craft from all over Southern California. But it was going to take a lot of planning and work to convince the federal government that building a harbor in Santa Monica would be practical and beneficial.

Only a few scattered events in the early 20's drew crowds to the Looff Pier. There was the 1921 mid winter expo and carnival that featured an aerial circus, huge electrical displays and an auto show, and a weekend in 1922 when Ted Miller the star rider of the L.A. Motorcycle jumped from the pier into the ocean. Unfortunately most events like the annual picnic held each February were quiet affairs. The 1923 event attracted ten thousand people who came for a free lunch. They were served from several hundred picnic tables loaded with food. Children were treated to free amusement rides that day.

Santa Monica's business people, after observing the Looff family's disinterest to add new pier attractions over the previous five years, gave a sigh of relief when it was announced on Feb 26, 1923 that they would sell their pier and that the papers were in escrow. A group headed by H.T. Johnson of Riverside and Capt. J.T. Denson of Los Angeles planned to invest $150,000 before the summer season. They planned to erect a dance pavilion to compete with the Rendezvous Ballroom that was under construction at the Crystal Pier at Hollister Street. They

View of the Municipal and La Monica Piers in 1924 shows the La Monica Ballroom at the west end of the pier and the Whirlwind Dipper roller coaster behind the carousel building.

The 80 foot high Whirlwind Dipper roller coaster's track was outlined by thousands of lights at night. The coaster, a Prior & Church 'bobs' design, had tight twisting turns along 3300 feet of track that made it one of the most exciting rides in Southern California.

Aerial view of the La Monica Pier in the summer of 1924. The enormous La Monica Ballroom is in the foreground and the banquet hall next to the billiard's building hadn't been moved yet to its new location next to the ballroom.

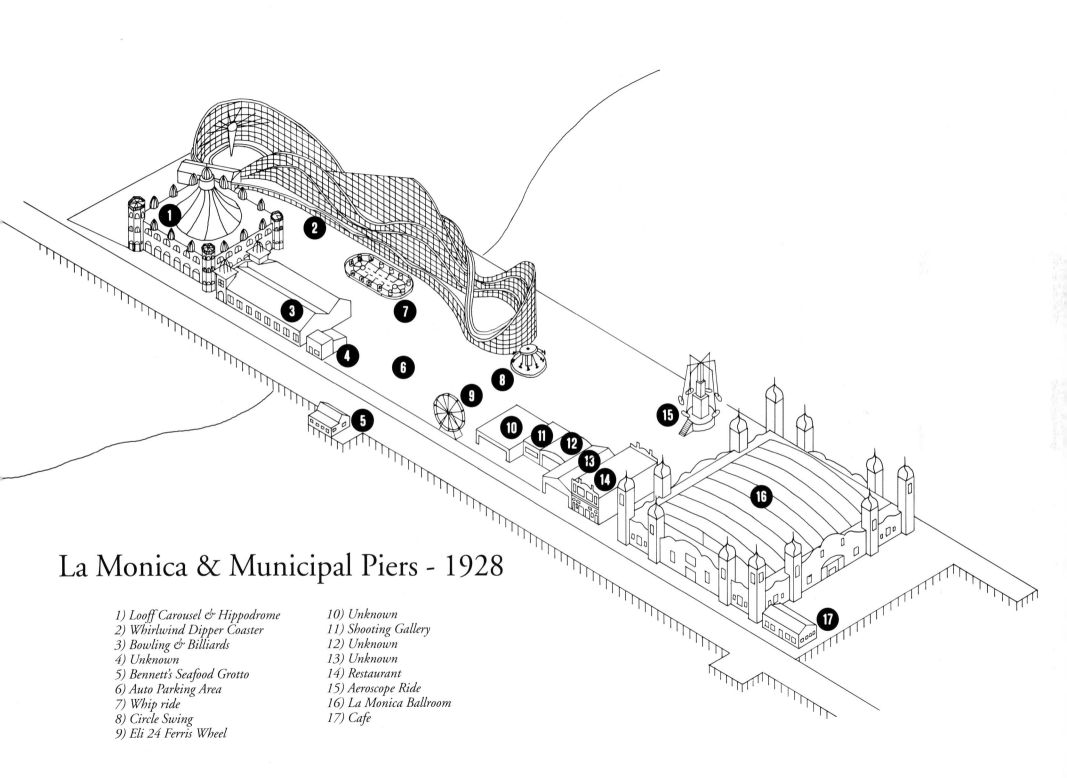

La Monica & Municipal Piers - 1928

1) Looff Carousel & Hippodrome
2) Whirlwind Dipper Coaster
3) Bowling & Billiards
4) Unknown
5) Bennett's Seafood Grotto
6) Auto Parking Area
7) Whip ride
8) Circle Swing
9) Eli 24 Ferris Wheel
10) Unknown
11) Shooting Gallery
12) Unknown
13) Unknown
14) Restaurant
15) Aeroscope Ride
16) La Monica Ballroom
17) Cafe

The La Monica Ballroom was the largest ballroom on the west coast. It's 15,000 square foot dance floor could accommodate 5000 dancers. The building's Spanish stucco exterior was crowned with a dozen towering minarets that were lit up at night. The Aeroscope ride was moved west of the roller coaster and raised on a pedestal.

also planned to extend the pier seaward another 300 feet and replace all the smaller buildings on the pier with larger ones. Unfortunately the deal fell through.

Finally, in mid September a syndicate headed by E.B. Conliss, D.B. Pascoe and C.D. Terry, all local businessmen, made an offer to the Looff estate that was accepted. The family owned 85% of the Santa Monica Pleasure Pier Corporation and they needed to invest their money in Santa Cruz, a more profitable California beach resort that was being expanded. The sale price of the pier exceeded $200,000.

The syndicate's Santa Monica Amusement Company had ambitious plans. First, they planned to lengthen the pier 325 feet out to the 1050 foot limit allowed by the pier franchise. This additional space would be used to erect the finest ballroom on the coast and additional parking for its patrons. A promenade would be built down the center of the pier leading directly to the dance pavilion. Next, they planned to remove all the concessions fronting the Ocean Front Promenade and rearrange several of the buildings on the pier. Frank Prior and Fred Church, Venice's famed roller coaster builders, were commissioned to design a superlative $75,000 twister coaster to replace the old Blue Streak Racer. Arthur Looff, who was hired as a consultant by the new pier corporation would supervise its construction. They also planned to concrete the pier's surface and install new pier lighting. They optimistically predicted that everything would be ready in time for the 1924 summer season.

E.B. Conliss assured the public that they would try to keep the pier's tradition of having quality amusements intact, and that they were retaining Kramer at his present capacity as pier manager. "We will endeavor to keep the pier free from rowdyism, but of course we can't keep the rowdy element out altogether."

The eighty foot high Whirlwind Dipper roller coaster opened on Sunday March 30, 1924 after six years of amusement inactivity. Mayor Steele was present at the opening ceremony to handle the brakes for the first car full of excited children. It was a thrilling ride that plunged down deep dips and up tightly banked turns along 3300 feet of track in an elongated pattern that featured a crossover reversing loop on one end.

The initial eighty foot drop, that left passenger's stomachs hanging as they hung onto the restraining bar with clenched fists, plunged into relative darkness as it raced through several layers of super structure. It then led upwards into a tightly banked hill that hurled passengers across the seat and pressed them tightly against each

other and the side of the car's upholstered seats. Before they could catch their breaths their car was hurtling downward then upwards again as the tracks crossed over the bottom part of the coaster's first drop. The ninety second ride, that continued up and down a dozen additional hills, subjected riders to a continuous series of accelerations, decelerations, jolts, and bounces. It was a very rough ride that gave everyone their money's worth. Naturally there were long lines all day.

The Whirlwind Dipper was a 'Bobs' design, short for bob sled, that Fred Church had perfected first on the Venice Pier then refined in his Ocean Park Pier designs. His newly patented cars with three point suspension and a shorter wheel base enabled the cars to negotiate the banked sharper turns that he favored. Each of the articulated cars, except for the first, had two wheels and were connected to each other by a ball and socket point. This allowed Church to design fast but compact roller coasters especially suited for the limited space on amusement piers. The Whirlwind Dipper was only 600 feet long by 115 feet wide at the ends, and 75 feet wide along the center.

The pier's reconfiguration continued during April and May. The Aeroscope ride was moved seaward of the coaster and installed on a new platform that lifted the flying boats higher off the ground. Designs were drawn for a new fun house and the building that housed the restaurant and banquet hall was scheduled to be moved next to the proposed dance hall.

The pier's owners interviewed numerous architects and selected T.H. Eslick to design the La Monica Ballroom and supervise its construction. He had achieved international fame in designing amusement palaces worldwide. Since the building would be the largest ballroom on the west coast, Eslick had to sink extra strength pilings down to bedrock to support its weight. He choose a Spanish theme for the La Monica's exterior and a modified French Renaissance motif for the interior of the huge 227 x 180 foot building. To add grace to the building, the ballroom's gray Spanish stucco exterior was crowned with a dozen towering minarets, each was twelve feet square and rising fifteen feet to twenty feet above the roof line. The minaret's caps were outlined with hundreds of lights at night.

The La Monica's interior was ingeniously designed to handle 5000 patrons at a time. The architect's simple yet perfect system of checking wraps, many spacious entrances to the dance floor, numerous ticket booths, a beautiful promenade and a mezzanine balcony furnished

with upholstery chairs and doge divans gave everyone a pleasant experience. Refreshments were available at the La Monica Fountain and Cafe located on the east side of the mezzanine level.

The ballroom's 15,000 square foot hard maple floor had beautiful inlaid patterns to break the monotony of its immense surface. Thirty-six thousand strips of maple in ten foot lengths were used to achieve the effect. Beneath it was a 'spring floor' made by layering the dance floor on a especially constructed subfloor.

Thirty six bell shaped transparent chandeliers were suspended from the ballroom ceiling by gold ropes. The wall decorations, painted by Russian artists, depicted a submarine garden. The effect gave patrons the illusion of dancing on coral. The final cost of the building exceeded $150,000.

The La Monica Ballroom opened with great fanfare on Wednesday evening July 23, 1924 at 7:30 PM. The wealthy, the famous, and numerous Hollywood silent screen stars arrived in limousines to attend the dedication of the structure by Mayor John C. Steele and his fellow Commissioners. It was like a movie premier with 25,000 curious citizens lining the pier to watch the festivities. Most of the people ventured inside sometime throughout the evening to dance to the sounds of the twenty member La Monica Orchestra. Don Clark, its director, had come directly from Paul Whiteman's Orchestra in New York City.

Customers, who bought dance tickets for a dime, danced the Charleston, fox trot, waltz, and pivoting, a dance where the couple turned continuously as they moved rapidly around the dance floor. At the end of each five minute dance, attendants used a big long rope to herd the couples off the dance floor and keep them separate from the new group coming onto the floor. Single women would watch from the side until an eligible male would ask them to dance. Couples, who usually came together, traditionally occupied the loges.

Roy Randolf operated his La Monica School for Dancing within the building. He offered classes primarily for adults in all aspects of ballroom dancing. In the late fall he staged a series of free Saturday matinees by and for children. Each week he featured a session devoted to folk and old fashioned dances of a particular country like Spain, Russia, China or Japan.

While the Santa Monica Amusement Company's initial success was attributed to the opening of the La Monica Ballroom and the Whirlwind Dipper coaster, it also benefited from the fire that totally destroyed Ocean Park's

Thirty young women competed in the 1926 American Legion Beach Post #123 sponsored beauty contest on the La Monica Pier during their annual summer Interpost Water Carnival and Mardi Gras.

The Rendezvous Ballroom on the Crystal Pier was located at Hollister Street; 1924.

Dancing in the La Monica Ballroom.

competing amusement zone in January 1924 and the growth of Santa Monica's nearby beach clubs. The Santa Monica Athletic Club approximately half mile north of the pier debuted in 1922. It was followed in 1923 by The Beach Club and the Santa Monica Swimming Clubs that were built side by side. These clubs provided a steady stream of wealthy clientele who would patronize the pier's amusements and dance hall.

In December Jack and Tilford Harter of the H & H Holding Company announced plans to build their two million dollar Casa del Mar beach club on the ocean front at Pico Boulevard. An eighty foot wide, 645 foot long pier in conjunction with the project would be built directly in front of the club. They obtained the Pico Pier franchise from the city in February 1925 for $500 and payment of 2% of the gross revenue after five years. The company expected to invest $750,000.

The growth of the Santa Monica Municipal Pier's fishing industry began to blossom in the mid 1920's. While there had been live bait boats like Mel Sheares' `Ursula' that serviced the pier as early as 1920, fishermen could only fish from the pier. Then in late 1921, Captain T.J. Morris began operating the first fishing excursion boats.

In 1925 Morris became head of a $75,000 corporation named Morris Pleasure Fishing Company. His operation had expanded to five boats; the Palisades that accommodated 75 fishermen, the Ameco (50 fishermen) and the Wiko (50 fishermen). The Myle and Lark were charter fishing boats that cruised for rock bass, barracuda, and yellowtail. In addition, he operated the fishing barge Norwahl that was anchored several hundred yards out from the pier. His smaller boats were used as water taxis to transport fishermen to the barge.

Morris had friendly competition on the pier. A.A. Hernage operated two fishing boats, the Colleen and Freedom from the same landing. The Owl Boat Company, which was active from 1926 until 1933 operated four day boats; the Guilio, Cesar, Virginia and Kitty A. By 1928, the three fishing operators had expanded their barge fleet to four; the Fox, Minnie A Caine, Charlie Brown and Norwahl.

New ticket booths for the fishing boat operators were built in 1925 at the municipal pier's second `T'. The old ticket booth at the winch house was removed for more room to load boats. F.S. Volk, the proprietor of the tackle and bait house also made improvements.

At the end of March 1925, the Southern California Steamship Company applied to the city to land their 660 passenger steamer `Long Beach' at the Municipal Pier.

The ship, which was equipped with a big ballroom, was to be part of a round trip excursion from Los Angeles via Long Beach and Santa Monica. Passengers would travel to Long Beach by rail, to Santa Monica by ship and back to Los Angeles by rail.

The most ambitious plan of the time was the Santa Monica Amusement Company's May 9, 1925 announcement that it was going to apply for a franchise to build a 500 foot wide, 900 foot long reinforced concrete amusement pier to connect with the north side of the Municipal Pier. The $5,000,000 project would take two years to build, but portions would be open in time for the 1926 summer season.

The pier's centerpiece would be an open air stadium over the Pacific that would seat 15,000 for orchestral concerts. There would be an aquatic hippodrome featuring a large swimming lake and an accompanying bath house for changing clothes. Amusements would include a fun house, a mountain slide, elephant house, shoot-the-shoots and ice skating rink. Plans also included a large cafe and a thousand feet of store frontage in a large shopping arcade. A huge million dollar hotel and garage space for 2000 cars would occupy the pier's inland end. The company in June ran an advertisement asking Santa Monicans to support a project that would put their city on the map.

The company's La Monica Ballroom continued to do fabulous business. Guest orchestras led by Paul Whiteman and Glen Oswald appeared throughout the spring and summer seasons. The La Monica Ballroom Orchestra directed by Carol Laughner was hired for the 1925-26 winter session. The east coast band was unique in that all its members could sing like a glee club. They were on hand when Hearst's Los Angeles Examiner sponsored its first dance contest. The newspaper offered a $5000 prize to the best couple who danced the Charleston.

One of the La Monica's most exciting nights was the Friday before Halloween 1925 when the ballroom was almost robbed. It started when four young men driving a car with red wheels held up the Montana Bus Lines office. The police set up a dragnet and located the car in the La Monica parking lot on the pier. Police headquarters telephoned Lincoln Hart, the ballroom's manager, to inform him that the dance hall was in danger of being robbed. He was advised that the police were on their way and to close if possible.

Plain-clothes men arrived shortly afterwards to round up the bandits. The manager opened up the arsenal and issued pistols to his responsible help. The night watch-

The three large beach clubs built in the mid-1920's south of the pier were from left to right in this photo; the Breakers, Edgewater and Casa del Mar.

Motion picture companies filmed numerous silent films along Santa Monica's beaches during the 1920's; 1927.

The Barnes Aerial Circus performed aerial feats as they flew between the Venice and Santa Monica Piers. The Ocean Park Pier is seen below in this 1922 photograph. (opposite page)

man had palsy so instead he was given a cutlass. Each man was responsible for guarding a ticket booth. The police arrived in force shortly afterwards. They even brought a shotgun squad for backup. For the next hour the La Monica was better guarded than the U. S. Mint.

The La Monica's orchestra began playing `Home Sweet Home', a piece traditionally used to signify the evening's end. But by then it was a well known fact that the La Monica was infested by bandits, and all the dancers were sticking around to see the desperadoes. Many women shivered with delight when they thought that they might have danced with a real bandit.

By the time all the dancers filed out, the four men who had driven the car with the red wheels had reached their vehicle and climbed in. The police shouting "Thar they are" and "Go git em men," closed in. The youthful dancers just looked up and laughed. That disconcerted everyone. Garfield Leon, Hart's assistant manager, explained that the young men were his friends and frequented the dance hall often.

On Monday February 1, 1926 waves from a huge mid Pacific storm began to threaten the Santa Monica Bay piers. The waves built up throughout the day until they were breaking during the night atop a fifteen foot high building at the end of Ocean Park's pier. The landing stage at the end of Santa Monica's Municipal Pier soon crumbled under the onslaught of the highest breakers since 1916.

The storm continued throughout the following day as the giant waves began pulling up pilings by their roots and hammering the standing timbers into kindling wood. The night watchman notified the owners that the dance hall's floor was buckling. Workers arrived immediately after midnight to remove everything of value including a $2000 grand piano. Even boats that had been dragged onto the pier for safety were taken off the pier to shore.

Word spread quickly throughout the city that the pier's collapse was imminent. Thousands swarmed the ocean front and atop the palisades to watch for the enormous wave that would send the La Monica to its doom. Police had to establish fire lines to protect the sightseers from danger. People watched in awe as wave after wave hurled tons of water against the few remaining pilings supporting the building. The structure shook with each blow, and the pier groaned as if it were about to break in two. If the La Monica fell into the sea it would mean an uninsured loss of $300,000. And if it took the entire Municipal Pier with it and broke the sewer pipes leading to the ocean, the loss would soar to $750,000.

Spectators gather on February 3, 1926 to watch the imminent destruction of the pier by waves from a huge storm.

Enormous waves from a February 3, 1926 storm nearly destroy the pilings beneath the La Monica Ballroom. When high tide crested that afternoon, only one-third of the pilings necessary to support its weight remained. (opposite page)

High tide peaked shortly after noon on Wednesday February 3rd. William Murdoch, a noted construction engineer, predicted that if the structure could survive until 1 P.M. that day, it would survive. By then it was supported by less than two thirds of the pilings necessary to support its enormous weight.

When the storm subsided slightly later that day, construction workers found the ballroom floor buckled beyond repair. It had sunk three feet on the west side near the orchestra pit. The three principal owners were making determined plans to save the ballroom, but they were philosophical about the outcome. They bought pilings to shore up the structure and ordered workmen to add supports to the trusses as soon as it was safe to work.

Reconstruction began on February 5th. Workers tore a hole into the side of the ballroom and moved a heavy pile driver inside. They began driving the sixty eight needed piles by 10 A.M. They hired Arthur Looff as a consultant. He suggested that for added safety and to strengthen the pier, that they concrete the pier deck adjoining the La Monica. The owners predicted that they would be open in about thirty days.

The owners blamed the city for the damage. They claimed loose pilings from the municipal boat landing did most of the damage because the pier dock was not fastened to the main pier properly. The city side stepped the allegations by saying that they weren't responsible for the storm.

The La Monica's interior was restored with loving care. The owners employed one hundred local artisans and construction workers. A.B. Rice, the famed dance floor builder laid down the new dance floor. The ballroom's decorations were the conception of the Russian artist V. Ulianoff and his partner John Thackento who painted the unusual motif, a mixture of Oriental, Russian and barbaric art. They used pale tints to blend in quietly with the lights and decorative schemes.

Thousands including numerous Hollywood celebrities attended the La Monica's gala reopening on March 25, 1926. Sally Rand, Follies girl and movie actress danced the Charleston and demonstrated various steps of the latest dance craze.

The winter storm season wasn't over yet. On April 8th high seas, some say worse than the awesome February storm, tore the fishing fleet loose from their moorings near the Municipal Pier. Captain T.J. Morris, Paul Brooks and Lee Gregory tried to prevent a floundering launch, the "W.K." from wrecking the Municipal Pier. They were washed overboard and the unattended boat was later

Palisades
Santa Monica Bay

A seaside colony of movie star homes was located north of the pier. Marion Davies $7 million dollar estate is in the foreground. The Gables Beach Club with the its spires was on the beach side at the bottom of the California Incline. The narrow coast road predated the Roosevelt Highway; 1924.

Workers put finishing touches on the lifeguard tower in front of the Deauville Club; 1926.

dashed to pieces south of the pier in front of the Edgewater Club. When Charles Trecy and Jack Dugan tried to rescue the drowning men, their small skiff was capsized by a huge breaker. Lifeguards rescued them but were unable to help the three fishermen who were swept south under the Crystal Pier and crushed against its pilings. Morris' body was found a week later offshore in El Segundo.

These two destructive storms prompted the Greater Santa Monica Club to revive their harbor plan to protect the pier. They hired Taggart Aston as a consulting engineer to prepare tentative plans. His plans were presented to members of the club and to Howard B. Carter, city engineer at their May 5th meeting.

The $1,750,000 project called for a 195 acre harbor between the Municipal Pier and the Crystal Pier at Hollister. The area, suitable for boating and a seaplane base, would be protected by a 5850 foot long breakwater wall built 2100 feet offshore in 23 feet deep water. The seawall would be sixty feet wide at its base.

A 55 acre waterfront park would be reclaimed from the sea by filling it in with rocks and earth dredged from the bottom of the sea. Most of the area would be used for recreational purposes such as docks for a small boat harbor, yachting club houses, an open-air swimming pool, and a pier at the foot of Pico Boulevard. The plans were given to the City Council in hopes that the city would float a $2,000,000 bond issue to defray construction expenses.

The previous winter's near disaster put the Santa Monica Amusement Company's future expansion plans on hold. Much of the company's profit from the first season, more than $75,000 went into rebuilding the La Monica Ballroom.

Then a serious accident that occurred on the Whirlwind Dipper roller coaster on May 23, 1926 rattled the pier's owners. Nineteen year old Diana Hamilton leaped from the car while it was on a turn and was taken to the hospital in serious condition. Her arm was later amputated and the three men that she was with were sought by the police.

A month later she sued the Whirlwind Dipper Corporation, whose stock was largely owned by the Santa Monica Amusement Company, for $75,000. She testified that the ride operator allowed three in a seat that was designed for two. The police took statements from her three companions who had all been drinking. They said Miss Hamilton became hysterical during the ride, stood up and threatened to leap from the car. She claimed that she

was thrown from the car as it rounded a turn. The judge ruled that, while the company shouldn't have allowed drunken customers on the ride, the coaster wasn't mechanically at fault.

Meanwhile the Greater Santa Monica Club's harbor plan generated a considerable amount of discussion that summer. The City Council proposed that a committee of two hundred be formed to stir up enthusiasm for the project. A petition placed in circulation in late August requested that the City Council take preliminary steps for a breakwater.

One group seriously proposed to finance the harbor by selling $1000 memberships in a breakwater club that would encompass all the beach clubs. Of course the promoters would get a 20% commission. That proposal stirred up a hornet's nest of opposition. The first to oppose it was Taggart Aston, the harbor's designer. He was adamantly against a community owned breakwater and he warned promoters not to expect the federal government to give them any support. R.J. Conners, the Edgewater Club's president opposed the harbor because it would end surf bathing in front of his beach club. But to achieve peace the Breakwater Club and the various beach clubs met on Sept 14, 1926. While they couldn't decide what the breakwater should look like, they did think that building one to create a harbor would be beneficial to the community.

Santa Monica's eleven beach clubs by the summer of 1927 were becoming a major political force in matters relating to the beach front. These clubs with a membership of 25,000 and an assessed valuation of $10,000,000 extended one and half miles from Pico Boulevard to the city's northern limit. The Casa del Mar, Edgewater and Breakers were located south of the pier, while the Deauville, Sea Breeze, Miramar, Club Chateau, Wavecrest, Santa Monica Athletic, The Beach Club, and Gables were located north of the pier.

Most of the clubs had swimming pools, beach cabanas, banquet rooms and extensive social and sports programs.

The Deauville, immediately north of the pier, was one of the more elegant clubs. Its enormous gothic castle style clubhouse, surrounded by gardens and esplanades, reminded one of the French Riviera. Its Continental Room, used for dancing and dining resembled a baronial hall. Each club attracted a different type of membership. While the Del Mar drew its membership from Santa Monica's and Los Angeles' business and professional people, others like the Santa Monica Swimming Club attracted a Hollywood clientele.

Evening Outlook newsboys are treated to a day of fishing off the Santa Monica Pier; 1927.

The 'Kittie A' fishing boat was operated by the Owl Boat Company.

Many of Hollywood's celebrities lived in Santa Monica's Seaside Colony located north of the pier. Silent screen stars like Mary Pickford, Douglas Fairbanks, Harold Lloyd, Marion Davies, Norma Shearer, Max Sennett, Bebe Daniels, Owen Moore, Jack Doyle, Edmund Goulding, and Richard Barthelmess maintained elegant beach homes and gave lavish parties. So did producers Louis B. Mayer and Jesse Lasky. The largest, containing 118 rooms and 55 baths, many imported from European estates, was the Marion Davies $7 million estate. It was built for her by William Randolf Hearst in 1928.

In September 1927 the Santa Monica Amusement Company, which owned the Looff Pier and controlling interest in the La Monica Ballroom and the Whirlwind Dipper, was sold to a syndicate headed by Dr. Frank J. Wagner. This didn't affect management or operations since Wagner was one of the four previous owners. The company was valued at $500,000.

Wagner presented a plan to the City Council on February 6, 1928 for a 200 foot extension to his amusement pier. He planned to sale memberships in his Santa Monica Yacht and Motorboat Club that would be located there. The club would offer members more than one hundred motorboats, each costing $7500 that were capable of reaching speeds up to 54 MPH. To avoid the unpleasant and dangerous feature of embarking and disembarking while boats were in the water, he planned to have the club's boats parked on the pier where passengers boarded them. A crane would lift them in the boat and lower them gently down in the water for a trip to the fishing grounds or a dash around the bay.

However, the fishing interests on the Municipal Pier saw Wagner's plan aimed directly at crippling their business. Wagner claimed that his boats were for club use only and that his activities would increase the public's interest in fishing. His club would provide its members with boats similar to those used in Catalina for deep-sea fishing for swordfish, marlin, albacore, barracuda, yellowtail, and tuna. The club would also hold yacht and motor boat races.

City Council granted Dr. Wagner permission to expand the pier at their February 20, 1928 meeting. The lease gave the city 2% of the club's gross receipts and included a provision for 197 feet of free public fishing space. Wagner announced that his Santa Monica Yacht and Motorboat Club would be organized at once, and piles for his pier expansion would be driven within the next few months at a cost of $86,000. But once again plans to maximize the pier's potential were thwarted

Santa Monica Beach looking north from the Crystal Pier was packed solid with bathers and their beach umbrellas every Sunday; 1927.

The Santa Monica Pier in 1927. The banquet was moved next to the La Monica Ballroom that year. The brick building in the foreground is the Deauville Club.

when Dr. Frank Wagner, the pier's principal owner, died of a heart attack in his office on June 27, 1928. He was fifty-five years old. Construction of his pier extension was even completed a week before his death.

His widow hired Ernest Pickering to manage the pier for her. Pickering had been very active in the area since he installed his first rides on the Abbot Kinney Pier in 1909. He had owned the Pickering Pier in Ocean Park from 1919 to 1923, then moved to San Bernardino to manage Pickering Park a small amusement area. He proved to be a capable general manager.

The La Monica reopened for the 1928 season with T.S. Eslick as the new manager. Each week featured novel attractions, surprises and personal appearances. The opening night's attraction was the beautiful transcontinental horseback rider, Miss Vonceil Viking, whose horse galloped from New York City to Los Angeles in 120 days. Management held a La Monica Club night featuring old time dances staged with an old time orchestra, Carnival night on the lines of the big annual festivals in Europe, and Collegiate Night featuring college dancing and prizes for the winning contestants.

The pier's new summer attractions obtained before Dr. Wagner's death were mediocre at best. They included concessions and rides in the City of Baghdad exhibit, an Eli 24 ferris wheel operated by A.V. Johnson, and a $50,000 hand carving exhibit by Professor Sterling of New York. Hailstorm, an Indian chief was hired to demonstrate the ability of his ancestors. He performed sacred tribal dances and skillfully used his bow and arrow. Pickering, who realized the Santa Monica Amusement Company's pier need more exciting attractions, made arrangements to travel east at the end of summer season to arrange for new amusement rides.

Aerial view of the Santa Monica Pier in 1930. The Crystal Pier is the small pier beyond, and the long pier in the distance is the Ocean Park Pier.

CHAPTER 4

Santa Monica Harbor and Breakwater (1928-1941)

The business community began to support Santa Monica's growing need for a breakwater and pleasure harbor by early 1928. Santa Monica's Chamber of Commerce was the first to publicly endorse the project at their February 24, 1928 meeting. The Beverly Hills' and Los Angeles' Chamber of Commerces followed a month later. In early April the Santa Monica group approached the Beverly Hills group about the possibility of forming a large assessment district to finance a breakwater since Santa Monica alone couldn't finance the project. By summer Breakwater officials reported that there was solid support among the public in several westside communities for a harbor and breakwater to be located in the vicinity of Santa Monica.

Creating the finest aquatic playground in the world required construction of a three mile long breakwater, 3500 feet offshore, from Santa Ynez Canyon to a point five blocks south of San Vincente Boulevard. Since the breakwater would cost a million dollars per mile, it was apparent that only a group of communities pooling their resources could finance the project. The formation of a harbor district to finance the breakwater meant that new state legislation would be required. State Senator Charles Lyon and State Assemblyman Walter Little submitted bill, #797, which would form an assessment district stretching inland to Western Avenue and south to Pico Boulevard. This would include the communities of Beverly Hills, Westwood and Hollywood. Bonds for the proposed project would then require a vote of the people within the district.

The Senate unanimously passed the bill on May 2, 1929 but there was a battle in the State Assembly. It finally passed on May 9th by a landslide vote of 51 to 1. It only needed Governor C.C. Young's signature for the bill to become law.

Opposition to the proposed harbor surfaced first in the Hearst newspapers, and to a lesser extent in the Los Angeles Times. Both owners were against the project because of their struggle with Alphonzo Bell, a large Los Angeles land owner. They feared out of jealousy that he might want to use the harbor for commercial purposes. The Los Angeles Playground Commission, whose members were opposed to any piers or breakwaters in Santa Monica Bay, objected too.

Workers unloading a large eight ton cap stone from a barge during construction of the breakwater wall; 1934.

It required 220,000 tons of rock transported from a quarry on Catalina Island to build the 2000 foot long breakwater. The 200 foot long pier extension that juts from the end of the pier was built by the Santa Monica Harbor Company in 1930.

Ten Santa Monica girls pose for a breakwater publicity photo just prior to its completion; 1934.

Governor Young was politically in a difficult position. William Randolf Hearst didn't want a harbor in Santa Monica and Young was tied hand and foot to the Hearst chariot. He knew if he signed the bill he would be crucified. A committee headed by Judge Arthur A. Weber, author of the legislation, went to Sacramento to appeal with the governor to sign the measure adopted by both houses.

But as the June 19th deadline approached, Governor Young said that his advisors felt that the bill was unconstitutional and that he feared the harbor's commercial possibilities. "The plain fact is that I do not believe that such a harbor could remain free from the commercial and disagreeable features which an expanse of water would naturally attract." He also felt that it was not fair for a mere majority of voters to place a financial burden on their district. Consequently he refused to sign the harbor bill.

The amusement pier business was competitive during the summer 1929 season. Ocean Park added a $3,000,000 five hundred foot extension to their pier, complete with a Chute-the-Chutes ride and numerous attractions. Pickering with much less capital made only minor improvements to the La Monica Pier. His aim was to attract families with children. The large Aeroscape swing was replaced with a smaller yet more exciting Captive Airplane ride. He also added a Frolic flat ride whose cars went up and down and in and out as they circled.

He offered numerous free children's activities. There was a Punch and Judy puppet show, movies, and ballroom dancing accompanied by the famous La Monica Dance Orchestra from 2-5 PM. On weekends Matt Gay, the world's highest diver, dove from a 97 foot platform into a twelve foot square tank of water.

Expositions held in the La Monica during the winter and following spring brought large crowds to the pier despite the beginning of the Depression. In November 1929, 5000 attended the opening day of an Automobile Exposition and in April 1930, 20,000 attended the Evening Outlook's three-day Household and Auto Exposition.

The sports fishing business remained viable at the beginning of the Depression. Operators kept busy transporting fishermen to four offshore barges anchored in the bay. These barges like the 76 foot Charlie Brown and 215 foot Minnie A. Caine were formerly sailing vessels with the masts removed so they wouldn't roll over in heavy seas. The larger barges had capacities of several hundred fishermen.

Regatta Week, August 5-12, 1934 marked the dedication of Santa Monica's new harbor and breakwater. Festivities included a week of yacht races.

Santa Monica's new harbor could accommodate several hundred yachts and small boats.

Paddleboard races were part of the Regatta Week festivities. (left)

On May 8, 1930 nearly one hundred fishermen were trapped on the barges when a sudden 40 MPH afternoon gale beat the seas into high waves. When the wind subsided that evening, they were rescued about 9:30 P.M. Many were badly seasick, but it could have been more serious.

A subsequent gale with twenty foot high seas on May 30th caused a major disaster on a 54 foot fishing boat with 73 aboard. The Ameco was about a mile and a half offshore at Santa Monica Canyon at 4:45 P.M. when a huge wave rolled toward the launch as it headed back to the Municipal Pier. The frightened women and children rushed to the boat's port side as the wave hit broadside. The unbalanced boat capsized immediately. Fortunately, the fishing boat Freedom was in the vicinity and rescued 35- 40 passengers. The next day the death toll was set at sixteen; three known dead and thirteen missing. All sixteen victims were later found drowned.

City officials were appalled by the apparent lack of safety regulations under which the Ameco's owners operated the boat. They revoked their franchise and in an effort to institute more stringent regulations regarding the operation of boats landing at the pier, offered the franchise to the highest bidder. Captain Olaf C. Olson, who also had a small landing on the Looff Pier, won the exclusive franchise. It brought the city about $800 per month revenue in peak season.

Olson's franchise allowed him to sublease dock space to other fishing boat operators. The Hernage family, Owl Boat Company, and Morris Pleasure Fishing run by Captain Morris's widow and brother continued to operate boats from Olson's two landings.

Charles Arnold soon joined them in late 1930, when he bought a 300 foot long, 43 foot wide all steel sailing ship called the Kinelworth. It had been used for salmon fishing in Alaska during the 20's. Since it was constructed in Scotland in 1887, Arnold renamed it the 'Star of Scotland', converted it into a fishing barge, and anchored it midway between the Santa Monica and Ocean Park piers. He operated a water taxi service to the barge.

A proposal to privately build a modest-sized harbor breakwater in front of the Municipal Pier was submitted to the City Council by Eugene Craven on June 14, 1930. His Santa Monica Harbor Company planned to construct a 2900 feet long concrete crib style breakwater beginning about 350 feet south of the pier and extending north. It would be connected by a 120 foot narrow, clearspan suspension bridge at the end of the Municipal Pier. A narrow wooden pier constructed atop the breakwater would connect to wharfs and piers suitable for docking pleasure boats on the leeward side.

Craven asked for a twenty five year franchise and offered the city 2% of the gross revenue after a period of five years. In addition, he would initially pay the city $500 annually for the use of their Municipal Pier as his entrance. This amount would rise to $750 per year after five years, then to $1000 per year after ten years. He agreed to start construction within four months of obtaining his franchise and would complete the first 1000 feet of breakwater within eighteen months. This first construction phase would cost $350,000. He offered to put up a $50,000 bond as a guarantee that he would complete the project.

The city advertised the sale of the franchise for a breakwater pier and harbor for boats to be held August 4th. There were a few protests by the Jonathan Beach Club and the Santa Monica Breakers Club who feared the loss of surf in front of their clubs, but the auction was held anyway. The sealed bid auction was won by Craven for $650.

The summer 1930 amusement season was exceptionally slow. Spending money was becoming scarce as more and more people lost their jobs. Money for new attractions was non-existent. Pickering, who had travelled East the previous fall to arrange for new attractions, cancelled everything. Business was so slow that the Santa Monica Amusement Company was in arrears on their franchise rent. They owed the city $1200. The Whirlwind Dipper Corporation went bankrupt at the end of the summer, and they tore down the roller coaster in October. The space was used to build a Tom Thumb Miniature Golf Course that was the latest fad. The courses, using playing surfaces of cotton seed hulls, were relatively inexpensive to build; about $25,000.

Worsening economic conditions affected the Santa Monica Harbor Company, too. The city began inquiring in February 1931 about the relative inactivity of the company's breakwater pier project. Craven testified that the men who backed the project had all suffered financial setbacks. The project wasn't fully capitalized and no stock had been sold. He stated that the company hoped to solve its financial problems in several weeks.

Meanwhile two contractors complained that they hadn't been paid for supplies ordered by the company for the temporary extension of the pier. One was owed about $3000 for pilings, and another $2500 for tools and other supplies.

It was becoming apparent that the only way Santa Monica would get its harbor would be through a state enabling act that would authorize its financing through a district bond issue. On May 5th the state legislature passed bill #1140. It was the same as the one vetoed by the governor the previous two years, but James Rolph Jr. was the new governor. He signed the bill on June 17, 1931 after he was convinced that local officials were serious about the project.

Santa Monica's city government moved rapidly to place the Breakwater Bond Measure before the voters. They favored a breakwater similar to the Santa Monica Harbor Company's concrete crib design. Theirs would be 2000 feet long, 2200 feet from shore and connected by a 120 foot suspension bridge from the end of the Municipal Pier. It would cost $690,000.

The bond election was set for September 11th. In a move to educate the voting public of the merits of the breakwater plan, the city prepared folders, stickers, and big posters. Fifteen billboards were erected throughout the city, and a model of the proposed harbor was placed on display on the city hall lawn. Harbor backers, confident of its passage, hoped to bid for the 1932 Olympic water contests. The city's engineer assured them that work could begin within thirty days of the election and it would provide work for 750 people, a good selling point in a city where unemployment was soaring.

Despite rising unemployment during the darkest days of the Depression, Santa Monica Pier businesses were fortunate during the 1931 summer season as crowds at the beach were larger than in the previous two years. Water temperatures hovered between a record 76 and 78 degrees Fahrenheit, only a degree or two colder than the waters off Hawaii. Hammerhead sharks were sighted in the bay for the first time. World wide weather was bizarre that summer; extreme heat and drought in North America with record rain throughout Europe. Inland Los Angeles temperatures hovered around the 100 degree mark throughout the summer, and residents headed for the beach to escape the heat. The Sunday July 26th, crowd that packed the narrow beach solid from Del Rey to the Santa Monica Pier was estimated at 450,000 people. Hundreds took a midnight swim near the pier.

On September 11, 1931 Santa Monica's voters overwhelmingly approved the Breakwater Bond Measure, 5429 to 1925. The Deauville Beach Club immediately reserved thirty boat slips. Some expected a rush of San Pedro based pleasure boats seeking anchorage in the new harbor.

The Santa Monica Amusement Company also wanted to get their property in shape for the expected Olympic visitors. Unfortunately the banks wouldn't loan them money since their pier franchise would expire in five years. In December they asked the city to extend their franchise until 1956. They felt that twenty five years would be enough to protect their investment.

Opposition to the franchise extension was led by sport fishing groups backing Captain Olaf C. Olson. Olson held an exclusive franchise on the city's Municipal Pier and wished to limit the amusement company's sports fishing facilities on the La Monica Pier. The city's engineering department was also against the extension because they didn't want their hands tied before the breakwater was completed.

Commissioner Helton met with Pickering and the company's lawyer. He blasted the pair with accusations that pier interests had for years "gotten away with murder and robbed the public." To appease him Pickering offered to give up the Santa Monica Amusement Company's interest in their fishing business that netted $2000 per year. An indecisive City Council merely postponed granting a new franchise until a later date.

It was ironic that Captain Olaf Olson's exclusive fishing franchise came under attack in January 1932 by the Owl Boat Company. Olson, who had free reign to deny landing privileges to any or all rivals, had decided not to sublease to Owl, a firm that had been in the sports fishing business on the Santa Monica Pier since 1926. The Owl Boat Company demanded that the city declare Olson's lease void. The City Council, wishing only to defend their right to grant an exclusive franchise, asked the city attorney to defend the case if it should go to court.

The city's delay in starting work on their breakwater prompted a private syndicate represented by Ralph Proctor to offer building the breakwater in exchange for a twenty five year lease. Their rental fees would be sufficient to retire the city's bonds in twenty five years and pay all interest charges. They expected to profit by selling boats and operating other harbor related activities.

The real issue was not cost but whether the harbor would be under municipal control. Commissioner Helton asserted that the cost of the breakwater would be $500,000 greater under private control than city control over the twenty five year period. He believed that the harbor would bring change to the ocean front development and the city shouldn't have its hands tied to exploit those opportunities. The City Council voted unanimously not to sell their yacht harbor to private interests.

The City Attorney meanwhile proceeded with the city's suit to cancel the Santa Monica Harbor Company's franchise. The franchise had to be cleared before the city could sell its $690,000 bonds. Negotiations had been going on since the previous November. The company originally demanded $21,000 to cover its expenses of building a 200 foot pier extension, but later lowered its demands to $8000. In April 1932, the city offered to pay $5,220.68 in an effort to settle the case out of court. This was the cost of building the extension less $1200 to tear it down. However, the company demanded an additional $1200 to pay debts for attorney fees, promotional, and other organizational costs before they would give up their franchise. They were at an impasse since Santa Monica couldn't legally pay those fees.

The state of California on April 15, 1932 gave the city the right to sue the harbor company on April 15, 1932

Actor Leo Carrillo was an avid sports fisherman. He is best known for his role as Pancho in the 50's TV series Cisco Kid.

Buster Crabbe, star of 30's movie serials Buck Rogers and Flash Gordon, was an honorary Santa Monica lifeguard; 1932

for return of its harbor franchise. While papers were been drawn up and filed, the Chamber of Commerce held a benefit to raise the $1200 to pay the company's debt. The money was placed in escrow and the city passed an ordinance to pay those funds. On May 4, 1932 the defunct firm surrendered their franchise rights for $5,220.68 plus $1200 raised by the city's business community.

City Council voted $5600 to begin preliminary work on the breakwater. A 100 foot barge owned by Robinson and Roberts of San Pedro arrived on April 30th to begin making soundings and corings of the bay. Borings at the site showed the breakwater site to be ideal. One week later City Engineer, Howard B. Carter ordered completion of the harbor plans. On June 15th the City Council ordered an ordinance authorizing the $690,000 bond issue. The city declined to advertise them until they were sure they would get a bid for their tax exempt bonds.

The breakwater's design called for 18 reinforced concrete cribs, each 111 feet long, 37 feet high, and 35 feet wide at the base. The deck, which was eight and one half feet above water, would have on the land side, a series of step-like elevations creating a marine stadium for thousands of people. 17,710 cu yds of concrete would be needed for the cribs, 6,670 cu yds for the superstructure, 991 tons of steel in the toe protection, and 1237 tons of reinforcing steel in the structure itself.

The contract and specifications covered sixty pages of single spaced type written copy. It controlled every phase of construction work. For example, it stated that the concrete must be prepared by an electrically operated mixing machine, and volcanic ash (Pozzulana) added to crystalize any free lime so the structure would be impervious to water. As the concrete was poured it specified that it must be tamped with an electric vibrator to pack it solidly in its forms, then must cure at least 28 days before it was moved.

Twenty six contractors studied the plans and the city hoped that at least six would bid. Carter estimated that the winning bid due August 12th would be under $500,000. The 5% bonds were bought by Bank of America National Trust & Savings on August 8th, so the city was confident that they could award the breakwater contract by August 15th.

Only two contractors bid on the project. Peter R. Gadd, Inc. bid $660,700 and Charles Sanborn bid $547,004.64. The Santa Monica commissioners rejected both bids as too high. At first the city offered to allow the contractors to write their own specifications and rebid, but the city attorney ruled that it was illegal to call for alternate designs.

Revised plans were drawn up that were expected to cut $80,000 from the cost of the breakwater. The cribs were more elliptical and the anchoring system changed so pilings could be driven through a collar on the outside of the base. Carter's estimate of $584,760 included a suspension bridge and mooring facilities.

One lone offer for $539,535 was made on August 31st by the Puget Sound Bridge Company of Seattle in partnership with W.F. Way of Los Angeles. The bid was accompanied by a $62,500 good faith bond issued by the American Bonding Company of Baltimore. Since the bid was $21,000 less than the estimate, the city awarded them the contract.

The contact was sent by air to the Seattle based company. Meanwhile harbor contract bonds were prepared; $134,895 for faithful performance and $269,770 for material and labor. By September 15th the prepared contract needed only Commissioner of Finance Frank Helton's signature who was vacationing at Gilman Hot Springs. A group took the papers to him and returned with them on the 17th. Puget Sound Bridge and Dredging Company had nine months to complete the breakwater once the contract was signed.

City Council approved the harbor builder's plans on September 25, 1932 as required by the contract. To avoid delay they authorized that the cribs could be cast at the contractor's San Pedro facilities instead of on Santa Monica's beach. Quiet waters were needed to cast the cribs and Santa Monica Bay was too stormy that time of year. Howard B. Carter was appointed as chief engineer in charge of supervising the contractor and the city prepared for a celebration for the arrival of the first block of the seawall on November 26th.

Plans for a breakwater fete proved to be a bit premature. The contractor encountered difficulties in driving piles down to bedrock at the graving dock. They needed to assemble a steam pile driver to complete the job. They figured that they would have the graving dock ready for pouring the first crib by the end of November but that too, proved optimistic.

The dock which was located only a few feet from the channel was over hundred feet long, forty feet wide and excavated to a point forty feet below sea level. The doors on the outer end resembled those of locks on a canal. The reinforced concrete cribs were to be poured out of the water, left to season for seven days, and later floated like a ship when the lock doors opened. They were to be towed to a safe anchorage to season for fourteen more days, then to their final position in the Santa Monica Bay.

Long Beach experienced a minor earthquake in late

December. The shifting ground along the Long Beach diversion channel raised the bottom of the graving dock as much as four feet in some places and caused water to break through and fill the enclosure. Driving another 200 piles down to bedrock took another two weeks, and then they needed to pour an eight feet thick cement flooring to counteract the earth at the bottom of the dock floor from pushing upwards. Workers didn't finish the graving dock until early February 1933.

Santa Monica's City Council took advantage of the delay at San Pedro to consider the Santa Monica Amusement Company's request to extend their franchise. Finally, after being pressured for more than a year, they agreed at their February 20, 1933 meeting to set a date for the pleasure pier franchise sale. Its terms would prohibit the operation of fishing boats or boats for hire from the pleasure pier, thus giving the city exclusive rights to supervise the revenue producing feature of harbor development.

The Santa Monica Amusement Company's winning bid of $480 on April 7, 1933 extended the lease another twenty-one years beginning June 7, 1936. For that the company agreed to pay 2% of gross receipts in return for the privilege of operating the property.

The graving dock in San Pedro was completed and W.F. Way's workers began pouring cement for the first harbor crib on Saturday Feb 25, 1933 at 4:07 A.M. The 111 foot long, 35 foot wide, 36 1/2 foot high unit was poured in one continuous session over an entire day. As the crib cement set, workers sprayed asphalt paint to retard the drying process. The pumicite in the cement mixture, used by the Italians for centuries for making cement of unusual hardness, would seal and protect more than 32 tons of welded reinforcing rods. There was a minimum of five inches of concrete between the rods and the seawater.

The first crib was floated out from the docks on March 9th and work was begun on the second crib. After it cured for two weeks it was filled partially with water until it rode low in the water and was stable for towing to Santa Monica. The crib was towed north at 2 1/2 MPH by the powerful Wrigley Tug, the Milton S. Patrick and accompanied by the escort tug Fossie. W.F. Ways' engineers and general manager as well as Norman S. Ross, Puget Sound Bridge and Dredging Company's business manager, were on board the tug.

Hundreds watched the first crib's arrival on Saturday March 26, 1933 at 2 P.M. With one tug positioned at each end of the crib, the 2000 ton concrete structure was first lined up so that it would be even with the steel tower marking the north end of the new sea wall. It was then

Delta dinghys were popular in the harbor in the late 30's. They were built by Tedford's Boat Service next to the carousel.

Santa Monica enlarged the 'T' at the end of their Municipal Pier and constructed a lower deck in 1934. The large building on the upper deck is the harbor office; 1937

The Santa Monica Municipal Lifeguard Headquarters was located in the La Monica Ballroom building beginning in 1935. The city service was formed in 1932.

moved to a point where it lined up with the center line on Colorado Avenue. After the crib was in place, it was anchored to the ocean bed with steel piling, then filled with crush rock from Catalina. Afterwards it would be capped with a reinforced concrete deck that would tie the entire wall into a unit. The first crib was actually the second from the end on the south side.

Everything was going well and the contractor expected to make up some of his lost time. They floated the second crib on March 28th and began pouring the third crib two days later. However, an April 3rd inspection of the first crib resting on the ocean floor showed a minor vertical crack on the outer side of the center section. Company engineers speculated that it was put down atop an unyielding obstruction. It would have to be raised for repairs.

A diver sent down on April 6th reported that the cracking was not caused by placing it on an obstruction as first feared, but by the action of powerful hidden currents that scoured away the sand on which it rested. The current was so strong that a trough extending 40 feet on both sides of the crib had been hollowed out, lowering the structure by three feet. A diver wearing 100 pounds of lead weights on his shoes was carried to the surface feet first. Further observations revealed that the crib wasn't sinking further and equilibrium might occur. But two days later the crib broke in the middle and was beyond repair.

The city hired D.E. Hughes, an army engineer, as a consultant to decide whether a plan could be adopted to deal with the currents, or they should abandon the crib design. He determined that there was no problem with the crib's construction, but the north-south currents were so strong that they scoured out the sand and clay beneath the unit until it cracked from its own weight. He recommended that a rock mound seawall be substituted. It would require about 200,000 tons of large rocks and could be built for about $500,000 with cheap rock available on Catalina Island.

Unfortunately with some of the money already spent, there wasn't enough money left to complete the harbor. They would have $33,719.69 left after building the rock seawall, but that wasn't enough to put a cement cap on the seawall, build a bridge to connect the seawall with the pier, and add facilities for mooring boats. The city had a difficult choice to make. They could terminate the contract with Puget Sound and call for new bids, or renegotiate the contract and hope to be credited with the $87,660.40 already paid. Termination could cost $165,000 plus the amount already paid.

Lifeguards taking their annual test; 1936.

The citizens' committee for breakwater construction asked the Council to hold the Puget Sound Company responsible. Many felt that the city should proceed with the crib design. Others felt that the city should shift to a rock wall design and pay them only an additional $480,000 to complete the entire project. The Evening Outlook newspaper hired their own consulting engineer, Major General Joseph E. Kuhn.

Criticism was especially heavy over Howard Carter's inexperience in breakwater construction and for his insistence to try an untested new design. They wanted him ousted as the city's chief engineer.

The contractor offered to complete the harbor using rock mound construction for $690,000 total. Their price included a six hundred foot extension of the city's pier to connect with the breakwater's concrete cap and parapet, and a 1600 foot long floating dock set 150 feet back from the breakwater. It could accommodate 84 yachts.

After the citizen's committee outright rejected the company's offer, on May 12th Puget Sound withdrew their proposal to build a rock mound breakwater. The committee then accused the City Council of hiding vital facts on the construction, especially the method of payment. Four days after the breakwater contract was signed, the City Council agreed to a change that paid the contractor for materials on hand before they went into the finished cribs.

The city's Commissioners and the two contractors failed to reach agreement after a series of meetings. The Puget Sound Company wanted to split the difference rather than go to court. But Edith Daniell, a Santa Monica taxpayer, was determined to prevent any compromise or change in the breakwater's design. She filed a lawsuit in Superior Court asking for an injunction to restrain the city from spending any funds for construction of a rock mound breakwater. She said that since it required maintenance to kept the seawall repaired, it would increase the city's indebtedness.

City Council, realizing that the controversy had become a political football, acted swiftly without any previous discussion at their weekly May 25, 1933 meeting. They ordered a 220,000 ton rock mound breakwater at a cost of $561,035.40. The contractor agreed to credit the city $87,660.40, part of the money spent to build the first few cribs. The Council's action left it up to the courts to decide if they had the right change the breakwater's design.

The contractor simultaneously filed a commitment to complete the pier extension for $11,122, marina for $21,378, and super structure for the breakwater for

The La Monica was used as the city's convention center from 1934-1937.

California Federation of Woman s Clubs convention in the La Monica; 1934. (opposite page top

Pier aquarium at the city's lifeguard headquarters. (opposite page bottom)

$22,125; a total of $54,624. The city would have $33,000 left after the harbor was completed.

The Breakwater Committee shifted the blame for the debacle from Carter, who they felt did the best he could considering he wasn't a marine engineer, to the city Commissioners for wasting $125,000. By changing the method of payment in the contract, they destroyed the only protection the city had in forcing the contractor to complete the breakwater.

The Puget Sound Company filed suit on June 7th for "declaratory relief" against the city of Santa Monica. The firm needed to establish the legality of the change order from City Council instructing it to build a rock mound instead of a concrete crib type breakwater. On the same day the Ocean Park Municipal League filed suit accusing the city of not opening the bids competitively for the new breakwater design.

The case was heard in Superior Court by Judge William P. Hazlett beginning on Wednesday June 14th. The harbor law suits were joined to speed decision. Daniell's suit was dismissed, and the Ocean Park Municipal League agreed to abandon theirs. On Friday, June 30, 1933 the court upheld the City Council's right to change the plans for the harbor breakwater. The judge said that the city had the legal right to require Puget Sound Company to proceed with the change order, and that the rock mound breakwater was reasonably sufficient for providing a safe anchorage for ocean going pleasure craft.

Work was scheduled to begin immediately with D.E. Hughes as the engineer in charge. A 110 foot long barge carrying 453 tons of stone quarried on Catalina arrived at 9 A.M. on July 6th. However, they didn't begin unloading the huge rocks until buoys marked the seawall's boundaries one week later. By July 21st 6000 tons of rock were in place and the northern portion of the rock wall was visible above the water.

Work progressed at a steady pace throughout the fall. The job at peak required fifty men at Santa Monica's harbor and another fifty men employed hauling rock or at the Catalina Island quarry located two miles south of Avalon. Small one ton or less rocks, forming the core of the huge stone pyramid, 102 feet wide at the base, 37 feet high and ten foot wide at the top, were dumped from barges. By mid December workers had dumped 194 loads of stone totaling 115,000 tons. The core was 1600 feet long and the job 52% complete.

On December 13th, during the first big rain storm of the season, the crew of one of the hopper barges prepared to dump a load of stone just after dark. Johnny McPherson, a thirty-one year old Ocean Park fisherman, was on

the rain drenched walk between two of the barge's five hoppers as the rest of the crew knocked loose the clogs holding the tripping gear that controlled the barge's false bottom. He slipped on the wet gunwale and lost his balance just as ten tons of rock thundered down into the water. He was caught in the load and undertow, then he disappeared. His body was found the next day under several pieces of core rock in twenty feet of water.

Another accident was thwarted on Feb 17, 1934, when a barge full of rock broke its mooring lines in heavy seas and drifted almost into the breakwater. For a time it was feared that it would head south and crash into the end of the pier. Fortunately the company had chartered the fishing boat Gloria H. to stand 24-hour guard and prevent this type of accident.

In March the city completed plans for doubling the size of the harbor and applied to the PWA (Public Works Administration) for a federal grant of $750,000. The plan was to add 2300 feet to the seawall, widen the crest from ten to fifteen feet and raise the entire breakwater from ten feet to fourteen feet above low tide. Five hundred feet would be added to the breakwater's north end before it arced inland to a point 600 feet offshore at the foot of the California Incline. The north end would be connected to shore by a 604 feet long, 24 foot wide pier.

The new harbor plans allowed the city to abandon their plan to connect the Municipal Pier with the breakwater via a suspension bridge. Originally they planned to lengthen the pier by 400 feet and have boats enter the harbor's south side beneath the suspension bridge. They felt that since this would be the only entrance to the harbor in the new design, they would need a more spacious entrance.

The city intended to use the remaining $35,000 in the harbor fund to renovate and enlarge the pier. The 75 foot pier extension built by the defunct Santa Monica Harbor Company would be removed and they would increase the area of the Municipal Pier's end 'T'. They would also add a lower deck with a landing stage on the harbor side.

Captain Olaf Olson's exclusive pier lease came under fire in City Council. He owed the city $11,300 rent for the period from Oct 21, 1930 to Oct 21, 1932 and he hadn't filed a statement for his 1933 earnings either. He claimed that business was slow because the new harbor had been delayed. The city on March 30, 1934 ordered him to vacate the pier.

Work on the breakwater was often delayed by winter storms and heavy ground swells. The contractor, in an effort to make up lost time, shifted to a twenty-four hour work day at the beginning of April. Men worked in four,

The Circular Swing ride was on the pier during the early 30's. It was situated west of the Whirlwind Coaster which was removed in October 1930.

Carousel building in 1934. Kiddie rides were located on the ramp leading to the Promenade. (opposite page)

Fourth of July always brought large crowds to the pier to tour visiting warships. The aircraft carrier Saratoga was anchored off the end of the pier; 1935.

six hour shifts. An electric power plant was put on the barge for night illumination. The barge, which was finishing the last of the breakwater's core only a few hundred feet from the pier, needed three battleship anchors and three rock anchors to prevent it from breaking loose.

The last load of core rock was dumped on April 11th. There was 171,028 tons of rock in place. About 30,000 tons of heavier armor stone, rocks weighing over four tons, were then lowered by derrick and placed on the seaward side to withstand the pounding surf. An additional 16,000 tons of cap stone, weighing eight to ten tons, were hoisted into place inside large metal banded crates. These large stones were used on the top and on the upper ten feet of the wall's seaward side to withstand the brunt of the worst storm's fury.

A Santa Monica engineer named Walter Young was inspecting the sea wall on April 16th when he was swept off the top of the breakwater by a huge wave. He narrowly escaped death as he was carried one hundred feet before being released by the surf's powerful undertow.

Santa Monica, in an effort to improve the pier's fishing facilities, assumed control over their Municipal Pier on April 17, 1934. They appointed G.T. Mills as deputy pier manager. With Olson out of business they wanted to lease the fishing and pleasure boating business to someone, but not on an exclusive basis. Two bids were submitted on April 30th. Both Ottie Carrillo and Morris Pleasure Fishing Inc. offered 10% of the gross to operate water taxis and live bait boats. Commissioner Sanborn recommended Carrillo but the City Council wanted competition.

The Puget Sound Company on May 10, 1934, reported to the city that their estimate of the rock required to complete the seawall was too low. The stone, when it was dumped from the barges, compacted more than expected. The company had figured that there would be more voids or pockets between the rocks. 184,000 tons of rock were in place but if it was to complete the breakwater to specifications, more than the 220,000 tons of stone called for in the contract would be required. The city still had $75,000 available for additional stone after all contracts were paid. The company, claiming bad weather, asked for a 42 day extension on their contract.

The city, preparing for the new harbor in May, ordered 125 new pier piles to enlarge the Municipal Pier. The $35,000 project involved increasing the area of the outer 'T' by widening it to 140 feet and building a lower deck eight feet above mean high tide to provide a boat landing stage on the north side of the structure. The lower deck would have space for a storage warehouse and utility station for the harbor. Reconstruction and resurfacing of the pier's deck would take two months.

By early July the contractors assured the city that the harbor work would be completed in time for the breakwater's dedication on Sunday, August 5th, and the scheduled Regatta Week that would follow. They had 210,000 tons of rock in place and only 10,000 tons needed to be put atop the breakwater, a job that would take less than three weeks. Work on the city's pier was almost done and only one additional week was needed to complete the project. The Corinthian Yacht Club wanted to start their pier addition for a clubhouse before the city moved the pile driving equipment.

Although the harbor wasn't even completed yet, there was strong evidence that the prevailing currents from the north were depositing sand inside the yacht harbor. Howard Carter and C.F. Nicholson, the city's harbor consulting engineer, were asked to prepare plans for three parallel groins extending out from the foot of California Avenue. Two temporary rock groins 150 feet long would flank a steel groin extending 300 feet out into the ocean.

The final few loads of rock arrived during the last week of July. In all, 223,719 tons of rock were in place and the company gave formal notice to city officials that they were finished. They said that once the city accepted the breakwater they would withdraw their tugs and construction equipment from the harbor.

On July 30th, the City Council members ventured out in a tug to make the final inspection, and on August 2nd they formally accepted the breakwater. It was agreed in the contract that the city would withhold 10% of the payment for 35 days to be sure of satisfaction.

Harbor rules covering an area of nine square miles, three miles along the bay out to the three mile limit, were posted the following day. Boats were required to have proper warning lights and reckless driving was a misdemeanor. Dumping garbage in the bay was prohibited and swimmers couldn't board or hold onto boats at anchorage. The later was to protect boat owners' property.

The city also set harbor mooring rates. The charge for open water anchorage was ten cents per linear foot per month. Owners would pay thirty five cents per linear foot per month for berths if they became available.

Regatta Week began on Saturday night with a dance carnival and barbecue at the Miramar. The breakwater was dedicated on Sunday August 5, 1934 following a breakfast for five hundred city officials and community leaders. Many of the breakfast speakers pointed out that the seawall marked the birth of a new era in Santa Monica. Congressman John Dockweiler said that he "recog-

Long lines of people awaited transport to the Navy ship Ranger; 1936.

Willmington Transportation's ship Cabrillo transported passengers from the Santa Monica Pier to Catalina Island during the summer of 1935.

Santa Monica Pier in 1937. The La Monica Ballroom's exterior was remodeled to resemble a Spanish fort. The circular track ride in the center of the pier was the Auto Ride. (opposite page)

nized at once that Santa Monica having displayed the initiative to make a harbor during times of Depression, was entitled to some assistance from other sources in order that the public might enjoy the full benefits of the improvement." He noted that space for yachts in the harbor would be inadequate and that the harbor would need to be enlarged. He pledged that he would lend assistance in obtaining that aid.

The afternoon ceremony on the sand at the foot of Colorado Avenue was a festive occasion. Eugene Overton, commodore of the South Coast Corinthian Yacht Club took charge of the festivities on behalf of the yatchsmen. There were speeches by Mayor Carter, County Supervisor Quinn and Congressman Dockweiler. The plaque ritual, conducted by Charles A Koenig, grand president of the Native Sons of the Golden West, was a fitting tribute to the hard work and dedication to all those who were involved in creating Santa Monica's new harbor.

Afterwards guests of honor and visiting officials were taken aboard several yachts and shown the new breakwater at close range. The afternoon festivities concluded with finish of the Long Beach to Santa Monica powerboat races at 4:30 PM, and fireworks illuminated the harbor that evening. The day's festivities marked a major milestone in Santa Monica's history.

Sailboat races for the 12th annual Pacific Coast Sailing Regatta filled out the schedule throughout the midweek and concluded the following Saturday when 1600 guests gathered at the Del Mar Club for trophy festivities and a dinner dance. The Regatta brought Santa Monica a considerable amount of publicity. The wire services carried daily stories of the yacht races and feature stories about Santa Monica's new breakwater. Pacific Skipper, a yachting magazine, devoted the entire August issue to the event.

Yachts from San Pedro and Newport began anchoring permanently in the new harbor. Many like Charlie Chaplin's fifty foot 'Panacea' were owned by celebrities. Johnny Weismuller, Leo Carillo, Roy del Ruth, Eugene Overton, Howard Hawks, and Morrie Morrison all leased space within the first year.

A survey of the new harbor a week after the regatta dispelled fears that the harbor would soon silt up with sand. The scouring action of the hidden currents deepened the harbor six feet in some places. The 25 feet deep contour line moved shoreward 125 feet, while the mean high tide line moved seaward 100 feet.

The final stage of the pier's renovation project began on September 11th with the aid of SERA (Social Eco-

The mackerel fleet of commercial fishing boats anchored on the south side of the La Monica Pier. They sold the fish to companies that made fertilizer.

nomic Recovery Act) federally funded workers. Workers painted the pier and turned all the planking. A storeroom and lockers was built on the subdeck and the deck itself was extended shoreward. Then they installed a ten foot boom and a small power winch for handling dories and shore boats. The city awarded a paving contract to asphalt all 14,000 square feet of deck for $770.

The city's wish for competition in the boating and fishing business on the pier was realized during the mid thirties when leases were granted to Morris Pleasure Fishing, Hernage and Bray, Kern and Tedford, and Charles Arnold. Most of the operators offered day fishing trips, transport to offshore fishing barges, or boat rentals. Santa Monica Bait and Tackle and later Frank Volk offered fishing supplies and live bait from storefronts on the upper deck. Both Union Oil and Standard Oil on the lower deck serviced the fishing fleet with gasoline and diesel supplies piped from tanks buried on the beach.

The harbor's expansion was on many politician's minds. Commissioner H.C. Sanborn breached the subject in late September of whether a $560,000 bond issue for enlargement and completion of the yacht harbor to four times its present area should be submitted to the voters. He said it could be made conditional upon the granting of direct federal aid equal to the amount. The Council voted to delay the proposal for future consideration.

Further study by Congressman Dockweiler revealed that the harbor project was entitled to aid from the PWA (Public Works Administration) only if bonds were shown to be self-liquidating by city revenue. He said that he would make an effort to interest the War Department and the Congressional Rivers and Harbors Committee to enlarge the harbor.

Sanborn still felt that voters should decide if they wanted a bond issue despite the prospect of 100% WPA financing. The city would still need to put up 25% of the project even if it were federally constructed. The inland communities in the bonding district, which included Santa Monica, Pacific Palisades, West Los Angeles, Westwood, Beverly Hills and Hollywood, said they were willing to cooperate with the enlargement of the harbor.

The city, in need of a convention center, leased the La Monica Ballroom in October to serve as a 4000 seat convention hall. It was a two year lease at $225 per month for the first year, rising to $300 per month for the second year, and an option for a third year. The building would also be used to house the lifeguard headquarters, offices for the harbor and city's publicity departments, and concessions catering to fishermen and yachtsmen.

In some ways it was a said fate for the famous ball-room, but hard times had hit the financially strapped Santa Monica Amusement Company. Pier patrons had little money to spend during the Depression and the company had to close virtually all their amusements except the carousel, shuffleboard and shooting gallery concessions. Ernest Pickering resigned at the end of the 1934 season when the amusement company couldn't afford his salary. The company eventually declared bankruptcy the following spring.

SERA carpenter crews began the remodeling job shortly before Christmas with lumber salvaged from motion picture studios. They began work on the lifeguard headquarters and sleeping quarters located on the northeast corner of the building. The guards planned to furnished their offices with used nautical gear from a salvage company in San Pedro; porthole fittings and nautical ladders. The tower nearby had a copula on the top so that a guard with a pair of field glasses could "see a dog fight on the beach a mile away."

Offices, concessions, and conference rooms facing inward were built in a square around the huge dance hall floor. Each conference room resembled houses of different countries and periods, complete with roofs and chimneys. The row of cottages on the east side included a Swiss Chalet, an English cottage, Pompeian reception room, Italian room, and a garden room. A stage accommodating 300, sixty feet long and forty feet deep, was constructed at the south end of the ballroom. Offices for the convention center as well as for the California Naval Militia, the Santa Monica Sailing Club, and lifeguard services were on the mezzanine level. Six store-fronts were built along the north side of the auditorium and leased out to defray rent of the entire building.

The lifeguard headquarters was ready by the end of February 1935. The move from the old headquarters on the pier in the northwest corner of the billiards building saved the city $40 per month rent. Heavy glass plate tanks for displaying fish caught in the Santa Monica Bay were installed on the mezzanine level just outside the life guard station. The lifeguards also installed a tank outside the building so they could keep a pet seal.

The SERA carpenters worked diligently through March and April to finish the convention center in time for the California Federation of Woman's Clubs convention on April 22, 1935. Despite the free labor and salvaged material, the renovation cost the city $10,000, a job that would have cost at least $50,000 under normal circumstances.

Plans began shaping up for steamship service from

The harbor patrol launched their new rescue boat Palama-Kai; 1937.

Members of the Manoa Paddleboard Club pose in front of their clubhouse located beneath the roadway opposite the La Monica Ballroom.

Fishermen on the Municipal Pier's lower deck; 1935.

Paddleboarders Bob Donnis (left) and Pete Peterson (right) at the Santa Monica Bathhouse located just north of the pier. Pete's mom owned the bathhouse and Pete later became a life-guard. The black woolen bathing suits that they wore were the kind the bathhouse rented to beach visitors; 1933. (right)

Santa Monica harbor to Catalina Island during the summer. The Wrigley interests approached the city about inaugurating an experimental line if the city was willing to build pier docking facilities. Commissioner Sanborn conferred with Captain W.H. Leisk of the steamer Cabrillo and determined that it involved extending the lower deck by eighteen feet so that tidal surges wouldn't throw the steamship against the pilings. They also needed to construct a ticket booth and waiting rooms. The estimated cost was $3500.

The Willmington Transportation Company applied for a 25 year permit, but the city decided to lease the pier instead of granting a twenty five year franchise. This would allow other commercial interests to use the dock since the Catalina boats would only use the facilities thirty minutes each day.

Many of the 101 yacht owners in the harbor protested the plan for the steamer to travel through the heart of the harbor after it left the dock. It would create a wake that could damage their boats. Instead the steamship company agreed to back the vessel away from the dock and depart by the south entrance.

Daily summer service to Avalon Bay started June 1, 1935. The 600 passenger, 611 ton steamer left Santa Monica in the early afternoon on a three and one half hour voyage to the offshore island. It returned the following morning. They expected to transport 40,000 tourists throughout the summer season.

The 1935 Fourth of July weekend was one of the busiest on record with 250,000 people cramming the beaches and piers. The aircraft carrier Saratoga was anchored in the bay and the throng awaiting the launches was the greatest ever assembled on the pier. Nine thousand people visited the Saratoga during the weekend and eight hundred paid passengers booked passage on the pier's day fishing boats. Some tried the pier's new Auto Maze ride located behind the carousel. The naval and military ball held at the La Monica that evening was attended by over one thousand people.

Passenger service business to Catalina was far below forecasts throughout the summer. By August 31st the boat company had lost $10,807.36 and they announced that they would discontinue service between September 15, 1935 and May 31, 1936. The company didn't resume service to Catalina the following summer, but in later years smaller boats like the express cruiser Norconian would offer limited summer service.

In late August a harbor bill introduced in Congress became law. It provided a survey for the breakwater expansion to be funded by the federal government. Since

The Santa Monica Pier was a popular place in the late 1930's.

Water taxis from the Santa Monica and Ocean Park piers took patrons out to the gambling barge Rex anchored beyond the three mile limit. Its slot machines were destroyed after it was closed down in August 1939.

Santa Monica wanted their harbor to look good for the harbor survey in November, they made some needed repairs. Two thousand tons of rock were added to shore up the seawall.

The city also ordered improvements to the Municipal Pier in February 1936. The work mainly involved improving the never used extension that was constructed by the South Coast Corinthian Yacht Club. The city installed a small boat landing and storage facilities there. They also installed a hoist opposite the La Monica and new restrooms nearby.

On February 18, 1936 City Council voted for the Nicholson plan, a $2,000,000 harbor expansion that would extend the breakwater on both ends by one thousand feet and increase the usable anchorage to 101.7 acres. The extensions and beefed-up seawall would require 640,000 tons of rock at a cost of $1,120,000. The plan also included a $524,000 passenger pier, 500 foot long, 300 foot wide, extending out from the present pier and a $132,000 transit shed. A small landing pier and groin costing $26,350 would be constructed at the foot of California Avenue to serve yachting interests. The city would spend $141,000 for dredging operations to deepen the silted harbor. The city first needed approval from the War Department before asking for federal funds.

City planners in March reconsidered their ambitious plans and scaled them down considerably to make the harbor fundamentally a yacht basin. The new breakwater would still be twice its present length, a thousand feet longer on both the north and south sides, and slightly wider and higher, but the pier wouldn't be extended. However, the pier would be widened so that small coastal vessels could dock on its south side. The cost would be only $800,000.

The project had the support of the Los Angeles County Board of Supervisors and surprisingly the Los Angeles City playground department. The city applied for a federal grant of $861,000 on March 12th to fund the project. Their report stated that 170,000 persons were carried on round trips originating from the Santa Monica Pier the previous year and that at least 200 more yachts could use the harbor if it had better anchorage. They estimated that the cost of moving sand southward at $30,000 per year.

But the U.S. War Department on April 27th recommended that improvement or maintenance of the Santa Monica Harbor at federal expense was not justifiable. The city asked for a new hearing and filed an appeal from the adverse decision of the Army's division engineer. They sent George Nicholson to Washington D.C. to make a

personal appeal on the city's behalf.

Ownership of the La Monica Pier finally had to be decided in Superior Court after the Santa Monica Amusement Company filed bankruptcy on June 14, 1935. Security First National Bank foreclosed on the property the previous summer. On April 11, 1936, the court awarded the bank title to the property at the pier's entrance along with its twenty year franchise due to expire in only two months. The court ruled that the new franchise granted to the amusement company by the city's previous adminstration was not automatically transferred to the bank. Judge Bowron held that at the conclusion of the present franchise, the bank might remove the pier but couldn't continue to use it under the current agreement.

The ruling left the city in a very strong position. They considered offering the bank a franchise to the eastern portion of the pier rent free if the city could retain the La Monica Ballroom. But the Santa Monica Amusement Company's lawyer muddled things on June 11th when he sent the city notice that they were to pay the La Monica's rent to the receiver for the bankrupt company. It was accompanied by a copy of the judge's decision that the real estate was owned by the bank, but the franchise was possessed by the company. On that basis the receiver laid claim to all rent dating from June 7th, the beginning of the new franchise. He warned the bank that if it attempted to collect rent, it would be prosecuted for contempt of court.

In December the city pondered purchasing the pier and the La Monica Ballroom from the bank for $122,000. Under the terms of the offer the municipality would pay the bank $602.22 monthly for seventeen years plus an estimated $51,000 in maintenance, insurance and taxes. At the end of the lease the property would belong to the city for one additional dollar.

The city said they would be interested only if they could make a profit owning the pier. A survey among the thirteen longest tenants revealed that they paid $1727.20 rent and that the auto park was the best source of revenue. Howard Carter was ordered to survey the condition of the pier and he found it to be in good condition. But the city was still worried that the pier's purchase might result in a court battle since the title to the pier might be in litigation.

Commissioner Plummer at the Council's December 20th meeting presented the city attorney's recommendation against acceptance of Security First's offer to sell the property for $100,000 on a lease purchase plan. He recommended that instead, the current franchise on the pier

be forfeited. The Council adopted a resolution of forfeiture. Meanwhile the bank demanded the city's rent for the La Monica that by the end of the year had accumulated to $2070. The bank promised to repay the money if the court ruled against them, but the city wouldn't pay because it could leave Commissioner Plummer personally liable.

In March 1937 the city made one last concerted effort to gain support for their harbor expansion by waging an intensive campaign in Washington D.C. While they awaited a decision on an appeal to the War Department Congressman Dockweiler considered a plan to obtain PWA or WPA financing for the project.

Finally, on April 5th, Dockweiler informed the city that their appeal to the War Department was denied. The board of engineers both for the Army and the Rivers and Harbors committee felt that the costs were excessive considering the benefits to be derived. They feared that the proposed addition to the breakwater might increase the present rate of sand accretion in the protected areas. They also felt that existing harbors at Newport and San Pedro adequately served the needs of the Los Angeles Metropolitan area.

Security First National Bank decided that since the city didn't want to purchase the pier, perhaps they should improve it for the summer season. In April 1937 they authorized $30,000 to build three new concession buildings, install a new pier electrical system, and asphalt the auto park. They removed the gingerbread towers on the merry-go-round building and refurbished the five apartments on its second floor. H.E. Walker was hired as property manager for the bank.

Another ten ton power hoist operated by David Baird of Pacific Yachting Supply was installed on the upper deck. This supplemented a ten ton hoist that had been installed by Robert Lamia on the lower deck the previous year. Both were capable of hoisting boats up to 45 feet in length onto the deck for servicing. Rent to the city was 10% of the receipts.

Lights marking the harbor entrances were installed in May. A red light on the north end and a green light on the south end set fifteen feet above the breakwater were visible from ten miles away. The lights were operated by sun valves that turned them on whenever darkness fell.

The $1,750,000 beach erosion suit finally went to trial during early summer. The beach clubs south of the pier were involved in what was known as the Carpenter case. Carpenter represented Pacific Mutual Life Insurance Company who had bought the old Del Mar Club in 1934. The club's southwest boundary was the mean high-tide line on what had been a very wide beach. The clubs alleged that construction of the yacht harbor breakwater interfered with south bound currents that normally deposited sand on their privately owned beaches in front of their properties and instead caused them to erode.

Another group of plaintiffs north of the pier were suing for a completely opposite reason. Those allied with Los Angeles Athletic Club, owners of the Deauville Club, claimed that the breakwater caused too much sand to build up in front of their property. The city's contention in both cases was that the property owners had no right to sue the municipality and that there was no erosion above the mean high-tide line.

Santa Monica, in an effort to solve the problem, had installed two six inch pumps and an air compressor under the pier in February 1935. They had hoped that the pumps would have opened a channel for the shore currents to move the accumulating sand to the beaches immediately south of the pier. It apparently had minimal effect.

The judge on August 16, 1937 declined a ruling and withdrew from the case. The entire matter was assigned to the appellate division of the Superior Court to be retried by three judges in the fall. But the fifteen litigants suffered a setback in mid September when the Pacific-American Fire Insurance Company, who was suing for $578,967.52, offered to sell their property to the city for $75,000. They owned 197 feet of frontage between the Grand Hotel and the old Edgewater Club. Their offer showed evidence that the plaintiffs hadn't suffered damage in anything like the amount claimed. The four main suits totaled $1,329,000. (The case would drag on until 1944)

Another lawsuit involving ownership of the Santa Monica Pleasure Pier began to drag on throughout the summer. Edward H. Marxen, trustee for the bankrupt Santa Monica Amusement Company filed suit in May against Security First National Bank and the city for recovery of the pier and $30,000 in damages.

The city's La Monica lease would lapse on September 2nd. The city was reluctant to renew it because of the pier's uncertain ownership. However, leaving it would weaken the city's position in the law suit. Besides, they needed the facility for conventions and its lifeguard service. With the bank willing to guarantee the city that it would pay any claims for rental to Marxen if he should win, the Council voted to renew their lease.

The bank then decided to remodel the exterior of the structure so that it would resemble a Spanish fort. The fancy minaret towers were cut in size. The bank, still not willing to give the city a lease that would protect its claim

to ownership, ran into an impasse with the City Council. Finally, in frustration, they voted on November 14, 1937 to abandon its lease except for the lifeguard headquarters.

The bank leased out the La Monica to Austin McFadden who announced that he would operate it starting in the summer as the Rollaway Roller Rink. He renovated the former ballroom so that it would be the most beautiful and up to date rink in the country. He purchased hundreds of skates and had his paid attendants help put on patron's skates without charge. Loges could be reserved at Rollaway for skating parties.

The city decided to dredge the harbor in the spring of 1938. They retained George La France as a consultant for $400 per month. The plan was to move 750,000 cubic yards of sand to the south beaches. By the end of May they had spent $19,000 on the dredge Anita but it was still not ready. When it finally began dredging in the late summer it could barely keep up with new sand accretions. The dredge was often stranded at low tide, and when the it operated the high tide often brought back the dredged sand. At an operating cost of $1000 per month, the project became an endless waste of taxpayer's money.

Someone calculated that at the rate the dredge was operating, only eight hours a day, it would take five years to dredge the harbor. They were supposed to dredge 750,000 cubic yards in a three year period, but sand was accumulating at 337 cubic yards per day. Thus by the time the sand was removed it would take an additional sixteen months to finish the job.

The late 30's brought back the popularity of the offshore gambling boats. Several of these boats began operation in 1929 beginning with the Johanna Smith that anchored five miles directly west of the Venice Pier. Water taxis would deposit gamblers at these floating casinos that sometimes offered entertainment and dancing in addition to crap tables and roulette.

In 1938 Tony Cornero bought the Star of Scotland fishing barge, a 51 year old four-masted barkentine, and converted it into a gambling ship. It had a superstructure especially designed as a luxury gambling casino. His investment, rumored to be $600,000, was financed by Bugsy Siegal and George Raft. He towed his boat exactly 3.1 miles offshore, and announced with radio and newspaper advertisements on May 4, 1938 that he was open for business. He offered a challenge, a $100,000 reward to anyone who could show that any game on the Rex was rigged.

It was a first class operation with good food, top name dance bands, unwatered booze and honest games. Gamblers had a choice of playing craps, roulette, blackjack, chuck-a-luck, high spade, wheel of fortune, Chinese lot-

tery, stud poker, and faro. There were tango layouts between decks and 150 'one armed bandits' lined the casino walls. Nick the Greek Dandolos, Carl Leemmle, and Fanny Brice were noted celebrity gamblers that added atmosphere to the floating casino. The operation was a success and netted Tony $300,000 per month despite a payroll of 200 employees including a dozen armed guards.

The McGough brothers' Santa Monica Boat Service began operating eleven water taxis to the gambling barge once the Rex was open for business. While local authorities and anti-gambling forces could do nothing because the gambling ships operated just beyond their jurisdiction, Commissioner Milliken served notice on Roy and E.J. McGough that the city would revoke their lease on the grounds that it did not permit the operation of taxis to the barge or anywhere else in the harbor. To counter it, the brothers filed an action in superior court for declaratory relief. They hoped to have the court rule that their lease contract permits operation of taxis to any destination.

The McGoughs remodeled and redecorated their waiting rooms on the lower deck of the pier adjacent to the former Catalina Island terminal. Milliken countered by shutting of the water and power to their building and he refused to allow them to post signs. The barge owners, however, placed a large neon sign on the Santa Monica Pier auto park that was owned by the bank. The sign had an arrow pointing to the water taxi dock on the adjoining pier.

The city continued to try to oust the McGough brothers from the pier despite three court restraining orders issued by Judge Orlando Rhodes. Commissioner Milliken made a motion at their May 15, 1938 meeting to eject them, remove their water taxi float and gang plank. Mayor Gillette voted 'No' because the Council had informed the McGoughs previously that it would approve a plan for them to use the old Catalina Island steamer waiting room if its proposed boat service to the island wouldn't "detour" to the gambling barge. Two days later the city, despite restraining orders, locked their waiting rooms, removed their float and raised their gang plank. This reduced their receipts because it delayed unloading their boats.

On May 25th Judge Rhodes ruled against the Rex. Los Angeles County law enforcement officers threatened to make arrests if gambling took place on the ship. Cornero shut down and moved first to Long Beach then back to Santa Monica Bay where he anchored off Redondo Beach on June 14th. The move pleased Santa Monica officials.

Santa Monica officials were preoccupied with construc-

Fishermen return from offshore barges with their catch. (above)

The Morris Pleasure Fishing Company operated the Star of Scotland fishing barge anchored between the Santa Monica and Ocean Park Piers.

The 'Scotty' transported day fishermen to the Star of Scotland.

tion plans to build a new city hall. But to obtain a PWA grant of $158,000, they needed to prematurely abandon their old city hall at 4th Street and Santa Monica Boulevard by January 10, 1939. City departments leased space wherever it was available. The Police Department transferred all their offices, court and the city jail to the La Monica Ballroom in early December 1938.

The city also enlarged the Santa Monica Aquarium located in the building. The nine specimen tanks were stocked with sea creatures provided by the local fishermen. The aquarium also had a relief map of Southern California and a chart showing all of the lifeguard rescues along Santa Monica's waterfront. There was also a marine library and lecture room on the second floor.

Sport fishing facilities were improved in 1938 when Preacher Scott Hume and his partner Bob Lamai began operating from the Municipal Pier's landing. They brought with them the boats Faith, Freedom and Pali, a charter boat Chi-Camoi, two bait boats Orca and Scotty and a small barge, Miss Dianna.

On the afternoon of January 2, 1939 a giant swell out of nowhere, washed nine fishermen, one a woman, off the seawall as it swept it end to end. The wave was the forerunner of a violent storm that battered the beaches the following day. The storm accompanied by some of the highest tides of the year washed away most of the sand in front of the Del Mar Club and reached the Promenade in places. Much of the harbor dredge's pipeline was smashed and it silted up the lagoon that the Anita had been digging out since the previous summer.

With the dredge damaged and only $2500 in funds remaining, the city decided to abandon the dredging. They had spent $35,000 for the dredge and work, yet not a single square foot of mooring area had been restored to the harbor. However, between 10%-17% of the total accretion had been pumped south. This, however, had not made a noticeable showing in restoring the denuded beach south of the pier.

Security First National Bank announced on May 15, 1939 that they had finally sold their La Monica Pier and Auditorium for $200,000 to a group of investors headed by Mrs. Harriet Ball, wife of a Texas oil man. The new owners said they expected to make improvements at the end of the summer. They planned to beautify the structures and give the city a real boardwalk on the pier. The city issued a twenty five year franchise to the investors on June 7th and told them that they expected to vacate their leased police department offices and jail in the La Monica when the new city hall opened in November.

The new owners bought the ornate Parker carousel from the Venice Pier and sold their 1916 Looff carousel

Children watched short films on moviolas in the arcade. (above)

Gymnasts worked out on the playground equipment south of the pier; 1936. (below)

to San Diego's Mission Beach park. Harry Hargrove's American Amusement Company operated the new carousel. The owners reoriented the pier's circular miniature auto ride on the main promenade but left the kiddie rides on the ramp adjacent to the carousel. One of the vacant buildings was leased out as a penny arcade. The La Monica's dance floor continued to be used as a skating rink and as a location for occasional special events.

Three shifts of workmen in late March had begun remodeling the old Star of Scotland landing on the Municipal Pier for use for water taxis to the Rex when it returned. Although the city was opposed, they couldn't interfere with that phase of the operation. The lease was originally granted to Captain Charles Arnold for transporting fishermen to the Star of Scotland when it had been a fishing barge.

The Rex returned on March 30th and anchored directly off the pier just beyond the three mile limit. Two signed petitions presented to the city had 250 names on one against offshore gambling and 4900 names for it on the other. The city disregarded the later since the circulators were paid ten cents for each signature obtained. The city attorney advised the mayor that transportation of patrons to the Rex violated the penal code, but after the debacle of the previous year decided to wait for assistance from state and county authorities.

The city, after watching the gambling ships flaunt their immunity for two months, finally lost patience and went after the water taxi businesses on the Municipal Pier. They initiated a lawsuit on June 28th against Charles Arnold and others serving the Rex from the Arnold landing. The city claimed that the lease only allowed them to operate taxis to boats devoted to fishing. The city wanted the lessees ousted from the pier.

Captain Arnold told the court at the hearing in late July that he no longer owned the pier landing. He had sold it when he sold the Star of Scotland to Tony Cornero. Frank Haskell was now managing the water taxis service to the Rex.

California's Attorney General, Earl Warren, had enough and finally decided to take action. He armed himself with nuisance abatement warrants and went after the gambling fleet. He had no difficulty shutting down two boats in Long Beach and the Texas off Venice, but the Rex didn't give in easily. Cornero got wind of the operation when seventeen unarmed plainclothes officers tried to sneak aboard the ship with the other customers. Bouncers spotted them easily and escorted them off the ship.

Warren rounded up a flotilla of State Fish and Game boats, manned them with deputies and ordered them out

Construction of the 650 foot ramp and overpass to the Santa Monica began in September 1939.

Fishing boats 'Annie M' (foreground) and the 'Sea Wolf' (background) were two of five boats that were beached by high winds and heavy surf on December 21, 1941.

to the Rex on August 1st. Cornero was ready and repelled the invasion with high-pressure fire hoses. The authorities laid seige for nine tense days while Cornero's men stood guard with sub-machine guns. His attorneys filed suit after suit charging Warren with everything from harassment to piracy.

Then Tony Cornero unexpectedly surrendered on August 9, 1939. He said that he "had to get a haircut." The war moved to the courts. The high court finally ruled on November 20th that the three mile limit in the Santa Monica Bay extended from an imaginary line connecting Point Dume to Point Vicente. The Rex was found to be operating inside the limit. Tony had to pay $24,900 in fines and court costs and all the gambling equipment on his ship was destroyed.

In late September construction began on a 650 foot bridge from Colorado Avenue to the Municipal Pier. After the Roosevelt Highway to Malibu opened in 1935, traffic in front of the pier at Appian Way caused a bottleneck. The completion of the tunnel under Colorado in February 1936 that routed traffic inland helped, but traffic engineers felt that the best solution was a concrete overpass. A bid was received from Contracting Engineers Company for $196,744 and the contract was approved.

The city continued throughout the fall to dredge the harbor despite a river of sand flowing south that built up faster than the dredge Anita could remove it. What confounded the experts was that the sand pumped out and deposited south of the pier in front of the Grand Hotel flowed north. They could lengthen the hose but it would reduce capacity.

They even considered letting nature take its course, abandoning the harbor and writing the bond issue off as a loss. The harbor was losing its popularity, not just from a decrease in anchorage space, but because it lacked docks. People didn't like to approach their yachts from a dingy tied up to a pier among dirty fishing boats. Besides, the city would need to spend at least $30,000 to plug up gaps in the harbor wall, particularly on the south end near the pier. No maintenance had been done on the seawall in the previous five years, and the wall was beginning to unravel.

Pier businesses asked the city for a 50% cut in fees in May. They pointed out that Santa Monica charged 10% of gross receipts while Los Angeles, Newport, Huntington Beach, Hermosa and San Diego charge 5%. When a 5% sales commission was added it made it impossible to advertise. It was signed by nearly all the lessees including Calvin M. Blackmore who was granted a lease in February to operate sail boat excursions from the former Star of Scotland landing. The city was sympathetic and lowered its fees to the fishing boat operators, but not the cafe owners.

Apparently the La Monica Pier's new Texas owners weren't satisfied with the financial return on their investment. They defaulted on their mortgage and Security First National Bank repossessed the property. The city reassigned the pier franchise back to the bank on March 28, 1940.

The Municipal Pier was redecked during the spring as a WPA project. It was finished in time for the opening of the pier's overpass on June 17, 1940. The Chamber of Commerce then began its campaign to popularize Santa Monica's pier as one of the city's major tourist attractions. At the least they wanted inform the public that the road to the pier was open. Just a year later the Santa Monica Pier Businessmen's Association would install a new arched neon sign at the pier's entrance at the top of the bridge.

Charles Arnold in 1940 decided to reopen his water taxi and fishing barge business. He leased the ex-gambling ship Texas from the government, renamed it the Star of Scotland, and parked it about a mile offshore in front of the breakwater in eighty feet of water. The 261 foot long ship had been an British navy Q-Boat in World War I.

He operated the boat at first as a fishing barge during daylight hours and as floating nightclub at night. The night club wasn't popular and folded after the first year. The barge, however continued to operate as a fishing barge for several more years until it eventually sunk off the pier during World War II.

One of the lawsuits in the beach erosion suit that began in 1937 went to trial that summer. The Deauville and Santa Monica Athletic Clubs were suing the city for $110,655 for damages for causing the beach in front of their property to widen. Howard Carter testified that the beach widening occurred naturally before the breakwater was built or because of the proximity of nearby piers. In fact it widened between 50 and 150 feet in front of their property between 1921 and 1933.

Judge Rhoades ruled in the city's favor deciding that the newly formed sand beyond the original mean high-tide line belongs to the city and not the club. The club appeared before the judge in October 1940 to ask for a new trial.

The state government in October 1941 allocated $162,500 to help Santa Monica complete its dredging project. The city planned to dredge 2,000,000 cubic yards of sand and install groins to slow down the southward flow of sand at a cost of $325,000. Unfortunately, war clouds were on the horizon and the project would be delayed nearly a decade.

Members of the Santa Monica Pier Businessmen's Association stand beneath their new sign at the top of the pier s new ramp; 1940.

Santa Monica Pier on the Skids (1941-1974)

The Japanese sneak attack on Pearl Harbor on Sunday, December 7, 1941 left the nation stunned. It was an event that in the words of Franklin D. Roosevelt, the world would long remember as a "day that would live in infamy." People living along the Southern California coast felt particularly vulnerable because the vast blue Pacific Ocean concealed a fleet of enemy submarines that could suddenly surface and shell their homes, businesses, and brightly lit piers.

Sam Reed, the city's harbor master, took the war threat seriously and the following morning refused to allow several boatloads of Japanese fishermen to put to sea. The harbor had become home base to 46 mackerel fishing boats when naval activities in San Pedro caused them to relocate to Santa Monica. After Reed sent a message to the 11th Naval District Headquarters, he received prompt instructions to prohibit any vessels from leaving the harbor. A naval patrol consisting of small power boats was immediately established and began patrolling the coast that afternoon.

The immediate threat was an expected air attack guided by Japanese spies living in the area. The FBI rounded up all those suspected of being a danger to the nation's internal security. Forty-five Japanese were arrested in Venice and West Los Angeles on December 8th, and hundreds more the following day.

The harbor fog horn was mounted atop city hall and was used to broadcast air raid warnings. American Legion members reported for duty as air raid wardens. The city was ordered to be blacked out at night, and the few cars that ventured out were driven with blue cellophane taped over their headlights. Santa Monicans took the blackout seriously during the first few days of the war. The area's first blackout was on December 11th at 9:50 P.M. when army headquarters flashed an emergency warning that unidentified aircraft were over Los Angeles. While air-raid sirens blared, the whole southland was plunged into darkness. When neon signs and other lights continued to illuminate downtown buildings, angry citizens moved through the streets and smashed dozens of lights that had been left on when store owners closed for the day.

A citizen's defense militia was formed along the beach front to guard against possible infiltration by enemy saboteurs. Men and later women stood watch in four-hour shifts at fourteen stations strung along Santa Mon-

Searchlights illuminated the Santa Monica Pier at night; 1946.

ica's waterfront. The beach, protected with barbed wire entanglements, was effectively closed during the day. Anyone caught on the beach at night was likely to be arrested.

The battery of the 3rd Battalion, 144th Field Artillery was housed at the Municipal Auditorium in Ocean Park. Other army groups manning anti-aircraft gun emplacements encamped at various open fields throughout the westside. Additional anti-aircraft batteries were set up at Clover Field to guard the camouflaged Douglas Aircraft plant that from the air resembled a suburban housing tract.

The first test came on February 25, 1942 when wailing air-raid sirens went off at 2:25 A.M. Huge searchlights scanned the sky along a ten mile front south of Santa Monica, then converged on a single spot in the sky. Moments later the anti-aircraft batteries opened up, throwing a sheet of steel skyward. Tracer bullets and thousands of exploding shells lit the sky in a spectacular fireworks show witnessed from streets and rooftops by several hundred thousand residents. Rumors abounded that as many as fifteen enemy planes were involved, perhaps from a secret inland enemy base. The public was willing to believe anything and everything about the enemy. At 7:19 A.M. the all clear sounded.

No bombs fell and no planes were shot down. Navy Secretary Knox reported that it was a false alarm. What they shot at that night remained a military secret throughout the war, but most people concurred that it was likely just a loose meteorological balloon.

Rules for operating fishing craft changed throughout the opening months of the war. At first passengers only needed to carry proof of citizenship with photographs and ID cards. But on April 24th all pleasure craft were ordered into port by the Coast Guard. They announced that only vessels used for fishing or those used for transporting passengers on regularly scheduled routes would be allowed to operate.

Santa Monica's mackerel fishing fleet resumed operation on May 11th under the Coast Guard's new rules. It was a fleet that lacked its traditional complement of Japanese-American fishermen because a paranoid government during the first months of the war rounded-up all citizens of Japanese descent and shipped them to inland detention camps for the duration of the war.

By summer most young men in the area between seventeen and thirty-five had either volunteered or were drafted into the armed forces. But the piers and beaches still played host to thousands of soldiers on leave from nearby military bases and the cadre of defense workers at

plants like Douglas Aircraft. Since most had never seen an ocean, the lifeguard service urged residents to publicize safety rules for beach visitors.

The area's normally brightly lit amusement piers were forced to curtail operations after dark because of dimout regulations. Santa Monica's pier, which had far fewer amusements, had less of a problem remaining open in the evening. Dance halls on Venice and Ocean Park piers offered one of the few forms of evening entertainment and were especially popular with swing-shift defense workers whose shift ended at midnight. By October the city passed laws where by people under eighteen couldn't attend swing-shift dances and those 18-21 had to leave by 2 A.M.

Santa Monica's mackerel fleet was busy during the war providing food for the nation's war effort. In October 1942 a three-ton weight limit placed on pier vehicles due to a weakening structure made fishermen angry. It interfered with their shipments to San Pedro canneries. They claimed that 10,000 tons of mackerel were lost through load limitations placed on the Municipal Pier. The mayor suggested instead that the fish be taken off the pier in small containers loaded in light trucks, then transferred into heavy trucks for the trip to the canneries.

A series of winter storms wrecked havoc on the fishing fleet. First the 60 foot fishing boat 'Palisades' ran aground off the California Incline on January 14, 1943, where it was pounded to pieces in the surf. Then a 56 hour storm in late January dumped seven inches of rain and created heavy seas in the harbor. Forty-eight boats washed ashore and ten more were sunk or missing. Damages ran to $80,000 and most blamed it on the Coast Guard's regulations that required that all boats remain behind the breakwater after dark. Worse yet, the local fish market was glutted and by the end of February local brokers refused to accept one fifteen ton catch. The price of fish fell from 21 cents per pound to 13 cents per pound in one week.

In February 1943, Security First National Bank sold the Santa Monica Pleasure Pier to Walter D. Newcomb, who was managing their pier under a lease agreement. Newcomb, who owned the pier's gift shop and arcade, had taken over management at the beginning of the war when Lt. Commander Harry E. Walker entered naval service.

The pier's fifty-five businesses including seven restaurants had great potential, but wartime restrictions with building materials made it impossible to make immediate improvements. Newcomb's plan was to develop it into an outstanding attraction once the war ended. On March

5th the city, finally relieved that the pier had a new owner, assigned Newcomb the bank's twenty-one year franchise that began on June 7, 1936.

Johnny "Tarzan" Weissmuller was a frequent pier visitor and came to the beach often during the war to enjoy an afternoon of paddleboard racing. He was walking on the pier on August 6, 1943 when he heard a fifteen year old boy screaming for help below. He leapt from the pier to rescue the boy who had tired on his return swim from a distant harbor float. It wasn't Weissmuller's first rescue for he had worked as a lifeguard in Chicago and was an honorary captain of Santa Monica's Municipal Lifeguard service.

The city was in a get tough mood when it came time to renew several Municipal Pier leases in October 1943. They ignored pleas from boat operators that their leases be rewritten because of war time restrictions Instead they offered five year leases with rents twice what they were previously; 10% of gross receipts. They also voted unanimously to cancel any leases that allowed liquor sales on the Municipal Pier. Olaf Olson had been operating a cocktail bar, but had recently vacated the premises.

As the war in the Pacific pushed the Japanese back further towards their homeland, the Santa Monica area became a rest and recovery area for returning soldiers and airmen. In late November the Army began leasing the beach club hotels, first the Grand Hotel, Del Mar and Edgewater Clubs. Later they leased the Miramar, Ocean Palms and Shangri-La to quarter 1500 men returning from combat service. The beach club hotels operated like a hotels rather than like an army base, and rotated about 2500 men per month through 14-21 day periods.

The La Monica Auditorium reopened in the spring of 1944 as the Palisades Dance Hall. Considering its proximity to their hotels, it was only mildly popular with the visiting troops. Most soldiers preferred either Ocean Park's or Venice's more exciting amusement zones that offered roller coasters, fun houses, theaters, games of skill, and various spinning rides in addition to several dance halls. Santa Monica's Palisades Dance Hall closed several months later with $3200 in unpaid debts. When new management tried to reopen in the fall, the head of the National Musicians Union refused to sanction his members from preforming there until the debt was paid.

Both Pacific Mutual Life Insurance's beach erosion lawsuit, better known as the Carpenter case, and Los Angeles Athletic Club's beach accretion lawsuit were retried in April 1944 by the U.S. District Court of Appeals. The court ruled in both cases against the plaintiffs and for the city of Santa Monica.

The court found that the city was not responsible for either the erosion or sand accretion caused by the construction of the breakwater. It also ruled that the city had a legal right to protect its harbor and the property of others within its boundaries from the action of the ocean. In the Carpenter case it found that all the eroded beach in front of the Del Mar Club had been artificially created from 1875-1921 by man made structures in the Santa Monica Bay and that they belonged to the state and city, not the upland owner. Therefore it was state tidelands that had been damaged. And similarly in the beach accretion case, the newly widened beach in front of the Deauville Club belonged to the state because it covered state and city tidelands property. Both plaintiffs appealed to the California Supreme Court, but the court refused on June 16, 1944 to grant hearings to them. The city's tideland claim was finally legally established.

Santa Monica still wanted to dredge its harbor in July, 1944. The city had planned to shift the sand to the south beaches between the Sunset Pier and Avenue 32 in Venice. $235,000 in funds were available; $162,500 from the state, $51,166 from the city of Los Angeles and $27,084 from Santa Monica's own budget. It was the second time that they advertised for bids and the second time that none were submitted. Contractors lacked equipment to do the job since the military had requisitioned the three remaining dredges along the coast.

As the World War II came to an end during the summer of 1945, Santa Monica and other beach communities began to plan for the future. City officials in July hosted the Congressional Rivers and Harbors Committee who came to study the Pacific Coast's beach erosion problems. They were shown the harbor area that needed dredging. The city, however, received no promises because the Congressmen were trying to work out an impartial solution to erosion problems that required different methods in different parts of the country.

Los Angeles County's Regional Planning Commission had much more ambitious plans for the ocean front along Santa Monica Bay. T.D. Cooke, their division engineer, unveiled plans on July 10, 1945 that called for the elimination of the Santa Monica Breakwater and all the amusement piers along the coast. The county planned to buy all the privately owned beaches, then widen the entire beach front by 600 feet at a total cost of $55,000,000. They proposed parking areas alternated with parks along the beach south of Colorado, and north of the pier where homes were, a landscaped park 100-200 foot deep in front of them, then sand fill for another 400 feet between the park and the ocean.

Santa Monica celebrated its first post-war 4th of July with its 1st annual Santa Monica Fiesta at the pier. Paddleboard races were held on the north side of the pier; 1946.

At first Santa Monica officials weighed the advantages and disadvantages of the county's proposal. They had to decide whether they should sacrifice millions of dollars invested in their breakwater, sport fishing and amusement piers for future benefits of a wider, more accessible ocean front. Both Los Angeles city and county were insistent that all man- made structures in the bay would need to be removed because they interfered with the free movement of sand by the prevailing currents.

Finally, after a month of deliberation, Commissioners W.W. Milliken and D.C. Freeman opposed the plan. They said they would only support a beach plan that would not destroy the identity of Santa Monica's waterfront. While they admitted the breakwater was in deplorable condition, they vowed to fight its removal.

The first postwar plans for private beach development were unveiled in mid-December when amusement interests announced that they were going to make Santa Monica the "Atlantic City of the West." John Lorman and associates contemplated building a $1,000,000 amusement zone on the Lankershim beach property between Arizona and California Avenues. It would include a dance hall, glass covered swimming pool, merry-go-round, ferris wheel, and twenty five other ride devices. The 1200 feet of beach property was zoned C-2 for general business, but they needed a C-3 designation for amusement activity. They expected to begin construction in April 1946 if they could get a zoning variance from the Santa Monica Planning Commission.

The proposed amusement zone immediately aroused protests from the Chamber of Commerce, real estate men, and especially property owners along Santa Monica's 'Gold Coast' who were not willing to accept an amusement park at their front doors. Producer Hal Roach, actor George Bancroft, and actress Bebe Daniels were among those who protested at the December 22nd hearing. Others sent representatives. Morton Anderson, a Santa Monica member of the State Shoreline Planning Association said that to permit a carnival construction on the beach would be a "return to the horse and buggy days and would wreck Santa Monica's development as a leading resort city."

The planners, too, felt that a Coney Island development would not fit into the city's overall development plans as a first class resort and beach community. At the conclusion of the two hour hearing David Fearon moved to deny the zone variance request by the Lankershim Corporation. There was no dissenting vote.

The city, in an attempt to return their Municipal Pier to a profitable operation, placed deputy city clerk Ralph

Spectators watched water sports events during the Santa Monica Fiesta.

Paddleboarders; 1946.

Paddleboard water polo; 1946.

Kruger in charge of all Municipal Pier leases in February 1946. He instituted new lease procedures that put expired leases out to public bid. The first was the Porthole Cafe whose lease would expire April 30th. Then when Bay Fish Market's lease came up for renewal in June, Kruger refused to renew it since the city's intention was to rid the pier of commercial fishing. But the Commissioners out of a sense of fairness overruled him and gave them a two year lease that would expire at the same time as those of the California Seafood and Santa Monica Seafood companies.

It was never the city's intention to turn their yacht harbor into a commercial fishing port, but when the harbor wall failed, yacht owners scurried for the safety of protected waters at Balboa and Newport Harbors. The commercial fishing fleet took their place. When the war ended it was difficult for private yachts to return since all but four of the 125 moorings were leased to fishing boat operators who paid higher mooring fees through subleases. The city didn't benefit since they had relinquished control years ago and received only 10 cents per lineal foot regardless of the rates charged. While the city did collect $6234.57 in fees from commercial fish buyers the previous year, the annual harbor deficit to maintain the harbor and pier was $70,000.

Beach front activities were beginning to return to normal during the spring. The Army vacated all the hotels and beach clubs that they had leased during the war, and those that were owned by insurance companies were sold to private investors. The Deauville Club, previously owned by the Los Angeles Athletic Club, was sold to a group of movie stars that included Joan Crawford, John Wayne, Fred MacMurry, Robert Walker, Frank Borzage, and George Brent. They planned to invest $400,000 and make it a beach cabana club with an Olympic size outdoor swimming pool. The Del Mar Club reopened in June and both the Grand and Edgewater Hotels remodeled in time for summer reopenings as a tourist hotel and beach club respectively.

Santa Monica scheduled its first annual Santa Monica Fiesta at the Municipal Pier to celebrate the end of the Second World War. It was the first Independence Day in five years that defense workers and returning soldiers could celebrate, and it became the biggest beach celebration in the city's history up to that time. Hundreds of thousands jammed the beach for an afternoon of festivities while fifty combat aircraft from Alamitos Bay Naval Air Station paraded overhead.

Foremost was the bathing beauty contest to crown Miss Santa Monica. Leo Carillo, a noted Santa Monica

Fourteen foot long Paddleboards of hollow mahogany on spruce frames were designed by Tom Blake and build by Tom Rogers in Venice.

movie actor was the master of ceremonies. Judges, mostly from MGM Studios, judged the thirty eight contestants and crowned eighteen year old Mary Joe Devlin as the city's beauty. Governor Earl Warren presented her with the trophy.

The Monoa Paddleboard Club opened their show with a fifteen girl paddleboard ballet, then held races and an exhibition polo paddleboard contest in the calm waters north of the pier. Entertainers like Johnny Weissmuller took part in a swimming exhibition and Stubby Kruger preformed his comedy act on the pier.

Acrobatic and gymnastic exhibitions were featured at the playground several hundred feet south of the pier. This area that had become known as 'Muscle Beach' was built in the early 30's as a Works Progress Administration "time-killer". The WPA built a weight lifting platform to provide work and recreation facilities for the crowds of unemployed and relief recipients who had nothing to do during the Depression. It was eventually taken over by the Santa Monica Recreation Department after the original users found jobs and moved on.

These exhibitions, that were usually held on Memorial Day weekends since 1935, featured weigh lifters, gymnasts, balancers, muscle control artists, and tumblers. Some of the better known performers included Wayne Long, Glen "Whitey" Sunby, Pudgy Stockton "queen of the barbells" and Beverly Jochner who was known as the strongest girl in America. She could lift three people weighing 350 pounds overhead. Russ Sanders, the gymnastic coach would fill out the program with high school and college athletes. The Fiesta, however, marked the first time that they staged a men's physique competition for the title of Mr. Santa Monica.

Business on the Newcomb Pier increased during the first postwar summer. Band leader Spade Cooley rented the La Monica Ballroom and his style of country-western music attracted large evening crowds. Then business was also helped somewhat by the elimination of the competing Venice Amusement Pier. It had been forcibly closed down in the spring when the Los Angeles Department of Parks and Recreation refused to renew the Kinney Company's tidelands lease. The closing, however, deprived Walter Newcomb of much of the income that he needed to remodel his aging pier and turn it into a modern tourist attraction. He had operated the merry-go- round and the popular Venice Fun House on the condemned pier.

While Newcomb was preoccupied with removing his attractions from the Venice Pier, he found a buyer for his Parker carousel located in the Hippodrome building. He

then moved his 1922 Philadelphia Toboggan carousel, PTC #62 from the Venice Pier into the building. He had purchased the carousel before the war for $25,000 from an amusement park in Nashville, Tennessee.

The new carousel opened on June 27, 1947 after a two month long renovation by famed carousel builder, Rudy Illions. It was a fifty feet in diameter, three abreast machine with two chariots and forty-four horses hand carved by John Zaler. It was illuminated by 750 electric lights and had a Wurlitzer band organ that played from punched rolls of carousel music. Robert Newcomb, Walter's brother, became manager of the ride.

Newcomb lost an incredible opportunity to move his beloved Venice Fun House to Santa Monica that summer. It was largely a problem of economics. While it would have been easy to move the slides, mirror maze and various fun devices, there was no suitable large building to house them. The potential cost of a large new structure on the pier combined with a shortage of building materials deterred him.

Pleasure boat enthusiasts who used the pier's facilities to launch their boats began to complain to city officials in 1947 that commercial fishing interests were hampering their access to the harbor. Besides charging an exorbitant hoist rate of $10 per round trip, California Seafood Company refused to operate their hoist for Sunday patrons. Boaters who launched their boats on Saturday had to return on Monday to retrieve their craft.

Representatives for commercial fishing interests, pleasure yachtsmen, and sports fishing groups met in the City's Council chambers and worked out a compromise. Myer Simon, president of California Seafood Company agreed to cut hoisting fees in half and provide Sunday service.

Santa Monica businessmen began to discover what Venice had long known since the beginning of the century. Numerous beach festivals and special events bring people to the beach where they spend their money. Thus it was no surprise when the city's second annual beauty pageant in 1947 was staged almost two weeks before the Independence Day festivities. It began with a mile long parade from the Santa Monica Pier to Ocean Park's Casino Gardens. A crowd of 100,000 watched eighty horseback riders, numerous movie stars in parade vehicles, and two bands march past. Spade Cooley, radio western star, acted as Grand Marshal for the event. A panel of movie celebrities judged Susan Brown as the city's most lovely beauty.

The Independence Day celebration at the pier was just a shadow of the previous year's festival. The Recreation

Department staged its 2nd Annual Muscle Matinee on July 4th. A crowd of several thousand watched Charles B. Grayling, a 24 year old studio technician, win the Mr. Santa Monica title. Later that evening thousands watched twelve members of the Manoa Surf Club preform a water ballet. There were no fireworks.

The Labor Day contest for the Miss Muscle Beach title was much more exciting and included a show by Pudgy Stockton's Beachettes and a Thrill Circus featuring outstanding Pacific Coast athletes. A sweating, yelling, whistling, hot dog munching, soda pop drinking mob of sun-burned men, women and their children gathered to 'ooh' and 'ah' at the nearly three dozen shapely contestants. The pageant was supposed to prove that a woman could pour beauty and biceps into the same bathing suit. Mrs. Vivian Crockett, a 22 year old housewife and free lance actress, won the title.

On September 3rd the State Board of Health quarantined twelve miles of beaches from the Santa Monica Pier south to Hermosa Beach. This left Santa Monica with only 1.7 miles of swimming beach. The problem once again was Los Angeles' antiquated Hyperion Sewage Plant which had run out of chlorine again and was dumping large amounts of untreated sewage into the bay. While Santa Monica and Ocean Park's beaches reopened the following summer, Venice's beaches remained closed until the new Hyperion Sewage Plant began operation in June 1950.

City officials gave considerable thought after the war to plans to rehabilitate their harbor. Accumulating sand inside the harbor had cut the harbor's anchorage potential from 525 boats to 135. Mooring spaces, like seats on the New York Stock Exchange, were selling between $100 - $750 depending on size.

City Manger Randall Dorton was the first to question the economic advisability of pouring additional funds into the harbor. He called the harbor "a luxury that the city was unable to afford and one that would never pay its way." The harbor revenue in 1946 was $43,520 while its operating cost and bond interest were $53,971.11. That left a $10,541.11 deficit. Rather than have the city spend $897,000 to enlarge and dredge the harbor to its original depth, he recommended the status quo as the least expensive option.

In 1948 fishing lobbyists in Sacramento launched a concerted effort to remove the ban on net fishing in Santa Monica Bay waters. It was necessary to pave the way for a commercial fishing port and small fish cannery at Santa Monica. Dorton, who was previously the city manager in Monterey, cited Monterey's unsuccessful

The Manoa Paddleboard Club performs a water ballet; 1946.

Members of the Monoa Paddleboard Ballet team pose for a photograph; 1946. (opposite page)

attempt to combine a resort community with a commercial fishing fleet and fish canneries. Santa Monica became vigorously opposed to the idea.

The mackerel fleet in Santa Monica harbor was at its peak from 1946- 1948. It consisted of 200-300, small 28-40 foot boats that used a floating pier dock to unload their catch and sell it to legal fish buyers on the pier. The fish were trucked to canneries in San Pedro for processing.

Bob Lamia, who was partners with Preacher Scott Hume in their sports fishing business, managed to force Scott out in 1948 by legal manuevers. He operated the boats Palisades, Resista, Ramona, Sea Biscuit, Mardi Gras, W.K. and a flat bottomed fishing barge Tradewinds.

Santa Monica's harbor finally received official recognition as a government approved small craft harbor on January 31, 1949. Its approval by the U.S. Army Corps of Engineers and 11th District Coast Guard entailed no change in local adminstration, but brought the hope of future government money.

The U.S. Army Corp of Engineers began hearings in the spring to implement Los Angeles County's shoreline beach plan. Beach erosion experts blamed Santa Monica's harbor wall and pier as the major causes of beach erosion south of the harbor and recommended that they be removed. Santa Monica was against the removal of the harbor wall because of the adverse effect it would have on the pier's lower deck. City officials, in a move to defend their harbor installations, studied plans to dredge 1,000,000 cubic yards of sand out of the harbor basin as a contribution to the $26,000,000 beach improvement program. Dredging would permit the accumulated sand to flow southward. It was a compromise that Los Angeles city and county officials were reluctantly, but willing to accept.

Santa Monica officials went to Sacramento and appeared before the State Parks Commission to ask for the remaining $256,000 of the $325,000 dredging fund that was set up in 1943. They planned to move the sand southward and widen the beach by 370 feet between the Santa Monica and Ocean Park Piers. State officials finally approved the plan on April 29, 1949.

Six months later the federal government approved the breakwater as a barrier to curb erosion of the north beaches with the understanding that the city maintain periodic harbor dredging to replenish its south beaches. The Army Corp of Engineers had previously recommended a groin system for stabilization but abandoned it for one that did without the unsightly and dangerous groins extending into the surf.

Tens of thousands of beach visitors jammed the beach north of the Santa Monica Pier on Independence Day weekend; 1946.

View of the Santa Monica Municipal and Newcomb Piers in 1947. (opposite page)

Standard Dredging Company won the $247,000 project to sluice one million cubic yards of sand to the south beaches. They began moving equipment onto the beach in front of the breakwater at the beginning of November. Three days later the company ran into a snag when they lost their huge 100 ton crane and barge that was used to unload 38,000 feet of pipe. The barge was intentionally beached to unload a second barge loaded with pipe. Trouble occurred when workers attempted to refloat the barge, only to find that it had been securely beached during high tide. When they tried to pull the barge free for relocation, its under planking was ripped to pieces and the crane lay toppled in the surf line.

Once 38,000 feet of steel pipe was in position, the company moved one of the largest dredges on the Pacific Coast into the harbor and set up a temporary bank of transformers to provide power. Rough seas several days later caused them to move the dredge closer to the pier and shore. Fifty additional boats and their moorings had to be removed to make room for the company's equipment.

The company dredged one thousand cubic yards per hour on a twenty-four hour per day schedule. By December 6th, 250,000 cubic yards of sand had been moved. Dredging even continued through rough seas and a 30 MPH gale which swept over the harbor wall, sank the city's harbor tug, and tossed other craft like giant corks at their moorings. They reached the half-way point by December 19th and completed the project on January 15, 1950. The newly dredged harbor was eighteen feet deep near the pier at low tide and ten feet deep further north.

The city in July 1950 began to operate Pound's Bathhouse on the beach on the south side of the Newcomb Pier. Its one-hundred changing stalls gave patrons a place to change clothes when they arrived at the beach and a place to shower at the end of the day. The state bought the land for $35,000 and the city bought the building for $15,000. The city hoped to eventually lease the building to a private concessionaire.

Spade Cooley 'King of Western Swing' and his country-western dance band, which performed in the La Monica Ballroom on weekend evenings, had grown to enormous popularity. KTLA, Channel 5, began broadcasting the band in 1948 on Saturday nights at 8 PM and by 1950 the show was the second most popular Los Angeles television program.

Cooley, who gained his nickname when he once drew a five spade flush in a poker game, came to Hollywood from Oklahoma in 1934. He showed up one day at the

Spade Cooley 'King of Western Swing' entertained dancers at the La Monica Ballroom beginning in 1946. He was televised live on KTLA on Saturday nights at 8 P.M. from 1948-1955. Vocalist Becky Garfield is on Spade's left.

The Santa Monica Pier became increasing popular after World War II when bandleader Spade Cooley began performing in the La Monica Ballroom; 1947. (opposite page)

Walter Newcomb bought a Philadelphia Toboggan Company carousel from Cumberland Park in Tennessee and shipped it to California before World War II. Walter Newcomb supervises unloading of the carousel horses.

The carousel began operating at the Santa Monica Pier on June 27, 1947 after months of restoration by Rudy Illions. It had been operating on the Venice Pier until it was closed in April 1946. Walter's brother Robert, at right, managed the ride. (opposite page)

gate of Republic Pictures with a fiddle and six cents. Roy Rodgers liked him and gave him a job as his stand-in. Eventually he formed his own band and his "barn dance" style entertainment caught on during the war. His theme song was "Shame, Shame on You." Spade's television guests included Tex Owens, Sons of the Pioneers, Roy Rodgers, Tex Williams, Frank Sinatra, Frankie Lane, Count Basie, Dezi Arnez, Ella Fitzgerald, Sammy Davis, and Jo Stafford.

The Santa Monica Pier obtained a unique attraction for its 1950 summer season. Fred V. McGann converted a former 110 foot long navy sub chaser into a toboggan slide by adding a wooden superstructure consisting of two thirty five foot high curved chutes. The barge was parked against the north side of the Municipal Pier. Customers, who rented two man toboggans at $1.50 / hour on weekends and $1.00 / hour on weekdays, slid down the chutes into the harbor waters below. The city received 10% of the gross plus $50 / month rent.

The Toboggan Slide barge, which off season was anchored behind the breakwater and away from the pier, broke loose on October 26th and grounded itself on the beach. Since the craft was in danger of breaking up, it was ordered out of the harbor and moved to San Pedro for the winter. It didn't return the following season, and any plans Newcomb might have had to add additional attractions were indefinitely postponed because of a Korean War imposed amusement building ban.

The Department of Recreation in the fall launched a two phase program for harbor improvement. The first phase was to improve access and launching facilities so boat owners could get their craft into the water. The second phase was to recap the breakwater at a cost of $64,800, then add additional wings to the Municipal Pier for more public boat landings. It was hoped that by attracting small boat owners back to the harbor, the harbor might return to a level of profitability.

City Council approved the first phase of their plans at their November 1, 1950 meeting and authorized paving of an access road to the water's edge parallel to the pier for use by boatmen to launch their boats. Trailer boat parking was to be provided beneath the pier. The funds, however, were contingent on a surplus in that year's current pier repair appropriation which was budgeted for deck repair.

The city, always short of funds, even considered transferring its lifeguard service to Los Angeles County control. It seemed the right thing to do since title to its beaches was transferred to the state in fall 1949, but the City Council voted against it, 4-3 on July 26, 1950. The

Mr. Santa Monica competition was held at Muscle Beach located just south of the pier in the late 40's.

seventeen man fulltime lifeguard corps, which was founded in 1932 and remained under the control of the police department, was put under direct control of the City Council.

But by January 4, 1951 the policies of Supervisor Frank Holborrow created a serious morale problem. He had set up an internal spy system. Captain George Watkins was asked to return to full command of the lifeguards to head off a threatened lifeguard 'revolt'. Three weeks later the city, for the ouster of Holborrow, threatened to shift them to county control.

Sane heads prevailed and instead a complete reorganization of lifeguard duties was effected. In addition to their guard duty, members of the corps were assigned equipment maintenance tasks and were required to teach classes on surf safety. Actually that was nothing new since they always assisted the Department of Recreation and the Red Cross in their summer water safety classes. Those nine week, weekday morning classes taught over 400 people aged 5-55 each summer how to swim and to protect themselves and others from water hazards.

Walter Newcomb, who anticipated in early 1952 that the Korean War imposed amusement building ban would be lifted soon, began negotiating with the city for an extension of his pier franchise. He explained that it was difficult to obtain financing or make plans for long term improvements when only five years of his twenty-one year franchise remained. The City Council was sympathetic but several members were worried that the city might be left with an orphaned pier when Newcomb's twenty-one year franchise ended in 1973. They short sightedly insisted that he agree to tear down his pier when his franchise ended. He agreed to their terms and was granted a new franchise beginning on February 26, 1952. The rent was $250 per month.

An unusual attraction opened on the pier in March 1953 when Henry and Mary Freedman leased the former penny arcade building for the summer season. Henry Freedman, who looked like a balding, bespectacled college professor, had recently returned from the Amazon River in South America where he caught electric eels and piranha fish. Their Tropical Fish Show and Electric Eel Aquarium featured six electric eels, one nearly five feet in length, displayed in large tanks.

Henry would invite the audience to hold hands in a broken circle and would give the two participants on each end the wires from the end of two electric terminals. Then, using a pair of protective gloves, he would remove one of the larger eels from the tank, place it on a table and touch the two terminals against the creature. The

Miss Muscle Beach 1947 was won by Vivian Crockett, a Santa Monica resident. Val Njord (center) and Jackie McCullah (right) placed second and third.

Santa Monica's Muscle Beach Contest was won by Pepper Gomez of East Los Angeles. He was a former fullback for L.A. City College; 1950.

Gymnastics and acrobatics were performed by club members at Santa Monica's Muscle Beach platform.

Four gymnasts perform a double handstand at muscle beach.

Ten year old Beverly Jochner, known as the strongest girl in the world, performs a bridge front bend stunt while Harold Zinkin, weighing 180 pounds does a hand stand on her stomach. She was able to support the weight on her shoulders of three people in a human pyramid weighing 350 pounds. (left)

audience often gasped as they received a shock when the current passed through them. Henry, to satisfy those in the crowd who were still skeptical, then used the eel's current to light an electric bulb held overhead. The show also included two sea lions that performed tricks for the audience. Admission was fifty cents.

The conclusion of the Korean War on July 27, 1953 in effect lifted the building ban on amusement and entertainment facilities. One of the first to take advantage of the situation was Roger Cunningham, president and owner of the Deauville Club. He announced that work would begin in ninety days on the largest and most beautiful yacht club on the Pacific Coast, one that could accommodate 1000 yachts. He planned to expand his club, which already had both an outdoor pool and the largest indoor pool on the west coast, by adding steam baths, a thousand car parking lot, and docks beginning on the shoreline in front of the club. It was an ambitious $7,000,000 project that would provide Santa Monica with a marina nearly twice the size of the one at Fort Lauderdale, Florida.

The City Manager, who was more concerned with the drifting sand that was silting up the harbor, didn't think Cunningham's marina was a solution to the problem. In fact, he thought his proposal bordered on the fantastic and assured detractors that "money like that doesn't grow on federal or private trees anymore." The proposed marina began to look more iffy when Cunningham closed the club in December pending the sale of the property.

Plans to make the Municipal Pier more of a tourist attraction was presented by O.J. Bennett, operator of the Sea Food Grotto, at the City Council's November 24, 1953 meeting. He wanted to build a $250,000 'Fisherman's Wharf' development on the north side of the pier. Thirty stalls, available for eating places, specialty shops and marine exhibits, would extend 560 feet seaward from Bennett's Grotto. The city engineer estimated it would cost $220,000 for piling and decking along the side of the pier. The city wasn't interested in paying for pier improvements.

The city in 1953 began to seriously consider building a new city auditorium to serve as a convention center. They paid Benjamin O. Rees a $3000 consulting fee to prepare plans and recommend a site. His report to the city in February 1954 urged that they consider a beach front site adjacent to the Municipal Pier. He proposed a $1,200,000 three story high auditorium, seating 2500 that would be built as part of the east end of the Newcomb Pier. It would span the promenade and provide an arcade of quality shops below to service tourist activities.

The structure at the beach level would contain facilities for beach activities and serve as a youth activity center.

The $2,000,000 project would require purchasing the Newcomb Pier and all of the ocean front properties across from it. The merry-go-round, bathhouse, and the promenade storefronts would be removed. Parking would be provided in the area between the new auditorium and a renovated ballroom.

The Chamber of Commerce was against a beach front site and instead supported the report's alternative site, the Civic Center area south of the courthouse. Although it would require moving the city's bus yards at a cost of $500,000, it was a more suitable site with sufficient parking and easier access. The Deauville Club was also offered as a possible alternative. It could accommodate 3000 people in the club's auditorium and the cost was only $610,000.

Finally, on June 15, 1954, the City Council by a vote of 4-3 choose the Civic Center site as the economically more feasible location. They felt that the added costs associated with condemning and acquiring the beach front property, rehabilitating the pier and building access roads would put the project over the $2,895,000 budget. Besides there was the possibility that state officials might object to their using state owned beach lands.

While the Newcomb Pier was saved by building the auditorium elsewhere, it suffered a severe setback when Walter Newcomb died unexpectedly in Paris of a heart attack on June 12, 1954. He was 63 years old. His widow, Mrs. Enid Newcomb, continued to run the pier, and her daughters Elizabeth and Betty helped her with the gift shop.

That summer was Spade Cooley's last year at the La Monica Ballroom. With his popularity waning, he moved to Ocean Park's Casino Gardens for his last year on television. After several years of inactivity in Southern California he achieved notoriety in 1961 when he went on trial for the brutal torture killing of his 37 year old wife in the presence of his daughter. He was sentenced to life imprisonment at Chino prison and died there in 1969.

George Gordon and his brother Eugene began doing business on the Santa Monica Pier in 1954. They leased the vacant arcade building where the Eel Aquarium had been the previous summer and installed a new penny arcade with extensive skee ball equipment. It was called Playland Arcade. They also began managing the carousel for Mrs. Newcomb.

The Gordon brothers had grown up in Atlantic City, New Jersey where their father, until George was thirteen, operated a carousel at Rendezvous Amusement Park.

They came to California in 1944 and after the war operated several game concessions on the Ocean Park Pier. The relatively undeveloped state of the Newcomb Pier after Walter Newcomb's death gave them the opportunity to escape from the intense competition at the Ocean Park Pier and thrive.

Others took advantage of the business opportunities on the pier. Mrs. Newcomb's daughter Elizabeth and her husband Richard Westbrook opened Sinbad's Cafe in the old banquet hall next to the La Monica Ballroom. Al Bond and his partner Jeane Crowne began operating Al's Kitchen where Dusty's Chowder House had been, and F. J. Favares opened the Surf View Cafe next to Mrs. Newcomb's gift shop. Edmond Friege took over Lewis Rea's boat sales and rental business at the end of the pier, and Pete Peterson, a former lifeguard, began an aquatic supply business on the pier.

Versal Schuler and his partner Jack Rea began operating their charter boat fishing business from the end of the Municipal Pier after Bob Lamia left. They previously operated out of the Ocean Park Pier's landing, so most of their customers were already familiar with their boats. Their company, Santa Monica Sports Fishing, operated the Bright 1, Indiana, Maiden 1 & 2, Delaware, Jesabel, Pegasus, and Kiaora. Both the Indiana and Kiaora were sixty five foot long vessels that could accommodate forty-five fishermen who fished for barracuda, halibut, bass and rock cod within three miles of the pier. Versal Schuler eventually bought out his partner several years later.

The commercial fishing business was dying out in Santa Monica harbor. Mackerel catches, like sardine catches in the Monterey area, began dwindling by the mid-fifties. It was primarily caused by over fishing and increasing levels of pollution in the Santa Monica Bay. Santa Monica officials were pleased as they had for years made a half-hearted attempt to curtail the fleet by not renewing pier leases that catered to the commercial fishing business.

Santa Monica during spring 1954 explored the possibility of financing its harbor rehabilitation with royalty income from offshore oil drilling in the bay. Ten oil companies informed the city that they wished to drill offshore, but the city wasn't sure if they should call for bids before or after the repeal of the 1939 anti-drilling ordinance was submitted to the voters. They decided in the summer that it would save time and might convince voters if they had a viable contract in hand. They approved a contract with General Petroleum on August 10, 1954 that offered royalties and a $500,000 bonus. The company planned to drill two test wells within five years.

The Deauville Beach Club immediately north of the Santa Monica Pier installed an Olympic size outdoor swimming pool in 1947.

While the electorate in the November 2, 1954 election wholeheartedly approved the auditorium bonds by a two-thirds majority, they trounced the offshore oil drilling initiative. 19,085 voted against it and only 5,576 voted for it.

In March 1955 Santa Monica's recreation director gave the Muscle Beach weightlifters an ultimatum. They either had to form a club that collected dues and carried liability insurance, or he would remove the weights from the beach. The problem started when a small boy picked up a barbell that was too heavy for him. It pulled him forward and the barbell hit another boy on the head. The injured boy's parents sued the city for $200. The city carried no insurance on the playground.

The Muscle Beach Weighlifters Club was formed with Dr. Paul Maclin as its president. Over one hundred members signed up and paid the annual two dollar membership fee. The club agreed to police the beach and get rid of troublemakers. The city was satisfied and made plans at a cost of $10,000 to rearrange the platforms and add bleachers for spectators.

The city, in an effort to clean up the city's image, decided to ban pinball games because they considered them games of chance. The Gordon Brothers Amusement Company, who operated Playland Arcade on the pier, were affected. Their lawyers agreed at the City Council hearing that multiple- odds machines were gambling devices, but pleaded that other pinball devices were not and should be retained. At first the city in May banned all pinball games, but relented in July. Then in September they overturned their ruling and left the courts to decide the issue because the police were not willing to enforce the regulation. The court upheld the ban and it wasn't until the early 1970's that pinball games were allowed back on the pier.

The Santa Monica Pier's new attraction for the 1955 summer season was the opening of the Hollywood Autocade in the La Monica Ballroom. It featured one hundred unusual automobiles ranging from a 1908 Moreland fire engine to Hitler's Auto-Union Horch given to his finance Eva Braun, to a $16,500 Dusenberg. One unusual car was a 1921 German Rumpler Drop Car, an amphibious vehicle designed to be dropped from dirigibles. The exhibit also included many motion picture star's cars like Jack Benny's Maxwell, Clara Bow's Rolls-Royce, and Rudolf Valentino's Lancia. Admission was 75 cents for adults; 25 cents for children.

Lamia's old charter boat office next to the Playland Arcade, which remained vacant throughout most of the previous season, was leased to Gordon and Beryle Brunk-

Looking south along the Ocean Front Promenade; late 40's.

ow by Mrs. Newcomb. They operated a wholesale and retail gift shop that specialized in plaster of paris statutes.

The Gordon brothers by spring 1956 were successful enough to open five kiddie rides in the unused area east of Mrs. Newcomb's gift shop. They bought a gasoline powered Stratton-Bridges train and laid track along the perimeter. The train, which accommodated twenty children in three cars, was operated by an engineer who sat in the five foot long locomotive. Other children's rides included a swing ride, boat and auto flat rides, and a trolley that ran on a figure eight track. The rides never made much money, especially during the long winter season. Consequently, they were moved to the San Fernando Valley after two seasons.

The City Council in the spring of 1956 began studying a report by city engineer Maurice King which stated that the Municipal Pier was in immediate need of repair or replacement. Replacement would cost $653,000, while making repairs that would extend the life of the pier would be only $285,000. In July the Council, by a vote of 5-2 (with Wellman Mills and Rex Minter opposed), authorized the repair work. Mills said they he felt that the expenditure was "throwing good money after bad" in view of the deteriorated breakwater. He questioned the advisability of having commercial fishing on the pier and advocated removal of the lower deck.

The Marco Corporation in late September was awarded the contract to replace fifty-eight pilings for $21,085. The city bought the pilings for $37,096. An additional $40,000 contract was put out for bid in November to rebuild the superstructure. It involved new decking, lighting, handrails and a new restroom. Work was completed by March 15, 1957.

Santa Monica began fighting the state's plan to take over its beach operations in August 1956. The city had been negotiating for more than a year for a long term lease but the state had its own comprehensive plan on the drawing board. Finally, the State Parks Commission agreed in the fall to grant Santa Monica local control with a twenty-five year lease. The city on November 14, 1956 approved the lease and instructed City Manager Dorton to retain the architectural firm of Welton Becket and Associates to prepare beach parking plans between the Ocean Park Pier and Santa Monica piers.

Santa Monica's beach front, like many beach fronts elsewhere, attracted numerous drifters, hustlers and petty criminals. But it was the runaways and perverts that were attracted to its famed Muscle Beach that worried city officials and the police department the most. Their worst nightmare occurred on November 21, 1956 when ten

Sea Scouts on their converted Navy boat Optimist #1. The skipper was G.A. Sprague ; 1949.

year old Larry George Rice's body was found lying in a pool of blood beneath the Santa Monica Pier. He died three hours later from thirty stab wounds.

Two teenagers identified a tall, bushy haired, toothless man with arms of a blacksmith as the man seen with the local lad shortly before the murder. When police found Stephen Nash, a thirty-three year old drifter and pervert, shortly afterwards, they discovered the blood soaked hunting knife on the man. He confessed to the sadistic knife slaying, and ten other murders in Long Beach and Sacramento.

When he was taken back to the scene of the crime the next day, nearly one hundred menacing people gathered and would have lynched him on the spot. Nash said that he talked to the boy for five minutes, then he pulled a knife. When the boy screamed he stabbed him in the stomach, then again and again. Nash was convicted and was executed in the gas chamber in 1959. The city, in an effort to prevent similar incidents, fenced off the area under the pier.

Welton Becket & Associates completed the master plan for Santa Monica's beach improvements in March 1957. The $724,000 project included parking for 2002 cars between the two piers, demolition of Pound's Bathhouse, and the relocation of Muscle Beach between Bay and Bicknell Streets. When the weightlifters objected and the Recreation Commission sided with them, city officials decided to let the weight lifting platforms remain near the pier.

Workers on October 7th began demolishing the old pier harbor office that was built in 1938. They began building at a cost of $10,000 a new eight hundred square foot building at the end of the pier that would house the harbor and harbor master's offices, sleeping quarters, and a garage. The lifeguard headquarters were placed directly beneath the new building on the lower deck. About a month later the Santa Monica Recreation Commission approved construction plans for a new lifeguard headquarters just off Seaside Terrace, south of the pier.

Santa Monica, in an attempt to keep its harbor functional, awarded the $278,000 contract to dredge 535,000 cubic yards of sand out of the harbor to Robert C. Watson. He began the job of moving the sand to the beach south of the pier on November 8th, and had completed 80% of the job when his dredge was beached by heavy winds and high tides during a February 4, 1958 storm. His dredge was damaged when the harbor tug freed it, and it was towed to Long Beach for repairs. The city became concerned that he wouldn't finish the job by summer and suggested that he switch to dragging the

Standard Dredging Company won the $247,000 contract to dredge one million cubic yards from the harbor and deposit it south of the pier. They used one of the largest dredges on the Pacific Coast during the two month project; 1949. (above & opposite page)

sand with huge cable driven shovels powered by shore machinery. Watson, however, decided to finish the job in May using smaller dredges and barely finished in time for the summer beach season.

The City Council took a major step in rebuilding their harbor when they retained George F. Nicholson, a marine engineer, to prepare a harbor survey for $10,000. They were encouraged by Rex Thompson, director of Los Angeles County Harbors and Marinas, who urged Santa Monica to take immediate steps to construct a small boat harbor because by the time it would be completed, Marina del Rey's harbor would be overcrowded. He believed in the use of revenue bonds to finance harbors.

Nicholson's harbor plan, which was presented to the City Council on February 11, 1958, envisioned a marina that would accommodate 1,665 small boats and parking for 3,280 automobiles at a cost estimated at $8,700,000. It was largely based on the city's engineering department's 1956 harbor master plan with several major revisions.

Plans called for an extension of the breakwater that would be extended 1600 feet on the north end and 768 feet on the south end. A viaduct at the north end of the enclosed area would support a two lane road leading out to the breakwater that would be widened to include restaurants, yacht club facilities, and parking. The Santa Monica Pier would be replaced by a filled 'peninsula' which could be ultimately developed for amusements and concessions. The plan also proposed facilities for servicing boat concessions that would operate trips to Catalina Island, extensive boat storage facilities, two landing areas, two fuel stations, and facilities for sports fishing.

Nicholson felt that to minimize funding of capital investment by the city, the three major mooring areas should be leased to private lessees on a competitive basis. These areas included a yacht club, restaurant, fuel floats, gasoline stations, Catalina and sports fishing pier, and the amusement zone on the 'peninsula'. All facilities including the mooring areas would be constructed at the lessees own expense. He thought financing could be obtained through a bond issue.

As Santa Monica explored the possibilities, it appeared that private financing was the only hope that they had to finance their harbor. State and county money was already committed on a first-come, first-served basis to various harbor projects, including the future Marina del Rey harbor. The private bond market was overflooded.

Mrs. Enid Newcomb Winslow, in the Fall of 1958, decided to form a corporation called Bay Amusement Company to manage the pier. The pier franchise was transferred to the company and she became its president.

Swimming and Water Safety classes sponsored by the Red Cross and Santa Monica Lifeguard Service taught 400 children and adults how to swim safely each summer. (above)

A typical summer beach crowd south of the pier. The beach had become narrow before dredging began in 1949. (opposite page)

'Mariners' was a boat oriented scouting group for teenage girls.

Various arcade devices in Harrington's penny arcade; 1947

She had recently remarried Charles Winslow. Her new husband helped her manage the company and run her gift shop, the skating rink in the La Monica Ballroom, and the parking lot. She consolidated her operations that year and sold the Philadelphia Toboggan Company carousel to George Gordon for approximately $20,000.

The Gordon brothers had already expanded their operations the previous year by opening a second Playland Arcade in the old Billiard's building next to the carousel. The new arcade offered archery in addition to the usual variety of amusement devices.

A scandal broke at Muscle Beach on December 10, 1958 when four musclemen were charged with statutory rape and having a sex orgy with two runaway Negro girls, aged twelve and fourteen. Three of the men, William G. Siddall, George C. Sheffield, and David J. Sheppard, former 1956 weight lifting champion, all lived together at an apartment on Appian Way. The fourth man, John J. Carper, was also charged with additional crimes. A warrant was also issued for a fifth man, but charges were dropped when the girls failed to implicate him.

City Manager Randall Dorton closed Muscle Beach the following day pending a hearing and a decision at the next City Council meeting. Councilwoman Alys Drobnick, who was always one of the area's detractors, said, "I don't think Muscle Beach is a proper recreational facility. I've been saying this for the last five years. It attracts a bad element to the area. If the musclemen want a weight lifting club its up to them to provide their own facilities". Then she added, "the Muscle Beach crowd has been bragging about how much publicity they have brought the city. I wonder how they are enjoying the publicity now." Other Council members like Frantz and Mills felt that the area needed more control by the recreation department, and it should be given more attention by the police.

A crowd of more than one hundred attended the two hour hearing on December 16th in the Council chambers. Police chief Otto Faulkner testified that Santa Monica has a "terrific sex deviate problem" and many are attracted to the city by Muscle Beach. He quoted statistics that arrests of pervert suspects each year were between 175 - 200. He concluded by saying, "I firmly believe that Muscle Beach is not an activity the city should provide. I also don't feel the city should provide a place for exhibitionists to show off."

One emotionally distraught mother said that Muscle Beach had corrupted her son and that other mothers were afraid to speak out. One letter read at the meeting asked the Council to take into consideration all the thousands of people who had benefited from Muscle Beach. "Don't close it - Think more of supervision", it implored.

Despite the fact that the courts eventually dismissed the four statutory rape cases for lack of evidence, the City Council indicated that it wouldn't allow Muscle Beach to reopen until it was rebuilt as part of the new Beach Park #4. The city's concern was not the $5000 cost of a new weight lifting platform but the long term expense of full time supervision at $1000 per month that would be required to keep the park safe. Even the decision to install $9,500 in adult gymnastic equipment (rings, bars and vaulting horses) in addition to children's swings and slides was controversial. Mayor Ben Bernard and Councilwoman Alys Drobnick said that they believed the installation of the adult gym equipment in effect restored Muscle Beach without the weight lifting platform. But the new park opened in August and as one lifeguard put it, "the creeps stayed away."

Winter and spring storms during 1959 wrecked havoc in what remained of the city's harbor. The January 5, 1959 storm was the worst in eleven years. Many boats were washed ashore by waves that were nearly thirty feet high. The harbor master, Pat Lister, narrowly missed being tossed into the swirling waters when a 70 MPH gust burst over the harbor office as he was surveying damages. The fierce winds tore off the restroom roof and knocked down pilings. DeLuca's Fish Market flooded when a wall collapsed.

Lister resigned two months later after being criticized by the City Council about his administration and maintenance of the city's harbor and pier. Robert L. Marples was appointed acting chief in April.

A second bad storm struck the harbor on May 3rd when high winds and booming seas caused two boats to break their moorings. They drifted south and struck the Newcomb Pier, causing $4000 damage as one ripped up planks with its mast. Lifeguards attempted to board the 38 foot Eva-Jim and push it free.

The accident renewed the debate over the harbor's deteriorated breakwater. The Harbor Commission in its request for $985,000 to repair the breakwater pointed out that if the last storm would have been worse; it could have wrecked the entire pier.

Harbor consultants, Stone and Youngberg, were hired in the fall to make economic studies to finance the crumbling harbor. They calculated the costs of seven plans ranging from harbor revenue bonds to private financing. It was suggested that the city should let the voters decide how they want to fund the harbor.

Meanwhile the City Council, on the recommendation

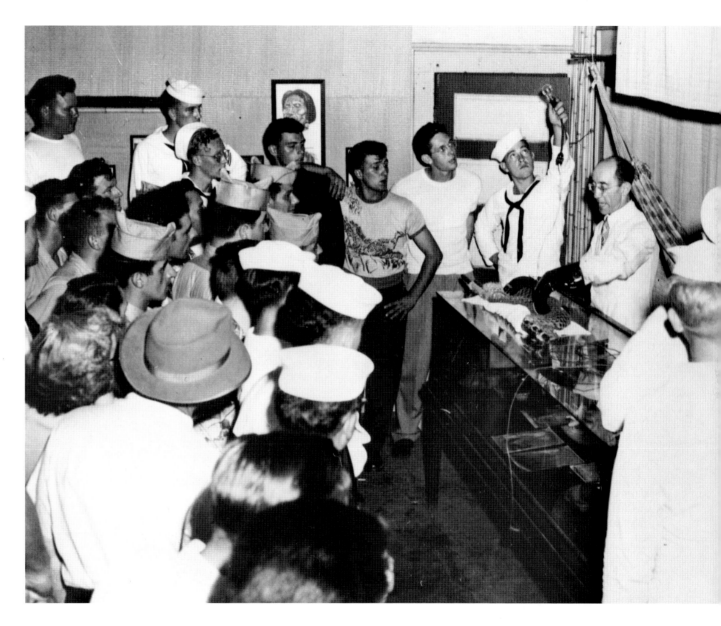

Henry Friedman demonstrates an electric eel's power to illuminate an electric light at his Tropical Fish Show; 1953.

of City Manager George Bundy, decided to keep their weather-beaten harbor open. It was felt that as long as they had a breakwater they were stuck with the harbor. In fact no money would be saved by removing the moorings, and $7000 would be lost in harbor fees.

A citizen committee, formed in November to work for the development of the Santa Monica harbor, planned to circulate an initiative petition asking that the 1939 anti-drilling ordinance be repealed. It would permit General Petroleum Company, which has a contract with the city, to drill in the Bay. The city's share of the revenue would finance the harbor. The committee had six months to obtain 15% of the voters signatures.

While the Chamber of Commerce supported the oil-petition, Mayor Barnard spoke out against it. He called the harbor plan "a pipe dream" and poorly timed. He asked, "Why should we remove a tremendous amount of beach?". He also pointed out that if Santa Monica permitted oil drilling, it would open the entire bay to drilling. The directors of the Chamber of Commerce weren't swayed by his rhetoric and voted unanimously 18-0 to back the tidelands drilling plan.

The oil issue seemed clear until John M. Stahl, a industrial developer who owned a large site at 26th and Colorado, threw a monkey wrench into the harbor project. He wanted to drill for oil on his land and planned to fight Santa Monica's anti-drilling ordinance to drill on-shore. He filed a lawsuit against the city on March 23, 1960.

The five hundred member Santa Monica Committee for Harbor Development decided to stage an all out drive in April to obtain 3000 more signatures on its petition to assure a special tidelands oil-harbor financing election. They had already gathered 5,100 signatures. They succeeded and on June 2nd submitted their petition with 8,446 signatures to the city clerk's office. The 6,104 valid signatures were more than enough to place the measure on the ballot and the election was set for August 23, 1960.

The 'Anti-Oil Crusade' opposition was accused of spreading a dense smoke screen of falsehoods and fabrications as the election drew near. Dr. Cyril Gail, leader of the Santa Monica Committee for Harbor Development, was subjected to a campaign of personal abuse by the members of the opposition. He was accused of trying to turn Santa Monica into an industrial city and was warned that his medical practice would be boycotted.

The Evening Outlook Newspaper exposed the group as being financed by the John M. Stahl Oil Company and called it "a cynical deception." Stahl's lawyers advised him

Mike Tomich's Water Ski School operated off the south side of the pier; 1950.

that his lawsuit against the city's anti-drilling ordinance had a better chance of winning if the offshore oil initiative was defeated.

The majority of the 46% of the registered voters who went to the polls on August 23, 1960 didn't want to risk having their beautiful view of the Santa Monica Bay ruined by unsightly offshore oil rigs. They rejected the oil drilling measure by a 2-1 margin; 6,360 YES and 12,149 NO.

One of the Harbor Commission's jobs was to improve small boat access to the harbor. They recognized that the area north of the pier was inadequate for launching small boats easily and recommended to the City Council in April 1962 that the dirt launching road there be paved and a ramp structure be provided. They also recommended that the city call for bids for an excursion boat service off the pier. The successful bidder would be required to install additional pilings and extend the landing platforms. Maximum recommended fees for motorboat excursions were fifty cents per person.

At the same time that the city engineer called for bids, the city manager began meeting with representatives of the Holiday Construction Company who submitted plans for constructing a small boat launching facility capable of handling 400 boats. The company proposed that a shallow water inlet and basin be dredged out of the area north of the pier, and the area under the pier be paved, covered and fenced to provide small boat storage facilities. They would install a mechanical launching frame that would enable boat owners to launch their boats from trailers and move them to shallow water without leaving their automobiles. Facilities would also include a snack bar, open air pavilion, and an enclosed playground for children. They asked for a long-term franchise. Unfortunately, the city and company couldn't come to an agreement and the offer was eventually dropped.

Santa Monica Harbor officials in May spruced up the pier with a new coat of paint for the 1962 summer season. They were expecting two million visitors. The pier's attractions included twelve restaurants and snack bars, merry-go-round, shooting gallery, two arcades, a roller rink, two fish markets, novelty store, two bait and tackle shops, and room for one thousand fishermen.

In July Mrs. Enid Newcomb Winslow permanently closed the La Monica Ballroom that she and her late husband had operated as a skating rink. The large timbers supporting the high roof were cracking and the roof was sagging dangerously. The building had become a hazard. The city wouldn't condemn the structure as long as it remained closed so she asked the police to rope it off. She

Powerboats await launching by Dutch Horton's crane located on the southwest end of the pier; 1956.

Fishermen on a bait boat harvest anchovies.

Fishing boats unloaded fresh fish destined for sale by the Santa Monica Seafood Company.

planned to tear it down after the summer and erect a Fisherman's Wharf style operation. The building was demolished six months later.

George Gordon consolidated his two arcade locations during the 1962 summer season into a single larger one by swapping his arcade location in the Billiard's building near the carousel with Beryl's Novelty Shop located in the building between his Playland Arcade and Sinbad's. Pete's Bait and Tackle Shop took up space in the rear of the building.

The pier's lack of amusement rides wouldn't be alleviated until the following summer when Rebhahn, Anderson and Brown installed their 'U Drive Cars' in the area behind the carousel building. Initially these gasoline powered carts surrounded by large rubber balloon style bumpers could be driven like bumper cars, but two seasons later they were converted to ride on tracks by a new owner. Kiddie rides would eventually replace the cars, but not until 1970.

The Chamber of Commerce revived Santa Monica's traditional summer sports festival on the pier with the sponsorship of the first Santa Monica Sports Festival in mid August 1962. The highlight of the seventeen day festival was the Malibu to Santa Monica outrigger canoe race. Other events included the National Lifeguard Championships, a Junior Fishing Derby, a surfboard ballet, and an aquacade at Santa Monica College. The festival would continue until the early 1970's.

Santa Monica's plans for building a large boat harbor in the early 60's were tied to plans to build a north-south causeway to alleviate the traffic along the Malibu coast. When the State Highway Commission insisted on a route either along the beach or inland along the foothills, it was feared that the route would either ruin the beach front or split Santa Monica at 7th Street and cut through prime residential districts both in Santa Monica and the Pacific Palisades.

The Harbor Committee, as early as the summer of 1961, pushed for a causeway route that would begin just north of the Santa Monica Pier. Jack Davis of Douglas Aircraft Company prepared preliminary plans that envisioned a series of islands that would support a road bed for the freeway all the way to Point Dume. A bridge would connect to the first island just north of the pier. The route was favored by both Santa Monica and Malibu residents.

The federal government, who took the plan seriously, ordered the U.S. Army Corp of Engineers in January 1963 to begin conducting wave tests for the proposed causeway. They studied beach erosion and wave action on

The Santa Monica Seafood Company owned by Mike DeLuca offered fresh fish caught along the California coastline; 1957.

a submerged reef and artificial dike in a one million gallon tank, twenty feet deep, fifteen feet wide and 635 feet long. They also tested the subsurface structure of the bay. The Army concluded in August 1963 that the causeway plan was feasible from an engineering point of view.

The state favored a coastal route for the freeway because it was the least expensive; $46,300,000 plus $17,900,000 for the rights of way. A mountain route would cost nearly twice as much as a seaside route. Both Santa Monica and Malibu sent a delegation to Sacramento to attempt to block the Highway Department's choice of a freeway route before the causeway route was given a chance.

The U.S. Army Engineer's final report in November, 1963 declared the nine mile causeway route feasible. They studied several alternate plans. While they found the cheapest plan to be the route along the present beach on a widened embankment at $121 million, the cost of a causeway without a new beach on the inner side of the mole was only $247 million. This causeway one half mile offshore would create a 3.3 square mile harbor with half its space devoted to mooring areas. They also considered plans for a structured causeway consisting of a series of eighty foot bridges, two parallel structures each with a roadway 64 feet wide. The cost was only $125 million. The causeway plan would be broken by only eight bridge openings to admit boats. The largest would be 1200 and 1500 feet long, while six others would be in the 550-600 foot range. They felt that the value of the recreational benefits alone would be $60 million greater than the cost of paying for an maintaining such a mole over a fifty year period.

Santa Monica's City Council was so impressed by the report that they appropriated $50,000 to promote and draw up preliminary plans. They hired Moffat & Nichols, a Long Beach engineering firm, as consultants. The plan submitted on October 27, 1964 featured a causeway that extended a mile out to sea on a series of man-made islands. The route, which enclosed 3200 acres, equally divided between water and land, ran from the Santa Monica Pier to just north of Topanga Canyon. Bridges would connect it to shore at Sunset Boulevard and Topanga Canyon. The islands would be 65% residential with the remainder devoted to schools, churches and parks. The project, which would need 200 million cubic yards of fill at a cost of $90 million, would be the world's largest earth moving project.

Assemblyman Robert S. Stevens and State Senator Thomas Rees introduced a bill in the legislature in March 1965 that would enable Santa Monica and Los Angeles

Numerous film crews used the pier and carousel as a set. Dennis Hopper and Linda Lawson star in the movie Night Tide; 1963.

County to establish an agency with the power to finance and build the causeway at no cost to the government. The State Lands Commission was opposed to the bill because they were concerned about the constitutional question of selling state tidelands to private enterprise. They wanted assurances that the tidelands would be leased, not sold, and that the project would be dropped if the Highway Commission rejected the route.

The bill passed in both the State Assembly and Senate in June and was sent to the governor. Both state controller Alan Cranston and the State Lands Commission urged Brown to veto the bill. After vetoing the causeway bill on July 22, 1965 he said, "every possible alternative to a marina causeway should be considered prior to committing the state in this direction."

The lack of a firm commitment by the state to proceed with the causeway plan caused city management to focus their attention instead on the city's deteriorating harbor. The City Manager calculated that the city could save $56,000 the first year and $70,000 afterwards if they terminated harbor operations. Sentiment in the City Council was against the administration's proposal and instead in July 1966 they talked about recapping the breakwater and dredging the harbor. Mayor Rex Minter proposed possibly placing a $2,000,000 bond issue on the future ballot to cover the costs. However, if the public didn't support the measure then he would recommend termination of the harbor.

The Council requested that the City Manager prepare a cost estimate for the revitalization of the harbor that would include either acquisition and rehabilitation of the Newcomb Pier, or adding to the north side of the Municipal Pier with concrete pilings. A large restaurant in Redondo Beach expressed interest in relocating if Santa Monica would modernize their pier. The city needed to place the bond issue on the April 1967 ballot because a $300,000 state grant in matching funds for dredging the harbor would lapse on June 30, 1967.

In December City Manager Perry Scott unveiled an ambitious $5.5 million dollar plan to rejuvenate and glamorize Santa Monica's harbor. He proposed construction of an offshore island 2,400 feet long by 325 feet wide on the inland side of the breakwater. It would occupy about half the space between the end of the Santa Monica Pier and a rebuilt and strengthened breakwater. The island would accommodate fourteen quality businesses such as restaurants and gift shops on the ocean side and parking for 914 cars on the shore side. The pier extended by three hundred feet would become a access road to the island.

Jack Rea, Versal Schuler's partner in a charter fishing business, feeds a pet seal; 1955. (opposite page)

He felt that his island proposal would only cost $1,000,000 more than the cost of restoring both piers, and that it should be submitted to the voters in April 1967. He calculated that the cost of the project over a 25 year period would be $10,789,000. Revenue from the fourteen leases and 914 parking spaces at thirty cents per day would yield $15,181,875.

The City Council was impressed with the proposal and hired Moffatt and Nichols, consulting engineers to see if the project was feasible before putting it on the April 12, 1967 ballot. Their consensus was that the project was feasible and that Scott's estimate was accurate if bids were solicited within the next twelve months.

Voters were confused. The state legislature was attempting to pass a new causeway bill authorizing a feasibility study. Scott assured voters that the island project and the causeway were compatible. Most voters, however, weren't interested in increasing the city indebtedness on a project that might be a waste of money. The harbor bond issue, which needed a two-thirds majority to pass, was defeated; 7,539 For, 7,615 Against.

Assemblyman Paul Priolo, who was sponsoring the causeway feasibility bill, said that a causeway between Santa Monica and Topanga would only cost $235 million. The bill, which required that the study be made by a special causeway commission established jointly by the cities of Los Angeles and Santa Monica plus the L.A. County Board of Supervisors, cleared the Assembly unanimously on May 22, 1967. The Senate passed it on Aug 6, 1967 and was signed by Governor Ronald Reagan on August 31, 1967.

But the city of Los Angeles, the following spring, began having second thoughts about the causeway. Edwin Piper, one of the city's administration officers urged the Los Angeles City Council not to approve the master plan agreement until the causeway's engineering was proved. Santa Monica's City Manager said, "it is just a back door way of saying that Los Angeles doesn't want a causeway."

Despite the appearance of pro-causeway forces at Los Angeles City Council's May 2, 1968 meeting, the causeway plan was dealt a vital blow. The Council, by a vote of 10-0, scuttled the master plan agreement, in effect nullifying the complicated causeway bill approved the previous year. Los Angeles felt that the state should have taken responsibility in financing the study. Assemblyman Paul Priolo, who expressed bitter disappointment, said, "the rejection vote washed out ten years of work by hundreds of people and thousands that supported them."

The fate of the Pacific Coast Freeway that would link

Sports fishing boat 'Bright I' operated by Santa Monica Sports Fishing.

with the Santa Monica Freeway and extend north through Malibu and south to Los Angeles's airport was decided several years later. Enormous public pressure, first in Venice and later in Santa Monica and Malibu, won supporters in the state legislature. Alan Sieroty's bill deleting the southern portion of the freeway was passed in 1970, and a similar bill introduced by Paul Priolo to delete the remainder of the highway was passed in 1971. Despite objections of the Santa Monica Chamber of Commerce, Santa Monica's City Council backed the freeway deletion bill by a vote of 5-2.

The defeat of the Harbor Bond Measure in the April 1967 election only postponed the city's desire to rehabilitate the city's piers. Mayor Herb Spurgin advocated purchasing the Newcomb Pier over a ten year period for $500,000. Councilman Virgil Kingsley, on the other hand, favored waiting for the lease to expire in February 1973. It was apparent that Mrs. Winslow was anxious to sell because her 25 year lease, when it expired, required her to demolish the pier at her own expense. Naturally she was reluctant to spend money to repair the pier deck or the pilings beneath and when damage occurred she fenced it off.

Ironically, while the general public in the mid to late 60's were becoming disinterested in Santa Monica's Newcomb and Pacific Ocean Park piers, many of Los Angeles' avant-garde artists and musicians were becoming fond of the dilapidated Newcomb Pier, particularly the pier's carousel. The seven unheated apartments above the carousel, since the early 50's, were rented by writers, actors and ordinary people. By the mid 60's it was home to people like James Elliot, chief curator at the Los Angeles County Museum of Art, graphic artist Clare DeLand, Coleen Creedon, Herb Albert's secretary at A & M Records, Jan Butterfield, public relations director for L.A. County, and artist Robert Irwin. Music people like Joan Baez, who lived nearby in Santa Monica often dropped by to visit Coleen Creedon.

Tenants living above the carousel could watch the ride below from their inside apartment windows. But the carousel's noise was often a mixed blessing. While most enjoyed music in their ears as they went about their daily chores, late risers were awakened by the sound of the band organ and the songs became repetitious throughout the day. However, living there was a unique experience.

It became fashionable in the late 60's to attend weekend parties hosted by James Elliot. Many upcoming artists would gather at the carousel and then venture off for an organized picnic at the beach sometimes near the pier, or often at Malibu. They would return at dusk after

the carousel was closed, decorate the area adjoining the carousel, and hold their parties. At other times motion picture studios and celebrities would rent the carousel for their evening parties.

The carousel attracted people from all walks of life, some who rode, others who just liked to watch it or listen to its band organ. In the early 60's President John F. Kennedy brought his children for a ride when he came to Santa Monica to visit his brother-in-law Peter Lawford who lived nearby on the beach. Marilyn Monroe visited the carousel several times at three or four week intervals just before her suicide. She would arrive by limousine and dressed in a drab raincoat and her face masked by sun glasses, she would stand for a half hour or more by the Wurlitzer to watch the carousel. Monroe was depressed and the carousel music renewed her. The carousel also renewed countless others, and would eventually become both the city's and pier's most cherished symbol.

Mayor Spurgin presented a new pier development plan to the City Council at their May 11, 1968 meeting. The plan, which would be financed by a private developer, would be similar to Port's of Call Village in San Pedro, a series of small single story commercial shops and small restaurants out along an enlarged pier. The merry-go-round, which would be relocated near the entrance to the new pier, would be the focal point of a small amusement center for children.

Parking would be provided with the construction of a two story 1200 car parking garage on the north side of the pier. The upper level would be for pier parking and the lower level for beach parking. The city would need to double the width of the pier's access bridge and add another lane along the pier. Spurgin assured them that an unnamed developer was ready to upgrade the pier and that he was currently in negotiations with the firm. The key point was whether the city was willing to buy the Newcomb Pier from Mrs. Winslow.

The city's reluctance to take any action upon placing both piers under city ownership was apparent. It wasn't until June 8, 1970 that the City Council once again asked the City Manager to prepare a report on the purchase of the Newcomb Pier, a report that he was instructed to prepare years earlier, yet did nothing. The impetus then was that the Newcomb Pier was attracting 'unsavory characters' and that residents were afraid to walk on the pier. Mayor Spurgin implored, "We either develop the pier as a tourist attraction, something the city can be proud of, or we can leave it the mess it is."

By the summer of 1971 the City Council was beginning to lean towards building a new pier and asked City

Manager Perry Scott to prepare a study. Instead he came back on November 10, 1971 with a fantastic plan to build a thirty five acre island off Santa Monica. He would use the breakwater as a base and connect the island to shore by an arch-type bridge. The island, which would be built by private financing and leased to a developer for sixty-six years, would cost $10,000,000. Both piers would be removed after February 1973, and many of the pier businesses could be rebuilt on the island. The cost of razing the piers would be between $180,000 - $250,000.

Scott had been holding private discussions with William Bates's Sherman Oaks based Mutual Development Corporation. They unveiled their plans with a formal proposal to the city on June 5, 1972. They proposed to build their 35 acre island with rock and nearly 2,000,000 cubic yards of sand that had been accumulating behind the breakwater. The cost of the initial phase of the project would be between $12 - $15 million. Two thirds of the island including a lagoon would be devoted to free recreation; fishing, biking, etc. A twenty-nine story, 1500 room hotel would be built at a cost of $18 million on the northern end of the island. A 60,000 square foot convention center would be situated near the hotel. There would also be a complex on the south end of the island that would include five restaurants, an ice hockey rink, bowling alley, four theaters, and numerous tourist shops. Underground parking would be provided for 5000 cars that would reach the island by a four lane bridge.

Bates said that construction, pending approval of the U.S. Corps of Engineers and the California Lands Commission, could start in the fall of 1973. They planned to use the existing pier during construction, but would be required to tear it down when they were finished. The city during the first twenty-five years of the sixty-six year lease, would receive 15% of the gross hotels receipts and 1.5% from the other businesses. Although the company would pay no ground rent during the first 25 years, they would pay $48,000 per year afterwards. The developer posted the required $50,000 security deposit with the city and the City Council scheduled a hearing at their June 13, 1972 meeting.

One hundred forty persons packed the Council chambers for the two hour debate. Opposition to the island was spearheaded by the Los Angeles chapter of the Sierra Club whose spokesman Ron Allin said the club's board of directors voted to protest the off-shore island. They felt that the proposed island would physically damage all beaches south of it by interrupting the drifting sand. Further the skyscraper hotel would interfere with a clear view

of the sea. He concluded his protest with the statement, "We consider this island to be an exploitation of the marine environment."

Councilman Nat Trives said that fishing would be improved and the Sierra Club should await studies by experts. Besides, he pointed out, sand is building up behind the breakwater and soon it will block all movement south.

Other opponents like Santa Monica resident Alice Chew labeled the proposal "another plastic shopping mall - the finest land developer is nature." Robert Hunn called the high-rise hotel a "blemish on the landscape." Samuel Wacht, the architect for the project termed some of the objections "Nonsense." "The project as proposed tonight can be nothing but an improvement for Santa Monica", he said. The opposition might have had some hope if Councilwoman Clo Hoover had been at the meeting, but she was away on business.

Despite the protest, the City Council by a vote of 6-0 decided to enter into an agreement with Mutual Development Corporation to build the island. Santa Monica as an act of good faith set aside $10,000 for preparing permit applications. The developer had already spent $100,000 on the proposal.

An anti-island group, 'Save Santa Monica Bay Committee' headed by Pieter van den Steenhoven asked the City Council in early August to hold a referendum on the island issue. City attorney Richard Kickerbocker explained that asking the voters to decide the island issue would be a futile effort since the city had already signed the contract. Both federal and state constitutions prohibited legislation that impaired the rights of existing contracts. He then cited numerous court decisions that invalidated any moves to break or change contracts made by governmental bodies.

The anti-island group's strategy was to stall for time while waiting for the passage of the California Coastal Protection Initiative (Proposition 20) on the November ballot. The state initiative would enforce strict controls on building near the coast. They decided to file a lawsuit anyway since it would at the very least raise a cloud of uncertainty over the proposed island. The group felt that it was unlikely that the developer would proceed until the legal cloud was lifted.

The Save Santa Monica Bay Committee filed their suit in Santa Monica Superior Court on September 8, 1972 to block the island on behalf of the taxpayers. They asked the court to invalidate the contract because the Council failed to prepare an environmental impact report before entering into the contract with the developer. The suit

The La Monica Ballroom was demolished in December 1962. (left)

also tried to prevent city officials from spending $10,000 for the city's share in preparing the EIR.

Sentiment against despoiling the California coast and particularly Santa Monica Bay ran high that fall. Even the Santa Monica Evening Outlook newspaper campaigned against the island. They said, "Major harbor improvement is a highly desirable goal, but linking it to the hoped for financial success of a towering hotel a few hundred yards offshore is a concept the public has made it clear they will not buy". They were right. Proposition 20 was passed by 55% of the state voters; 61% of Santa Monica's voters. The next day Perry Scott said that the island plan looked doomed as a result of the coastal initiative since the developer would need to submit its plans to the regional Coastal Commission to obtain a permit.

On December 22, 1972 the Santa Monica City Council announced that it would reassess its stand on the island within the next thirty days. Two Council members were ready to cancel the contract while five others were worried about the city's financial obligation for the developer's expenses if the contract were cancelled. They were all anxious to see the EIR that was being prepared by the developer. Mayor Anthony Dituri said that he was hoping for "something to happen to get the city off the hook" on its contract.

On January 3, 1973 the city asked Superior Court to dismiss the island suit because it wasn't legally valid. They explained that since the island needed additional permits from the U.S. Army Corp Engineers and the Coastal Commission, the court petitioners had not exhausted all available remedies.

Two hundred Santa Monica island foes jammed the January 9, 1973 City Council meeting as a result of a misleading radio report that the island was on the agenda. Actually the real issue before the Council was a request by Bay Amusement Corporation for a temporary extension of their Newcomb Pier lease that would expire on February 28th. The extension was approved on a month to month basis with a rent increase from $250 to $750 per month. Ernest Barbey acknowledged that his firm would tear down the pier once the lease was terminated.

The Council, responding to an angry crowd, agreed to an island plan hearing to be held at the Santa Monica Civic Auditorium on January 23rd. Leonard Clunes, who had been coordinating the petition drive to place the island issue on the April 10th ballot, charged that his

The Municipal Pier's lower deck was a popular fishing area; 1964.

group opposed the pier's demolition. "We have a legal right to the pier", Clunes shouted from the back of the Council chambers. "Remember there is an election in April," several members of the audience jeered. A group of young people let out repeated yells of "Save Santa Monica Pier" as the anti-island group left the meeting.

Many members of the anti-island group were young anti-war activists, UCLA students drawn to Santa Monica's Ocean Park neighborhood by low rents and beach front living. The pier provided the perfect focus for these radicals who were strongly conservation oriented and perceived Scott's plan as an outgrowth of a business-dominated municipal government. They put their hearts into the effort to defeat the island and save the pier. By January 15, 1973 they had accumulated over 7000 signature on a petition to place the issue on the April ballot.

The long awaited environmental impact report was unveiled on January 19th. The 150 page report generally gave the project favorable marks, but predicted some adverse effects. The study concluded that the island would be "an imaginative, balanced, and unusually beneficial private and public development. The most serious environmental effect would be the disruption of the southward drift of sand along the beach, but the effect can be overcome by dredging."

Councilman Arthur Rinck broke rank with supporters of the island and announced his opposition to the proposed plan. He said he wasn't going to support renovation of the existing piers either. "I'd like to see both piers removed and the beach returned to its natural state." He also said that the removal of the piers would make the beaches safer since it attracts many undesirables.

Over a thousand people packed the Civic Auditorium for the January 23, 1973 Santa Monica Island hearing. They heard a testimony from the project's few supporters and numerous opponents. Finally at 1 A.M. when the crowd had dwindled to about 300 people, the Council members, faced with mounting election pressure, voted 4-2 to scrap the island plan. By rejecting the development plans and returning the deposit, the Council's action amounted to termination of the contract.

The boisterous partisan crowd was jubilant over the demise of the island plan, but then their joy suddenly turned to anger when Councilman Arthur Rinck made a motion to demolish both piers. He said that he interpreted the passage of Proposition 20 as a "mandate from the people" that they are opposed to construction of any kind near the water. The motion without discussion quickly passed by a vote of 4-2. Those who voted for the pier's removal were Robert Gabriel, James Reidy, Arthur Rinck

and Mayor Anthony Dituri. John McCloskey and Clo Hoover were opposed. "Think of the people who want the pier," pleaded Mrs. Hoover. "You can't destroy what they want."

The following day City Manager Perry Scott spoke out in favor of removing the Santa Monica Pier. He in particular lashed out at the Bay Amusement Company who for the past twenty years had been only paying $250 / month rent for twenty odd businesses on the pier. He said that city taxpayers had been subsidizing the business operators on the pier. He pointed out that records around the state show that piers have not been good paying propositions and that is why most have disappeared over the years. Scott added, "There's a very substantial use of the pier by those who don't spend money. I'm talking about the kids and the elderly who come out to dangle hooks. The pier might be charming to some folks - but I wonder how much the general public should pay for that charm."

The pier's merchants began to rally to rescue the pier from demolition. They formed a group called 'Friends of the Santa Monica Pier' and began meeting daily at Al's Kitchen. Larry Barber, the restaurant's cook, became head of the group. In one of his first interviews he stated, "We believe the pier is too central to the identity of Santa Monica to be destroyed. It's like family. You don't get rid of your grandmother because she is a little old."

Jack Sikking, the manager of Al's Kitchen was the mastermind behind the group's strategy. He realized that Santa Monica's media was against the pier, so instead he decided to concentrate on getting the message to the people through newspapers and radio in Los Angeles because they were more sympathetic to the pier. The group was in desperate need of funds for their media blitz so Joan Crowne, owner of Al's Kitchen took out a $17,000 mortgage on her home. Sikking used the money to produce and distribute an illustrated 'Save Santa Monica Pier' booklet that showed the public that they would be losing a unique historic landmark if they allowed the city to tear it down.

Diane Cherman was co-chairman of the 'Save Santa Monica Pier Citizen's Committee', another group trying to save the pier. She solicited funds from the pier businesses for a drive that included petitions, brochures, radio and newspaper advertising, and 'Save Santa Monica Pier' car bumper stickers. Their goal was to pressure the City Council to rescind its order to have the pier removed.

The four Councilmen who voted to tear down the piers refused to be intimidated by public pressure and apparently weren't aware that they were out of tune with what the public wanted. They were convinced that they

acted in the best interests of the city. "The pier is a tired, old and dingy thing and the economics of fixing it up are not worth it", the Mayor asserted. "After it is down maybe the people will support a bond issue to put up something else. I'm not in favor of the taxpayer's subsidizing the businesses that have been drawing the criminal and drug elements to the city."

An overflow crowd of 350 people that spilled into city hall hallways, attended the February 13, 1973 City Council meeting. Most of the people who were fighting to save their pier were frustrated by Council rules where members of the audience could be heard only if the Council majority opens an issue to full discussion. Dianne Cherman, active in the 'Save-the-Pier' campaign, approached the microphone with a stack of petitions, but Dituri ruled her out of order. Council members ignored the noisy protests of the crowd by tabling a motion to open the pier controversy for a public hearing. And by a vote of 4-2 also refused to consider a proposal to put the pier preservation issue to the vote of the people on April 10th.

One impassioned youth expressed the feelings of most of the crowd best when he yelled, "Tear down the pier and you tear out the very heart of Santa Monica." Other young people held placards like the "Pier belongs to the people." One sign that drew the biggest accolade read, "Remove (City Manager Perry) Scott, not the pier." The police eventually ordered all the signs removed.

The Council did agree to listen to a presentation on restoring the pier by Larry Barber, head of Friends of the Santa Monica Pier. He and seven others outlined a plan that included restoring the dome on the carousel, adding a museum and first class restaurants, converting the parking lot into a park, and adding a dance stand plaza. They also proposed an art gallery, theater, and children's rides.

Jerome Sarrow, attorney for Bay Amusement Company, reminded people after the conclusion of the meeting that "the Council's action by no means indicates that the piers will go down as they need a permit from the South Coast Regional Coastal Commission created by Proposition 20. Even if they got permission, it is subject to a veto at the state level, as well as possible legal action challenging the issue of the demolition permit."

The following day the Los Angeles Times covering the filming of 'The Sting' at the merry-go-round on the Santa Monica Pier interviewed Robert Redford. "The pier is fun", he said. "It's a landmark. Everybody likes to visit the pier. I think it should be made into a museum. Not just out of nostalgia, but for a sense of history."

The public kept the pressure up and vowed to defeat

The pier's merry-go-round was used extensively during the filming of The Sting; 1973.

three of the four Councilmen who voted to raze the piers and were up for April reelection. So it wasn't much of a surprise on February 21st when Robert Gabriel, James Reidy and Arthur Rinck said that they would rescind their order to raze the Municipal Pier but not the Newcomb Pier at the next Council meeting. While they admitted they misjudged the public as a reason for changing their minds, they said they were most influenced by the imaginative proposal made by the Friends of the Santa Monica Pier. They suggested a citizen's committee be appointed to study the ocean front and come up with a recommendation to save the Newcomb Pier. If the committee could do that by September 4th, there would still be time to rescind the demolition order.

The Municipal Pier was reprieved by a 6-0 Council vote at the February 27, 1973 meeting, but it failed to quell the clamor over the issue. A jeering, overflow crowd of pier businessmen and pier patrons demanded that the Council also cancel its notice to Bay Amusement Company to tear down the Newcomb Pier. Instead the Council said they would at its March 13th meeting appoint a fifteen member citizen's committee that would draw up plans for both piers. The Mayor asked that nominations be sent to him.

The pier merchants hired a publicist to protect their holdings and demanded that three of their members be named to the citizen's committee that would study the pier and harbor area. They decided to spend thousands of dollars in a "Don't Dis ap-Pier" campaign to stop the removal order, and threw their support to three candidates in the April election; Rev. Fred Judson, Mrs. Donald Swink and incumbent John B. McCloskey.

Councilwoman Clo Hoover, who wasn't running for reelection but favored revitalization of the piers, zeroed in on City Manager Perry Scott, who, she said, considered piers to be "honky-tonk." Scott had been a long-time opponent of the pier. "We have permitted a paid employee (Scott) to dictate what Santa Monica should be," she charged. "He has gone overboard in selling the pier removal to his majority."

Election politics was on everyone's mind throughout March and early April. Harmony reigned among the various pier groups until March 30th when the Save the Pier Citizens Committee was evicted form their headquarters at Sinbad's on the pier by the Santa Monica Pier Businessmen's Association. A dispute developed over two flyers that the committee distributed for candidates Renee Gould, Richard Palmer and Garth Sheriff. The pier businessmen accused them endorsing candidates instead of saving the pier on its own merits.

Camera crews film a scene from 'The Sting' on the carousel's staircase - Robert Redford and Eileen Brennan; 1973.

Robert Redford and Paul Newman pose for photographers during the filming of 'The Sting.'

While only 44% of the voters went to the polls on April 10, 1973, those who did vote were intent on throwing out of office those Council members who voted to tear down the city's beloved piers. Incumbents Robert Gabriel, James Reidy, Jr. and Arthur Rinck were defeated, and they would have ousted Mayor Dituri, too, if his name would have been on the ballot. The populace instead elected Fred M. Judson, Donna Swink, John McCloskey and Pieter van den Steenhoven, a group who were all strong advocates of tighter control of any future harbor development. The voters by a margin of 78% also approved an initiative that would require voter approval for future major development in the Santa Monica Bay.

The new City Council elected Clo Hoover as Mayor, and as their first order of business, by a vote of 6-1 decided not to renew Perry Scott's contract. They postponed a decision on the Newcomb Pier despite complaints by the Citizen's Committee that they couldn't make a fair study of the pier rehabilitation until the order to tear down the pier was rescinded.

Finally on May 8, 1973, to the relief of everyone, the Council voted 6-1 to rescind the order to raze the Newcomb Pier. Anthony Dituri, who obviously hated the pier, was the dissenting vote. The Council, seeking a future bargaining tool in negotiating the extension of the pier lease, insisted that Mrs Winslow sign a statement that her firm still had an obligation to remove the pier under the terms of the twenty-one year lease.

Several weeks later Mrs. Winslow asked for a long term lease on the Newcomb Pier. She wanted an outside agency to draw up plans for the pier's improvement and that the plans be paid for equally by her Bay Amusement Company and the city. She felt that if the plans weren't acceptable to both parties, then the city should acquire the Newcomb Pier.

An initiative petition drive was revived in June to put the preservation of the Santa Monica and Newcomb Piers on the ballot. The Citizen's Initiative to Preserve the Piers was chaired by Richard Palmer and Garth Sheriff, two unsuccessful candidates for City Council. Councilman Nat Trives criticized the group for stirring up the public into wondering if the present Council was planning to tear down the piers since the election of a pro-pier majority assured their preservation. Garth Sheriff said the initiative was to protect the piers from future Councils. The group had collected 2000 signatures for Proposition #1 before the election and only needed 7000 to place it on the November ballot. They did reach their goal by the end of the summer, but withdrew the initiative when a large percentage of the gathered signatures were found to be invalid.

The city received numerous unsolicited proposals to take over and revitalize the Newcomb Pier. Perhaps the most promising was from the owners of the Redondo Beach Pier. Hal Pollock proposed a partnership with the development firm of S. Epstein and Associates who would demolish all the buildings on the pier and build two 5000 square foot restaurants. In return for a fifty year lease, they offered the city a minimum of $25,000 per year and 3% of the gross. The City Council tabled the proposal on June 13th along with dozens of others.

People already doing business on the pier submitted five proposals to the City Council in July. Four of the five proposals were for operating the pier on an interim basis while a long range plan for the beach front was drafted. The fifth was based on a long-term lease. Mayor Clo Hoover was in favor of continuing the present lease on a month to month basis.

Bay Amusement Company offered the city $1750 / month for a five year lease. They, however, wanted the provision that they had to tear down the pier removed from the lease. They said that if they were awarded the lease, they would spend $125,000 for repairing and maintaining the pier over the lease period. They had no plans for expanding the pier's attractions.

Mrs. Winslow's daughter and her husband, Richard Westbrook submitted a separate proposal under the corporate name Sinbad's. They offered to pay $2000 / month rent or 10% of the gross tenant rent, whichever was higher. They proposed to spend $100,000 to renovate the existing buildings, and assured the city that their tenants would spend an additional $150,000 for new rides and games. After the master plan was finalized in five years, they proposed a 33 year lease at $1000 / month or a percentage of the gross. They would agree to, if awarded the long-term lease, to start a $900,000 construction program that would include new buildings and parking facilities. They also proposed to sell the family's land at the entrance of the pier to the city for half of its market value estimated at $500,000.

Other less ambitious proposals were made by Howard Kleinman of Fiesta Concessions and George Gordon who owned the merry-go-round and arcade. Kleinman offered the city $6000 / month rent graduating to $10,000 over a five year period and proposed spending $100,000 to renovate the pier. Gordon only offered to give the city $2500 / year with 10% each additional year afterwards if he were given a lease to operate it.

The fundamental question was who actually owned the pier. While Bay Amusement Company said that the city recognized its ownership in its 1952 tidelands lease agreement, the city in asking for bids from private companies to manage the pier, felt that it owned the pier. However, the city knew that if it had accepted Bay Amusement Company's bid, it would have forfeited any presumption of ownership and would have given up the lever it had in the destruction clause in its lease with the company. Then again it was obvious that if the city awarded the lease to anyone outside Mrs. Winslow's family, they couldn't access the pier without Mrs. Winslow's land at the entrance. It was a dilemma that obviously could only be solved by the city's purchase of the Newcomb Pier.

The Beach Commission came to the same conclusion when the pier sub-committee released their twelve page report in September. It urged the city to buy the Newcomb Pier and renovate it, but cautioned that they didn't expect the pier operation to contribute significant net revenue to the general fund. They felt that a great deal of the pier's charm was due to low cost, low key commercial development, and that Santa Monicans didn't want a high density, intensely commercial development on the piers.

An open character to the pier was urged, one oriented to pedestrians. Since it was obvious that the pier couldn't be developed with parking on the pier, they recommended that parking for 1500-2000 cars be built adjacent to the pier. They felt that the pier should have no amusement rides because they would encourage use by unsupervised adolescents who by their presence would discourage the elderly and low income people from using the pier. However, they recommended that the merry-go-round and existing pinball machines should be retained to keep the young people interested in the pier.

Despite a climate of long-term business uncertainty on the pier, Maynard Ostrow and his partner Harold Kleinman in August 1973 opened a bumper car ride on the site of the defunct La Monica Ballroom. It was Fiesta Concessions second business on the pier. They had previously converted an unused area west of the Beachcomber Gift Shop in March 1972 into a games area. It featured numerous games like the 'Ring the Coca Cola Bottle Game' and the 'Ball in the Basket Game' where customers competed for stuffed animal prizes by tossing balls or rings at various targets. Fiesta's games area had competition on the pier. Various operators since 1956 had been operating skill games like the 'Milk Bottle Game', 'Tic Tac Toe Game', 'Fish Bowl Game' and 'Sling Shot Game' in a location immediately east of the fortune teller.

A structural survey of the pier, which Koebig and Koebig prepared for the city in January 1974 at a cost of

Santa Monica Pier in 1973. It was the last year that Sinbad's Restaurant operated.

$25,000, revealed serious structural deficiencies. Officials immediately closed the pier to traffic beyond the parking lot because the seaward end of the pier was in serious danger of collapse. There were twenty completely deteriorated pilings at the turnaround area and marine borers had attacked the new pilings that had been replaced five years earlier. They found the wooden pilings on both piers to be heavily infested by marine worms and the decking on the Newcomb Pier to be structurally unsafe. They estimated that the full reconstruction cost of the Newcomb Pier and its deck in 1977 dollars at $4.6 million, but immediate repairs to the Municipal Pier would cost the city only $300,000.

The City Council at their January 8, 1974 meeting authorized $280,000 for Municipal Pier repairs. They also instructed City Manager James D. Williams to develop plans for restoration of the adjoining Newcomb Pier beginning with a legal showdown with the pier operator. They decided by a vote of 6-0 to give Bay Amusement Company notice that they were in default of their lease with the city for failure to keep the pier in good condition. They told them that unless conditions were corrected within sixty days, the city would exercise its legal rights under the terms of the lease.

Repairs to the Municipal Pier were expected to be completed by summer. Fifty nine pilings needed replacement and 120 that were considered unnecessary were scheduled to be removed. Others were to be encased in concrete. But at the end of January repairs were postponed because the city couldn't find a supply of pilings.

The Newcomb Pier's carousel narrowly averted destruction on Monday March 4th, when a fire started in a trashcan at the southwest corner of the building broke through a window and spread through a maintenance room up to the second floor. Kathie Ellen Patterson, who lived on the promenade below, saw the flames and raced up the carousel's outside staircase to warn tenants in apartments above. Meanwhile Colleen Creedon's husband, who lived in the southwest corner apartment, ran downstairs with a fire extinguisher to battle the spreading flames, but to no avail.

Four fire engines from the nearby firehouse on 6th Street arrived only minutes later at 9:30 P.M. It took them thirty minutes to extinguish the blaze and rescue tenants and pets. The fire chief said that in another five minutes they would have lost the entire building. Luckily the carousel suffered only minor water and smoke damage but two upstairs apartments were gutted and four others were damaged. The fire caused $75,000 in damages.

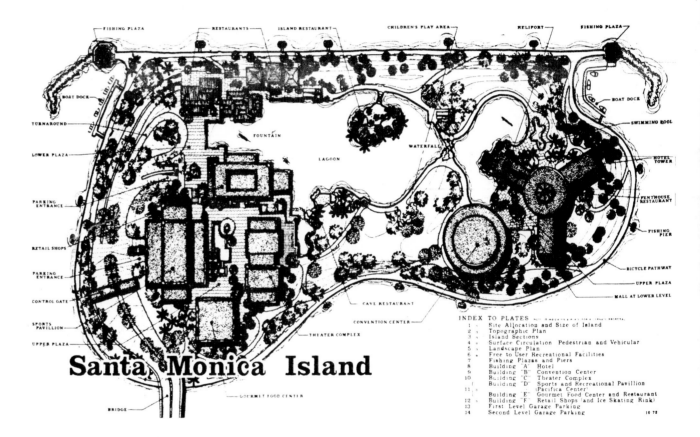

Map of the Santa Monica Island plan in 1972.

The fire was deliberately set. Numerous witnesses said two sixteen year old youths, one with long blond hair, were seen near the trash bins only moments before the fire started. The two perpetrators vanished and were never caught.

The city hoped to begin its pier repairs on May 1, 1974. They accepted a bid in April of $172,000 by Commercial Diver's of Long Beach to replace pilings and remove the extra ones. The city purchased 85 pilings to replace the rotted ones for $33,000 and applied for a Coastal Commission permit to remove the unnecessary pilings. They also extended the Bay Amusement Company's deadline for beginning their pier repair work.

But Santa Monica, after four months of unsuccessful negotiations, lost patience on May 7, 1974 when they gave Bay Amusement Company three days notice to cease management operations. They intended to follow it with a lawsuit for damages for failure to maintain the pier in good condition. City officials then notified the pier's businessmen that they should pay their June rent to the city rather than to Bay Amusement Company.

The city filed a lawsuit in Superior Court on May 23rd to take over the Newcomb Pier and collect $4.6 million for repairing the dilapidated structure. They also asked for $12.4 million in punitive damages and $10,000 / month for Bay Amusement's failure to cease operations as of the May 10th deadline.

Once the City Council informed Bay Amusement Company that their rent as of July 1, 1974 would increase 1000% to $10,000 / month, the pier operator sued the city over the rent dispute. Bay Amusement filed a lawsuit in Superior Court on June 4th, claiming the city has no legal right to increase the rent from $750 / month to $10,000 / month because of provisions of the lease. The lease stated that they could occupy the pier for six months after the lease ended without any payment of rent. Since they contended that the city's action was "malicious and unreasonable" they asked for $65,000 in damages for loss of subtenants rents, $30,000 for loss of business and $25,000 punitive damages for Enid Newcomb Winslow, the firm's president.

Superior Court Judge Laurence J. Rittenband on June 21, 1974 heard both sides of the pier lawsuit. While the city claimed that Bay Amusement had not kept the pier in good condition, Edgar L. Fraser, their attorney, countered that there was no point to keep up maintenance in recent years because the company knew it was obligated to demolish it within six months after termination of its lease. However, the city wanted the structure to remain despite obligating Bay Amusement Company to demolish it. "Our position all along has been that we're ready willing and able to demolish it. If the city wants the pier, we'll give it to them tomorrow. All we're asking for is a release from liability," Fraser said.

City attorney Richard Kickerbocker said Santa Monica wouldn't want the pier in its current condition because it has "negative value". The cost of repair is so great that if the city took it over, it couldn't afford to maintain it. It was plainly obvious that the demolition clause in the 1952 lease had been self-defeating because it discouraged maintenance and replacement of the infested pilings over the last decade.

When the two litigating parties met in the judge's chambers the following Monday morning, Judge Rittenband urged a compromise after he told the city that they were not entitled to collect damages from Bay Amusement Company. The central issue in the negotiations was the price asked for Mrs. Winslow's property at the entrance to the pier. She had the land appraised for $380,000 several years earlier. The city then offered $200,000 as a compromise in exchange for Bay Amusement's obligation to tear down the pier. The city agreed to pay for the pier over a five year period with 4% interest on the unpaid balance.

The City Council voted 5-0 to approve the pier pact on June 28, 1974 and vindicate Mrs. Winslow. The city immediately took over the pier's operations the following day. Since it was now liable for injuries, the city installed chain-link fence around all unsafe areas of the Newcomb Pier. The area, including the damaged merry-go-round, comprised about one-third of the pier. They said the unsightly fencing would be removed as soon as repairs could be made.

The Carousel narrowly escaped destruction on March 4, 1974 when a fire set in a nearby trashcan nearly burned the building down. (opposite page)

Pier repairs in 1974 required replacing numerous pilings at the end of the pier including several beneath the Harbor Patrol office. This required driving a pile through the roof and floor of the building.

CHAPTER 6

City Owned Pier (1974-1990)

The city, aware that their newly acquired pier would require money to rehabilitate, hired for $5500 an outside consultant, Economic Research Associates, to prepare a financial plan. Their July 22, 1974 report recommended that Santa Monica issue $1.1 million in twenty year general obligation bonds to be repaid from the various pier businesses. It would require that much money just to bring the Newcomb Pier up to building code requirements.

The group studied the demographics and spending habits of the 2.4 million yearly visitors and found that 70% were either young people age 12- 18 or senior citizens. On the average each visitor spent only 74 cents during their visit, compared to a three dollars average on highly commercial piers. Since the citizens didn't want the pier's character changed, the consultant recommended that there be only limited new development; possibly two added restaurants and a few new shops. In addition, they felt that the city should retain control as the master lessor and require existing tenants to renovate their businesses. The report cautioned that it would be financially unsound to expand the undeveloped parking area completely into an area of shops and restaurants.

In August the city authorized $22,542 to repair the merry-go-round building. George Gordon, who owned the carousel, had the horses repainted. He reopened for business on October 11, 1974. At the same time work on the Municipal Pier's structure continued, and by mid October the pier was no longer in danger of collapsing.

On October 18, 1974 Santa Monica unveiled a $2.1 million plan to rehabilitate the pier. It would include a new 9000 square foot restaurant and retail development, and could be financed by $1.1 million in revenue bonds that didn't need voter approval. In addition, the plan recommended that the city clear the blighted area near the pier by acquiring for $1,000,000 two run-down apartments and four dilapidated houses in the crime infested area south of the pier.

Councilman John McCloskey raised doubts about the pier plan when it came up on the November 5th Council agenda. Since he didn't feel that the income generated from the pier was enough to pay off the revenue bonds, he made a motion to refer it back to the administration for a better projection of revenue. It was estimated that bond financing over a twenty-five year period at 7.5%

Clint Eastwood and Sondra Locke try their luck at games on the Santa Monica Pier; 1978.

interest would cost $1,482,000 in interest and other expenses above the costs of the structural repairs. With Nat Trives absent that night, the motion remained deadlocked in a tie vote.

The $1.5 million program for restoring the pier and clearing out the blight around the pier was approved by a 6-1 margin at the following Council meeting. McCloskey remained opposed. The city decided to issue revenue bonds for the two and one half year project, and spend $500,000 from a federal grant to buy the Seabright and Purser Apartments, breeding grounds for crime.

The Council's action guaranteed that the quaint, small town character of the pier would be preserved, and that it would not be developed into a grandiose commercial venture. Clo Hoover said, "the plan shows the City Manager really listens and responds to what the city wants." She referred to City Manager William's plan to keep such low revenue features as the merry-go-round and other amusements while, making plans for quality restaurants and shops that would yield more income to the city. What Santa Monica needed was a prime tenant that would have become a catalyst for the whole pier.

Frank Gehry & Associates was chosen in January 1975 as the architect for the pier. The Beach Committee's choice was unanimous because Gehry's proposal showed the needed sensitivity to the special character of the pier and its environment. The City Council, by a vote of 5-1 with McCloskey dissenting, authorized the City Manager to negotiate a contract with Gehry.

The City Manager's office began exploring alternate means of financing the pier's rehabilitation. They discovered that since the pier was classified as a recreational facility, there were several federal funding sources that could be used to fund structural repairs to the Newcomb Pier. In February the City Council voted to apply for $371,000 in Community Development Act funds to be used mainly for "cosmetic" improvements. They planned to use $20,000 to pay the architect's fee, and $235,000 for special lighting, painting and landscaping on the pier. The Council also authorized a salary of $20,000 for the hiring of a property management consultant to manage the pier facilities and to negotiate leases.

Meanwhile the group called the 'Citizen's Initiative to Preserve the Piers' was campaigning again on behalf of Proposition #1, the initiative to preserve both piers for all time. It took them two years to get the initiative placed on the April 8th ballot. Opponents claimed that the measure would obligate future generations to subsidize the pier if it became unprofitable. The opposition also pointed out that if it were approved the measure would make

Fishermen on the Municipal Pier's lower deck; 1975.

The bait boat New Sunbeam and the Nordica were anchored in Santa Monica Harbor; 1980.

any design changes to the basic structure rather limiting, and that it's litigation clause would not only enable neighboring cities to sue, but would give the pier lessees a legal club to be used against their city landlord.

Proposition #1 won on April 8, 1975 when 64% of the voters supported the measure. Santa Monica's citizens, by a margin of 10,540 to 5,823, voted to assure that both the Santa Monica and Newcomb Piers would be preserved indefinitely. The measure permitted any resident of Santa Monica or its surrounding communities to file a lawsuit to stop a violation of the ordinance. The ordinance, however, did not preempt enforcement of existing health and safety regulations regarding both piers.

Los Angeles County decided to dedicate the Santa Monica Pier as an official L.A. County Historical Landmark on Pier Day, Sunday May 18, 1975. It was the opening day event for Santa Monica's centennial year, and James Hayes, chairman of the L.A. Board of Supervisors did the honors. Thousands attended the event that included an art contest and a beachwear fashion show featuring styles from 1875 to 1975. The Jaycees sponsored pie eating, bubble gum bubble blowing, corn eating, and whistling contests. Radio station KIIS broadcasted the Jerry Mason show live from a 8- x 50 foot hot- air gondola tethered to the pier.

The pier hosted another large crowd in August for the city's 14th annual Sports and Arts Festival. The eleven day festival in late August featured swimming and paddleboard races, fishing contests, and life guard competition. A Keith Williams big band concert was held on the pier on August 24th.

The city's application for a $361,000 Community Development Grant for pier improvements was approved at the end of July. Gehry's plans budgeting $215,000 for the pier's facelift, were approved in September by both the City Council and the Coastal Commission. Plans included a $43,590 wooden boardwalk between the carousel building and Moby's Dock restaurant, new stairs on both the north and south sides of the pier for easier beach access, forty new benches, and additional pier lighting. The pier's businesses would be repainted in a multi-colored schemes used during the 20's, and decorative lighting would be added to outline the profiles of the buildings. Work began in January 1976, and the project was completed by June.

The use of nearly $500,000 in federal community development funds to replace the pier's rotted pilings became controversial in January 1976 during a series of public hearings. Councilman John McCloskey, who opposed it, said that he would rather spend the entire

Three fishermen pose with their halibut catch.

The Nordica was owned by Pete Peterson.

Day fishermen departing from the Santa Monica Pier.

Girl displays her catch on the Indiana.

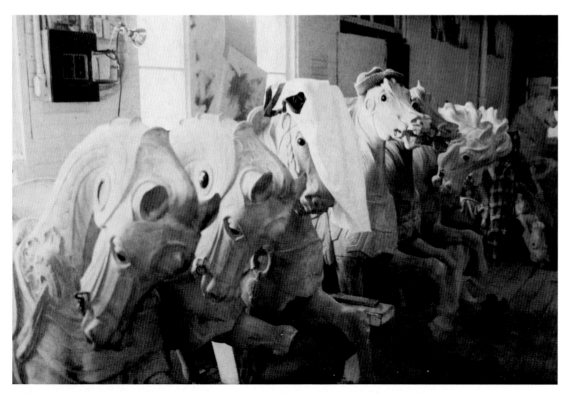

Tracey Cameron applies paint to a horse's saddle. (above)

Restoration begins on the carousel when the horses were sent out to have their paint stripped; 1981. (top left)

Stripped horses await sanding and repair before painting (left)

$802,000 grant to subsidize housing for the elderly. "The pier", he said, "is no historic monument and besides it carries no fire insurance." Mayor Nat Trives said the pier fell into the category of recreation for low and moderate income persons so the city could spend federal funds for upgrading it. The City Council on February 10, 1976 voted to spend $500,000 from the federal grant to repair the Newcomb Pier pilings. They would need to apply for funds for one additional year to finish the job.

After the funds were officially granted in June, a group of residents challenged their use by mounting a letter writing campaign to HUD officials. They claimed that Housing and Community Development block grants should only be used for providing housing for low income people. But HUD officials were satisfied that the money was used legitimately. City grants coordinator, Martha Brown Hicks, explained that federal grants were not intended to fund poverty programs, but rather were designated for community development.

The pier repair contract was awarded to the John L. Meek Construction Company for $469,950. Their job, which began after Christmas, required replacing 28 rotted pilings and repairing 120 others with concrete encasements. The work took six months.

The city's Landmark's Commission in 1976, after studying the pier's history, declared the pier a historic landmark. The commissioners did so primarily to control changes on the pier. Landmark status meant that the city was required to apply to its Landmark Commission for certificates of appropriateness to make alterations.

In January 1977 the city decided to buy the merry-go-round to assure that it would stay on the pier forever. Initially George Gordon Enterprises wasn't interested in selling their carousel, but the lease on their Playland Arcade building was up for renewal. While it broke Gordon's heart to sell the carousel, he had little choice if he intended to remain in business on the pier. The Council voted 5-2 at their February 23rd meeting to pay $100,000 for the ride,(payable in five $20,000 payments) and give him a five year lease on his arcade. The minimum annual rent on the arcade was set at $36,316 or 15% of the gross, whichever was higher. He was also given a contract with a ninety day cancellation clause to continue to operate the carousel on a month to month basis. The city lowered the price of a ride to a quarter to increase ridership, and received 12% of the ticket sales plus $856 per month rent. The lease arrangement was estimated to bring the city revenue of $13,000 per year.

The city approved several other leases and rejected one at the same Council meeting. Fiesta Games' lease called

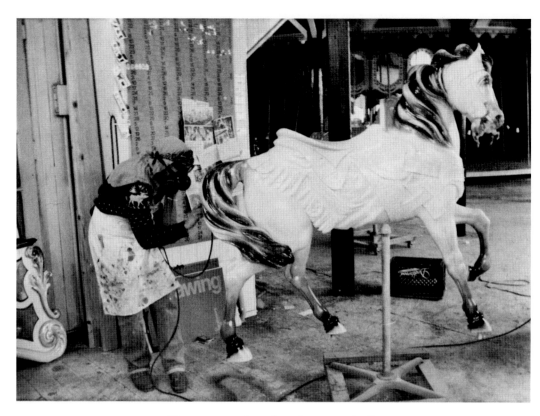

Tracey spray paints a horse's mane and tail.

Horses are placed in position on the carousel platform.

for a minimum annual rent of $20,256 or 15% of the gross, and Surfview Cafe's lease was set at $4212 or 10% of the gross. They rejected Fiesta's Auto Scooter's lease after members objected to the street frontage location of the ride.

The city applied for a third year of Housing and Urban Development (HUD) funds to complete the pier's structural repairs. However, behind the scenes political maneuvering through Representative Robert K Dornan's office nearly jeopardized the funding. Four members of the Santa Monica Housing Commission, headed by Arthur Rinck, tried to divert the funds to a loan program to rehabilitate housing for the elderly. They asked that Dornan investigate whether the Santa Monica Pier qualified for the block grant. Others like newly elected Councilman Perry Scott, an avowed fiscal conservative who was always against the pier, also objected.

When Councilwoman Christine Reed found out in April, she wrote Dornan a letter warning that if the city's current application for pier funding were denied, the first two years of funding would have been wasted. She explained that HUD had already allocated over $1,000,000 for restoring the pier, and that the $600,000 anticipated in the following fiscal year would complete the restoration effort. Dornan explained that he supported the pier and didn't realize that his inquiry into the Santa Monica Community Development application would jeopardize the pier. He called Reed to tell her that pier funding for the third year was assured.

With pier repairs nearly completed, developers in 1978 began to submit various proposals to the city for new businesses on the pier. The first was Jack Knight who planned to construct a 5000 square foot, 258 seat restaurant called Captain Jack's. It was to be located at the east end of the pier along the Promenade and would include indoor and outdoor dining areas with an open roof garden dining area. His proposal was approved by the Council on January 24, 1975. They gave him a twenty year lease with a minimum rent of $8196 against 10% of his gross receipts. A rent relief provision during the first five years was included in his lease to enable Knight to recover the cost of pier repairs.

The Entertainment Facilities Department was now in charge of the pier. It was headed by Jeremy Ferris, who was the director of the Santa Monica Civic Auditorium. In order to produce more revenue he actively sought new developers to renovate existing buildings and build new ones. One of his first priorities was to open bids to renovate the carousel building. He also sought proposals to use the vacant Sinbad's building as a Jazz Club and

searched for a developer to build two community theaters that would share a common concession stand. Ferris estimated it would take at least five years before the pier became self supporting.

His first move in March 1978 was to permanently close the pier to all vehicular traffic beyond the pier parking lot. The move, for the first time, was endorsed by the Santa Monica Pier Lessees Association. Most of the traffic, a high percentage of cruising teenagers, used to drive out to the end of the pier, not stop or patronize any of the pier businesses. It was wearing out the roadway.

Plans were unveiled in June for a three million dollar pier development project that included a water slide, public bathhouse, two restaurants and a disco. Actually three separate developers were involved, but the partnership of Jack Knight and Roy Cruickshank were responsible for the bulk of the project. They planned to spend $2.5 million on renovating the carousel building, installing a waterslide ride, and a bathhouse near the building.

Plans for their proposed Carousel Park included opening an ice cream parlor, cookie store and pizza parlor surrounding a restored carousel on the ground floor. The building's second floor would be converted into a 125 seat restaurant with a cocktail lounge. A water slide would be constructed on the burned out east side of the building. Its seventy foot high tower would have six chutes each running 440 feet down to a large wading pool on the Promenade level. A public bathhouse, located below the carousel building, would have fast food service available on site.

Robert Morris, owner of 'Gladstone's 4 Fish Restaurant' proposed to build a restaurant on the far south-west corner of the Newcomb Pier, an unused area of the pier. His two hundred fifty seat restaurant, that would have the appearance of a rusty steel building, was budgeted at $700,000.

A third developer, Doug Badt, proposed a chic discotheque ballroom named 'Disco La Monica' for the billiard's building next to the carousel. The building, which would be enlarged to 8500 square feet, would feature disco dancing in the evenings and ballroom dancing from the 40's and 50's on weekend afternoons. During the week the facility could be used for group luncheons. Rent would be $5000 / month.

Santa Monica's City Council by a vote of 4-3 quickly approved the projects at their July 17, 1978 meeting. Naturally Perry Scott was one of the three dissenters for he objected to the provision that relieved lessees of the responsibility for maintaining the pilings and common

area. He called the waterslide a "reincarnation of the old Pacific Ocean Park." Christine Reed defended the vote by saying, "I don't think the pier is going to turn into a POP. We're trying to get a pier to be a place where families get together."

Knight and Cruickshank were given twenty-five year leases for all seven businesses. They agreed to pay the city $164,856 rent annually during the first five years for all seven projects. Gladstone's lease was set at a minimum annual rent of $50,000 until the cost of the pier was recovered, then 6% afterwards.

The city's projected revenue for the pier when all the pier projects would be completed the following year (1979-80) was $450,000. They anticipated revenue of $296,000 from the four areas that the previous year only returned $15,000 in rent to the city. The city collected only $270,000 pier rent in 1976-77, and $350,000 in 1977-78.

Approval for the project was sought from the South Coast Regional Coastal Commission at their September 11th meeting. Approval was denied. Commissioner Ruth Galanter, in defending her position, stated in classic doublespeak, "It's not necessarily that there's anything wrong with any of these uses, its just the question of the mix of types of uses." She said that she had received sixteen written protests and several calls from residents who opposed the project. She was particularly worried about parking facilities.

The pier project was put on the Coastal Commission's agenda again in October. Only a handful of opponents attended the ninety minute meeting. Apparently the commissioners were satisfied for they approved the project unanimously.

But the pier's opponents weren't satisfied. Three of them, Henry Curtis from Ocean Park, John Longenecker from Beverly Hills and Colleen Creedon, who had lived above the carousel before the fire and didn't want to give up her home, appealed the decision to the State Coastal Commission in Sacramento. Commissioner Hank Doerfling, the South Coast body's representative, argued that the three planned developments would "improve public access to the parts of the pier that are not available now." He said that the development, all being made by private investors, are necessary for the preservation of the pier, which in some places had deteriorated badly and without improvements would continue to do so.

Ten members of the fourteen member Coastal Commission voted on December 12, 1978 not to reopen the matter to a full dress hearing despite the appeal by the three people. The Commission believed that the three

opponents raised no substantial issue. Unfortunately the three month delay in obtaining a coastal permit would prove to be crucial in completing the project.

Pier businessmen, reflecting a spirit of renewal, were optimist during the spring of 1979. Final engineering and architectural plans for the new development were nearly completed, and all the new businesses were expected to open in eight to ten months. The new restaurants and disco were expected to bring more night life to the pier.

Businessmen were sprucing up the pier. Moby's Dock restaurant was remodeled and the Boathouse restaurant expanded. George Gordon tripled the size of his Beachcomber gift shop. One group of businessmen made a proposal to lease and remodel the vacant Sinbad's building. There was even talk, to alleviate parking problem, of installing a miniature railroad to transport visitors from distant beach parking lots. Finally, pier lessees increased pier advertising and publicity using matching funds from the city.

The Carousel Corporation, who had taken over the carousel lease in June 1978, was planning its renovation. George McIndoe, the Scottish carousel manager who was hired by Jack Knight because of his expertise in carousel maintenance, expected to supervise the job. Knight felt that it would cost $250,000 for the restoration, while McIndoe was certain the cost would be almost double that amount. Barbara Williams, who would become head of Friends of the Santa Monica Carousel, doubted that McIndoe was qualified for the job. She asked several local carousel restorers to submit bids, but Knight never responded. The city, who owned the carousel, would in the end have to approve Knight's restoration plan and the person selected to do it.

The National Carousel Association became more involved and held their annual conference in Santa Monica on the weekend of September 14-16, 1979. Its president, Fred Fried had a long talk with Santa Monica's City Manager regarding the merry-go-round's restoration and several other carousel restorers examined the machine. John Davis, owner of the Griffith Park carousel, ventured a figure of $70,000 for the restoration.

In December the city, squeezed for funds by Proposition 13, decided they would no longer subsidize pier parking by splitting validations with the merchants. The pier lessees became even more upset when the city began charging monthly parking fees for lessees and employees. Clarence Harmon, owner of Moby's Dock restaurant complained bitterly that the city wanted to drain the pier for all the revenue it could get. He pointed out that else-

The first destructive storm began on January 27, 1983. (left) 153

The pier's lower deck begins to break up during the day.

where in town, restaurant customers could park for three hours for free, but when they went to the pier, they were forced to pay one dollar on weekdays and two dollars on weekends.

It was the same month that Richard Koch, who owned the Westwind Sailing Club and School, sued the city. He accused the city of trying to back out of their assurances that he would operate a sailboat concession on an "exclusive basis." His five year lease took effect in 1978.

In March 1980 the financially troubled Carousel Corporation finally choose Dick Norton and Tracey Cameron, both from Connecticut, to restore the carousel for $125,000. Norton would repair the mechanical elements of the machine and the band organ, while Cameron would strip and repaint the horses, six at a time so that the carousel wouldn't have to close during the long restoration. She wouldn't begin the job until after the first of the year, but Norton wanted to begin immediately to get the machine operational by Memorial Day. It had been closed since the beginning of the year.

As the summer 1980 season neared, Universal Marine, operating out of Long Beach, approached the city about operating a harbor excursion concession. They wanted to conduct eight thirty-minute cruises daily along the coastline. They offered the city 5% of an estimated gross of $75,300 over a ninety day summer trial period. Their proposal was contingent on operating that summer. The city, which rarely makes immediate decisions, turned them down.

When the planned discotheque in the Art Novelties location collapsed, the Powerhouse Group made a proposal to turn the location into a forty-eight seat theater that would show films of local history. They would also planned to operate a twelve seat motion simulator that took passengers on simulated roller coaster and bob sled rides. The project, which would require Coastal Commission approval, would be for the 1981 season.

The city meanwhile was becoming concerned about the lack of progress on the Carousel Corporation's waterslide and carousel renovation project. The company's contract required that all seven leaseholds be in operation by September 1, 1980. The firm didn't ask for a permit to begin work to demolish the fence and burned out ramp adjacent to the carousel until August 7th. The Council members, who were impatient because the original leases had been approved two years previously, blocked the permit.

Jack Cummings, the firm's vice president and general manager, said that the main reason for the delay had been

Television crews record the storm's destructive fury.

The lower deck, portions of the upper deck, and the Harbor Patrol office were destroyed.

the high interest rates that had soared as high as 23% at one point, and inflation that increased the project's costs to $3 million. He explained that the development had financial backers at the beginning but lost them when the project stymied for four months through appeals before the Coastal Commission. He assured the Council that his project had sound financial backing by a third group of investors and his project would be completed by May 1981. His firm was ready to pay the city their $173,000 annual rent on September 1st. "If our project is not permitted to proceed', he said," I doubt if there will be any other developers who would be interested in the pier."

Santa Monica didn't flinch. City Manager Charles Kent McClain on September 5th formally terminated the lease with the Carousel Corporation. He explained that the firm had defaulted on their agreement to open on September 1st. The City Council hoped for some sort of reconciliation and set November 12th as the deadline to reopen negotiations. Otherwise they instructed the administration to find a contractor to renovate the merry- go-round which had been closed most of the year.

It became plainly obvious that Santa Monica needed to rehabilitate the pier if they were to attract new development. Plans for three recent developments were cancelled because perspective developers found it financially unfeasible to replace the pier's understructure. Acting Mayor Ruth Goldway said, "you can't expect private parties to spend money on new pier projects unless the city makes a commitment to repair the pier." It was estimated that it might cost $3,000,000 to replace all the pier's rotted pilings and another $200,000 in annual maintenance costs.

The pier as usual needed another $400,000 in repairs. The city had just spent $330,000 to repair the area where the bumper cars stood and now one third of the area beneath the parking lot needed to be replaced. A spot check at the turn around area on the pier revealed eleven pilings that were 50-75% deteriorated. $472,944 of the pier's net revenue was available for the job. The Council approved the work on October 29, 1980, and as usual, Perry Scott was opposed.

The City hired Tracey and Steve Cameron of Hartford, Ct. to restore the artistic portion of the carousel for $80,000, and Dick Norton of Bristol Ct. to restore its mechanical elements for $40,000. Tracey was the artist who would repaint the horses and carousel and her brother Steve would do all the carpentry work on the horses. They had previously restored the carousel at the San Francisco Zoological Gardens and one for the Ringling Brothers Circus.

The horses were loaded on a truck in December short-

A second storm stuck the Santa Monica Pier six weeks later. On Tuesday evening March 1, 1983, 15,000 square feet of pier deck and buildings west of Moby's Dock, and 37,500 feet of the pier's parking lot were swept into the sea.

ly before the Camerons arrived and sent to a paint stripping shop in Glendale. There they were immersed in a stripping compound to remove three or more layers of paint. When returned the stripped horses were found to have sustained much damage to their legs and feet, and there was considerable wear in the saddles. Steve used auto body filler in small damaged areas and carved wooden parts for the larger areas needing repair. The horses were then gently sanded.

One of the four corner "sun parlors" in the carousel building was sealed off as a spraying room. But shortly after painting began, the fire department during a pier inspection shut down the operation. They claimed that the paint in the air created an unsafe, highly combustible condition. The horses were then trucked, a few at a time, to the municipal bus yard's official spray paint chamber where they were given two coats of clear sealer, then a coat of gray primer. While they were still wet, their hooves, noses, manes, tails, and legs were air brushed with automobile paint. Then their saddles, blankets, and other trappings were hand painted in bright colors. Finally the horses were painted with a clear high gloss finish to protect them from rider wear.

The carousel framework, central housing, panels, and upper rim were steamed cleaned in December while the horses were at the stripping shop. The 29 different stencil designs on the PTC carousel's mirrors and outside rim were copied onto patterns. The original designs were reapplied after the framework's surface was sanded, primered, and painted.

After months of painstaking work, the doors of the carousel building reopened on June 6, 1981 to allow 275 members of the National Carousel Association to preview the restored carousel and band organ. NCA president John Hayek presented the organization's Preservation Award to Santa Monica's Mayor Ruth Goldway.

The carousel's official grand opening was on August 14, 1981. The fund raising event, which was attended by over 500 people including guest celebrities Jane Fonda, Herb Albert, Daniel Travanti and others, helped to raise money to renovate the building. The carousel which was operated by Harvey Gaylin and Barbara Williams remained open seven days a week through September 30th, then was open only on weekends and holidays. 65,000 people rode the carousel during the initial six week period.

Major repairs authorized in October 1980 were nearly completed on the pier by mid summer. Since 1975 the city had spent $3.1 million on the pier, with $2.7 million coming from block grants.

Santa Monica recruited and hired Susan Mullin to manage the pier in August 1981. Her recent experience was in marketing men's shoes in the New York and Los Angeles areas. Mullin was listed as a department administrative analyst in the city hierarchy, but in reality she was the acting manager of the Santa Monica Pier. She immediately began meeting with the newly appointed fifteen member pier task force to formulate plans so that the city could apply for a share of $20 million in state funds set aside for improvements in urban waterfronts.

The Carousel Corporation, angry that their contract was terminated with the city nearly a year earlier, on August 18, 1981 filed a $6 million lawsuit. Their claim was based on the loss of the fair market value of their planned projects and fees expended for architectural services. The city attorney called the claim "nonsense" and said that the city would reject it because it had no merit.

In September 1981, the State Coastal Conservancy granted $30,000 towards restoring the pier. The funds were used to conduct public workshops to prepare a plan for expanded commercial and public recreational facilities on the pier. As a condition of the grant, the city was required to name a citizen's advisory committee to recommend objectives and review alternative use concepts.

The pier task force, initially chaired by activist Ernie Powell, included several professional planners, two pier business owners, and other citizens who had a long-term interest in the pier. The group meet weekly at various city park meeting rooms.

The task force, with a grant from the Coastal Conservancy, held three public workshops during the spring and summer. The first on April 2nd was attended by seventy people. The consensus was that everyone wanted the parking removed from the pier, and generally most wanted the pier to remain as it was. But there were those who suggested imaginative ideas. Several wanted a roller coaster and ferris wheel, others a children's park, an aquarium museum, a movie theater, a music center, and possibly even a people mover or a train that would travel from Palisades Park down the pier ramp.

Finally, after six months of meetings and three public workshops, the pier task force in conjunction with the California Coastal Conservancy in September published a 125 page analysis of the past, present and future of the pier. Task force chairman, Paul Silvern, told the City's planning commission that the report only suggested a "range of uses" acceptable to the citizens and cautioned that it should only be used as a framework for future pier development.

The report recommended that the city spend $7.9 mil-

lion in repairs and new attractions for the pier, and that $2.5 million of that amount be spent on a new parking structure to replace parking on the pier. It suggested new commercial development on the pier should match the existing open, low cost, friendly atmosphere while at the same time produce sufficient income to cover the pier's maintenance. It included a plan that preserved the carousel and Sinbad's and added a pavilion to house entertainment events. The report also envisioned an amusement area on the eastern end that could possibly include a ferris wheel, children's play area, family arcade, and bumper cars. Plans for the pier's west end included revamping the harbormaster's office and add an open-air marine display on the upper level and an "experimental" marine life learning center on the lower level.

The Coastal Conservancy made a firm commitment to the pier with an interest-free $500,000 loan to the city. The money would be spent on the eastern end of the pier for a children's park and playground, strengthening the pier for a pad for a ferris wheel, and for completion of the renovation of the carousel building.

Although emergency roof repairs were made to the carousel building when rain water poured onto the newly painted horses the previous winter, the building's renovation began in earnest in September 1982. Work included replacement of all the building's windows including frames, sills and glass on all four sides. Since little was salvageable, a wood working shop was set up inside to replace most of the frames. The old stucco was removed from the exterior and structural repairs were made before applying three new layers of stucco to the building. A color scheme of peachy-orange stucco with dark blue trim, thought to be the original, was chosen for exterior surfaces by the Landmark's Commission.

When the carousel closed in January 1983 for mechanical renovation, huge scaffolding was erected inside to add a sprinkler system. The horses were moved upstairs for touch ups while all the mechanical parts in the central housing area of the carousel were steam cleaned. The centerpole, sweeps and support rods were all painted, and a new commutator that provided electricity to the lights on the rotating carousel was replaced. The carousel's platform was then balanced and refinished before reinstallation of the carousel horses. It was a project that required months of work.

Winter storms along the Santa Monica Bay were nothing new, after all, the pier's lower deck had been damaged three times in the previous ten years. But the storm that began building up during the wee hours of the morning on Thursday January 27, 1983 not only had huge churn-

The wreckage from the Santa Monica Pier was washed ashore south of the pier.

ing breakers, but occurred during the year's highest tides. The swells at sea were only eight to ten feet at most, but their sixteen to twenty foot faces that broke on shore rapidly eroded sections of the beach from Malibu to Redondo Beach.

The buildings on the end of the pier were still above water at 7:30 AM but high tide hadn't peaked yet. A maintenance man described the situation. "The whole pier was rocking and rolling. Boards started popping. The end of the pier started to sag. It looked like it was going to go so we hot footed it out of there." Shortly before 9:20 AM, while hundreds of sightseers atop Palisades Park watched in the driving rain, the northwest corner of the pier broke off and fell into the pounding sea. The harbormaster's office and all the structures on the lower deck were lost. The remainder of the pier's ocean end, especially in the area near Moby's Dock Restaurant and the Tackle Shop was dangerously close to collapse.

Hundreds of scavengers attracted by the debris washed up on the beach south of the pier searched for souvenirs. Lucky ones claimed wetsuits, typewriters, even underwater cameras lost from the harbormaster's office. Crowd control was a problem throughout the day and evening as the area was as crowded as during Fourth of July. The police chief, who had closed the beach and pier by Thursday afternoon, reported that the biggest question that people asked was, "Can we go down to the beach?" Everyone wanted a souvenir of the Santa Monica Pier.

On Friday, after the storm had subsided, City Manager John Alshuler proclaimed, "Rumors that the storm damaged pier was in imminent danger of collapse into the sea are exaggerated and speculative. "He announced that the pier and south beaches would remain closed to the public throughout the weekend while city engineers assessed the pier's structural integrity.

Engineers blamed a flaw in the construction of the pier's lower deck for most of the pier's damage. When it was built in 1935, it was set too close to the water to be adequately protected from the high surf. It also provided support for the harbormaster's office built above it in 1957. They recommended that either the deck shouldn't be rebuilt or it should be raised four feet. They felt that the most of the pier could be reopened to the public within a week.

The City Council at their February 1st meeting supported the fishermen's pleas to restore the pier to its original condition. They appropriated $200,000 in general fund reserves to begin demolition and salvage operations on the pier. They needed to remove 10,000 square feet of the battered and broken lower deck and 5,600 feet of the pier's top deck.

A new estimate claimed $2.5 million in damages to the pier. This included damage to pilings, upper and lower decks, harbor office, small boat dock, commercial boat facilities, railings and stairs, structural damage to Moby's Dock and Sinbad's and water damage to the carousel building. Damage could be as high as $5.3 million if damage to all private property was included.

Southern California beaches were designated a federal emergency area and the pier became eligible for federal funds. The government would pay 75% of the pier's restoration costs but they would insist on preventative measures like restoring the breakwater to avert further damage, or rebuilding to a design that did not depend on the breakwater. Meanwhile a huge thirty ton crane was moved onto the pier's ocean end to remove the damaged lower deck.

Unfortunately a second storm, more powerful than the first raced towards the Southern California coast. It arrived on Tuesday afternoon March 1, 1983 accompanied by 40 MPH winds and fifteen foot waves. Worse, it coincided with the year's extreme high tides.

The storm built up quickly in the late afternoon, too late to move the crane off the pier before quitting time. The crew, however, felt that it would be prudent to move the crane back about fifty feet from the far end where they were working. The first hint of trouble came at 8:30 PM when the pier began vibrating and beams began to fall into the raging surf. Members of the City Council were informally meeting in the Moby's Dock Restaurant when Don Arnett, chief of Parks and Recreation, ordered it closed. Two employees of the restaurant, in a hurry to leave, left their cars behind.

As the huge waves began to pound relentlessly against the weakened pilings, they snapped one by one until the huge thirty ton crane toppled into the surf at 10:45 P.M. The sea then used the crane as a battering ram to smash the pier further and further back towards shore. Within fifteen minutes, just before the tide reached its peak at 11:06 PM, Peterson's boat launch crane, the Santa Monica Fishing building, a rest room, 160 feet of pier deck, three cars, and a large refrigerator truck were swept into the sea.

Councilwoman Christine Reed, who witnessed the collapse, said; "You could feel and hear this crud chewing away at the pilings until the cars were engulfed. Then the cars in turn became battering rams against the south corner of the pier. You could hear the glass smashing and the metal crunching." By midnight, less than two-thirds remained of what had been a 1200 foot long pier. Everything west of Moby's Dock was gone, and the restaurant was barely supported by a few lone pilings.

Damage to the pier was many times worse than from the first storm. 15,000 square feet of the pier deck west of Moby's Dock, and 37,500 square feet of pier parking lot, 20% of the pier's total area, was swept into the sea. Debris was stacked ten foot high on the beach south of the pier all the way to Pico Boulevard. One of the lost vehicles could be seen under the south side of the pier. It was wrapped around a piling. A construction company spokesman, who came to survey the damage, declared their crane a total loss.

Vestal Schuler, whose Santa Monica Sport Fishing office and tackle shop were washed away, blamed the city for what he called negligence to recap the breakwater before repairing the pier. All that he had to show for the twenty-seven years that he operated the popular sports fishing landing were memories and two boats.

Santa Monica wasn't the only city to suffer pier damage. The piers at Seal Beach, Malibu's Paradise Cove, and Mission Beach were swept away and others along the coast were damaged. Much of the coastline was badly eroded and many houses in Malibu and Ventura were swept out to sea. President Reagan, who surveyed much of the damage from a U.S. Marine helicopter, hovered over the pier on Friday morning. The coast was declared a federal emergency area for the second time within a month.

Assemblyman Tom Hayden and County Supervisor Dean Dana inspected the pier on Saturday and reassured Santa Monica officials that they could expect financial help. Hayden planned to introduce a bill in the legislature to provide funds for repairing all the piers along the coast.

The city estimated the damage at $8.5 million. Mayor Ruth Goldway acknowledged, "Now it will be more difficult to restore the pier. The financial burdens for the city may be greater." The City Council met in an emergency session and authorized $35,000 for the construction company to shore up the area around Moby's Dock. They waived competitive bidding requirements and awarded the contract to John L. Meeks Company.

While city crews worked all weekend to clean up the debris on the south beach, construction crews made emergency repairs in an effort to shore up Moby's Dock building. They drove sixty foot piling through the restaurant's ceiling and bar floor down into the sea. But more money was needed as there was virtually no pier platform beyond its back door. On March 8th an additional $216,368 was allocated for pier emergency repairs. It would eventually cost an additional $35,000 to haul 6,400 cubic yards of debris to a landfill in Sylmar.

City officials had to decide if simply restoring the pier

to its previous state would be adequate or whether it would have to be strengthened, better protected, or replaced. Cost was naturally a factor in the wood versus concrete debate. While wood rot normally set into creosoted piles within five to fifteen years, concrete cost one and one half to twice as much. Consequently the pier's future would be largely determined by the amount of money available from the state and federal governments.

Meanwhile the Task Force recommended that the architectural competition for the Carousel Entry Park should still take place at the end of March. The three day competition among five design teams chosen from twenty-three applicants was open to the public at the Civic Auditorium. The public was allowed to talk to the designers and provide ideas. The Santa Monica design team of Moore, Ruble, Yudell and Todd won the competition with a $320,000 design and a $30,000 commission.

In May the City Council decided by a 4-2 vote that a non-profit corporation be formed to manage the restoration and operation of the storm damaged pier. This Pier Restoration Corporation would have a nine member board that would be appointed by the Council. In addition to its responsibility for the pier's operation and maintenance, it would work with private investors interested in pier businesses. Its goal would be to put the pier on an even keel financially, thus enabling the pier to break even. Both Cristine Reed and David Epstein, who voted against it, were of the opinion that the non-profit setup would just add another layer of unnecessary and unwieldy bureaucracy.

The pier lessees were in favor of the non-profit organization. Many of the owners shared the fear of George Gordon, the association's president, that a private for profit pier operator might mean high rents, high-priced concessions, and evictions of current businesses. Maynard Ostrow, who owned the bumper cars and some game concessions, added; "The only way I see you making tremendous amounts of money on the pier is to put very high-scale development on there. I think you shouldn't ruin something that's so unique and beloved the world over."

The City Council voted to sign three year leases with the tenants whose businesses were unscathed by the storm. Initially they overruled the City Manager who wanted to terminate leases with the destroyed businesses. While they felt that they had an obligation to those lessees who had fallen on hard times, it certainly wasn't practical with the pier in ruins. As a result their leases

A series of summer Twightlight Dances beginning in June 1984 were held in a huge blue and white tent and the end of the pier.

were terminated by the Pier Manager. However, Oatman's Rock Shop, which had been on the pier's lower deck since 1965, was granted vendor status to operate its business on a month to month basis from a temporary booth.

The city, in an effort to both show the public that the business end of the Santa Monica Pier still stood, and to assure them that they planned to rebuild, scheduled a fund raising "Save the Santa Monica Pier Week". They hired Louise Kieffer and Peggy Clifford to produce the event. They enlisted the help of Group W Cable who contributed $5000 for the rental of the sound system and lights for the concerts, and General Telephone Company who contributed $25,000 in goods and services. Most of the money was used to buy 'Save the Pier' T-Shirts, visors, and buttons that were sold on the pier during the festivities.

The opening ceremony on May 23rd featured thirty Arabian horses and a numerous celebrities. Mayor Ken Edwards welcomed a crowd of five hundred and afterwards released 1500 balloons that filled the sky for a moment before drifting towards the south shore.

The pier hosted thousands who wandered through the art exhibit and crafts fair, watched street entertainers, or listened to some of the twenty bands that performed each day from noon to 4 PM. Many took part in the numerous contests on opening day. Fifty four anxious mothers exhibited their offspring in the Baby Contest. The winner of the brief pie eating contest almost inhaled the pie in one piece. A Build a Pier contest challenged participants to construct a model pier out of ice sticks that they purchased at twenty-five sticks for a quarter. There were also hoola hoop and boogie board contests, and a kite festival staged by Colors of the Wind.

Quality entertainment rounded out the ten day event. Many attended a film festival that featured movies that were filmed on the pier; Elmer Gantry (1960), Inside Daisy Clover (1965), The Sting (1973) and 1941 (1979). Others danced in the La Monica tent to several popular rock bands. The major fund raiser on the final Saturday night was an outdoor variety show, "A Salute to the Pier". It was a magic night of entertainment by bluesman Ry Cooder, singer Christine McVie from Fleetwood Mac, Billy Burnett's Band with drummer Mick Fleetwood, a 50's style swing group called Blue Indigo, and an all-star comedy show lead by Buck Henry. The appreciative audience was generous when a bucket was passed during the performance. Entertainment on the final Sunday included the L.A. Chamber Ballet and Ollie Mitchell's Sunday Band.

View of the Santa Monica Pier from the ramp; 1983.
Santa Monica Pier from Palisades Park after the storm; 1983.

Carousel Park and the pier's temporary fun zone; 1989.

Santa Monica Pier's PTC #22 carousel; 1988.

The entire 'Save the Santa Monica Pier Week' was a huge success. Money was raised from ads in the printed program, fees for craft fair booths, sales of 'Save the Pier' items, and donations during the various performances. In addition, a mailing to numerous motion picture celebrities from a list furnished by Jane Fonda and Tom Hayden, brought in additional contributions. A total of more that $40,000 was raised to help rebuild the pier.

The city, which was anxious to begin the pier's reconstruction in the summer, hired Richard Troy, Ben Gerwick, and Harry Harris as consultants. Their job, as experts in coastal marine construction, was to help select an architectural and engineering firm to begin design reconstruction of the pier. At the same time city officials were expecting to hear whether the federal government would approve the $4 - 6 million dollars in damage claims for the pier. The newly-approved state budget already included $1.3 million to restore the Santa Monica Pier.

Applications for the proposed nine member Pier Restoration Board were sought through the summer. The Council was seeking people with expertise in development finance, commercial leasing and development, coastal issues, recreational facility management, and urban architectural design. They wanted five of the members to be from the business community and two to be architects.

On September 13, 1983 the City Council appointed twelve candidates to an expanded board. David O' Malley, who was later elected Chairman, was an architect and president of Welton Beckett Associates. Herb Katz was also an architect and Mary Houha, was a planner with the L.A. City Community Development Agency. Local businessmen included David Anderson, president of General Telephone, Chris Carlson, a tax partner in an accounting firm, Chris Harding, an attorney, and Wayne Wilson, a management consultant. Other members were Ruth Goldway, former Mayor of Santa Monica, Judy Adbo, Ernie Powell, Henry Custis, and William Spurgin.

They began meeting in October in the conference room atop the General Telephone Building. Their first order of business was to study and discuss a reconstruction financing plan. Approximately $2 million was committed by the state Coastal Conservancy and Wildlife Conservation Board. The federal government agreed to pay for 75% of the of the anticipated $4.2 million reconstruction cost, but they would not pay an additional two million dollars to make it stronger. In addition they stated that they would not release any funds unless Santa Monica bought insurance for the federally funded work.

City officials agreeing to that, obtained a quote of $21,000 per year with an $84,000 damage deductible.

The firm of Daniel, Mann, Johnson, and Mendenhall was chosen out of a field of five firms to perform preliminary engineering and design studies to reconstruct the pier. Their proposal and several others raised the question of what was to be done about a breakwater that was ineligible for federal funds.

Phase one of the $283,640 contract, which would take five months, included an engineering and environmental analysis. The firm would study two or three alternate designs and would resolve whether the lower deck should be replaced and how to insure that the pier would remain safe from future storms. The second phase, which would take seven months, included development of a design, an environmental impact report, and final work drawings to begin construction.

The City Council also voted in January 1984 for $238,000 in additional emergency repairs so that the remaining pier could withstand anticipated winter storms. The work done by John L. Meeks Company was aimed at preventing the pilings from breaking away and acting as battering rams during storms. They added metal straps and wooden bracing to many of the pilings, and replaced twenty-four pilings deteriorated more than 50%. Divers, bouncing ultrasonic signals off the pilings, were able to accurately determine their inner strength.

Sinbad's restaurant was physically moved back forty feet, then forward forty feet to repair the pilings beneath it. Workers found several gold pieces that had fallen through the floorboards. Pier patrons were surprised when two hidden 20's era signs on the Playland Arcade exterior appeared. Few realized that Sinbad's had been moved to its present location from its old location next to the billiard's building when the La Monica Ballroom was built in 1924.

The search for the $60,000 / year director of the Pier Restoration Corporation narrowed as spring approached. The PRC board advertised nationwide in the Wall Street Journal, the New York Times, and in amusement park journals for someone who had broad experience managing pier facilities. They eventually interviewed fifteen candidates and finally selected Gail E. Markens, a bright, articulate, self assured 33 year old woman who had been an assistant commissioner of New York's Ports and Terminals Department. In her former position Markens managed construction projects for twelve retail and wholesale food distribution facilities and negotiated leases for those facilities. She was also involved in projects ranging from summer concerts to food concessions on the city's piers.

New Pier Corporation's games area at night; 1990

Tourists try their luck at the Frog Game; 1990

She held a master's degree in Urban Planning from Columbia University.

Markens on the first day of her job on April 9th, walked to the end of the pier, looked out on the water and announced to no one in particular, "Hello, I'm here." When asked by reporters what her intentions were, she replied, "First I want to bring people down here. I'd like to see it restored. It needs to be spruced up. We need to work with tenants to make improvements." She added that when she visited the pier for her two interviews, "I talked to people, people on the pier, people on the board, city people. The more I talked, the more I understood the importance of the pier, the history of it, the life of it."

Optimism pervaded the pier offices above the carousel. The first phase of the design plans for the pier's entry park at the Promenade were completed by the architectural design team who had won the design contest in March 1983; Moore, Ruble, and Yudall in a co-venture with the landscape architectural firm Cambell and Cambell. They proposed a 5000 square foot children's park with passive features such as a concrete boat and dragon for them to play on, a two hundred seat bleacher structure to accommodate volleyball spectators, and an extension of the pier deck east of the carousel connected by stairs and ramps to the Promenade below. Four thousand square feet of commercial space would be built beneath the pier deck near the carousel. Metal framed pavilions, which would flank the bleachers, would carry the theme of the carousel building to the south side of the pier. The $415,000 project, that the city hoped to start in the fall, was to be funded by an interest free loan from the State Coastal Conservency. Naturally obtaining a Coastal Commission permit, completion of the working drawings, and negotiating the city's bureaucratic maze would delay completion of the project nearly two additional years.

As summer approached it appeared that H.E.G. Enterprises, a Seattle firm, was going to obtain the Moby's Dock lease and build a new restaurant there. Eve Harmon, the previous tenant, had been evicted earlier for non- payment of rent. The Seattle firm would need to rebuild most of the structure but planned to finish it in the style of early 20th century waterfront structures; weather stained wood exterior trimmed with blue awnings. Its Fisherman's Restaurant would specialize in mesquite-broiled fresh fish from the Northwest as well as local fish. Seating would be tiered to offer views of the ocean, and outside seating would be protected by glass wind screens. The city asked for 6% of the gross. The restaurants projected sales of $2,000,000 could add

Crane putting in pilings during the pier's reconstruction; 1989.

$145,000 to the city's coffers. But when the firm discovered that the building wasn't salvageable, and the city tore it down, they had to redesign it. The city, however, wasn't very cooperative and never approved their plans. The project went into limbo. A gentlemen's agreement between the PRC, the Fun Zone developers, and the Seattle firm will eventually compensate them for expenses.

The carousel, which had been undergoing the final phase of interior renovation since December 1983, remained closed after the Memorial Day weekend. The city had awarded a contract for $178,523 to John T. Ingram and Associates. They were to install a new tongue and grove hardwood floor, rewire the building's electrical system, paint the interior of the ground floor, and install a security system. It was a job that was supposed to take less than five months, but after an initial flurry of work, the crew would disappear for weeks at a time.

The carousel's managers, attempting to work around the inconvenience, hopped to operate at least on weekends. But as summer approached the contractor pulled the building's entire electrical system. Then, anxious to finish the job and get paid, he decided to work throughout the summer.

After carpenters installed the building's new oak floor, they discovered that the floor was two and one half inches too high and didn't allow enough clearance beneath the carousel when it was fully loaded. Workers had to jack up the carousel and put shims under the center pole and its big struts. Finally the carousel managed to open in mid-August on the closing weekend of Los Angeles' 1984 Summer Olympics.

The Pier Restoration Corporation in July 1984 asked Santa Monica's Superior Court to settle whether Roy Cruickshank, who had operated Skipper's in the northwest corner of the carousel building, had a right to run his fast-food business there. His firm, the Carousel Corporation, once held the lease to the building, but when it failed to restore it by September 1, 1980, the city demanded that he vacate. He managed to hang-on and technically held lease rights to 25% of the building.

Skipper's temporarily moved out of the building in February 1983 while the city renovated the structure. The city agreed to compensate Cruickshank for his inconvenience and gave him $6000 one year later. But his business, more than a year after the June 15, 1983 completion date, was still in limbo and he operated from a popcorn cart in front of the carousel. The Health Department wouldn't give him a permit without defined business boundary lines which were in dispute. He offered to

sell the business to the city for $70,000, but they refused his offer.

The lawsuit as usual dragged on for more than a year. The city, who was anxious to settle and terminate any existing or former leaseholds in the carousel building agreed to buy Skipper's out for $90,000. It was the amount that Cruickshank would have earned during the lengthy remodeling and for the damage that the remodeling caused to his place of business. The city also eventually settled their lawsuit with the Carousel Corporation a few years later so that there would be no cloud on the property. They agreed to pay $86,500 to the firm in April 1988.

The Pier Restoration Board had planned in August 1984 to decide on one of the two pier design proposals. The first, a $14.4 million plan, included a wooden pier protected by a rebuilt fifteen foot high breakwater. The second, a $13.6 million plan, envisioned stabilizing the existing breakwater at six feet and building a 545 foot long promenade perpendicular to the pier that would serve as a second breakwater. It would be used for walking and fishing.

Instead, PRC told the City Council that they needed more time and another $289,400 in engineering and environmental studies to reach a decision on how to rebuild the pier. They leaned toward the promenade plan because it provided more space and harbor uses, but they were concerned with its effect on the shoreline. The three months of testing that the PRC requested would simulate wave action on the breakwaters and would determine how the promenade would affect the sand drift along the shoreline. Testing would have normally been done on the chosen plan, but tests on both plans cost just $23,000 more. City Council agreed and voted the funds at their September 4th meeting.

But in January 1985 the city scraped its consideration of both $14 million pier reconstruction plans for two new plans that were several million dollars cheaper and that would retain the pier's pre-1983 appearance. The PRC asked its consultants to develop new plans because it was concerned over costs, the drastic change in the pier's configuration and the ominous appearance of the promenade or a fifteen foot high breakwater on the horizon. It had become obvious that the project had grown beyond the city's ability to afford it, especially since the expensive breakwater was ineligible for federal funding.

Their choice was between a $10.2 million plan for a pier made of timber and concrete, that would be protected by a six foot high breakwater extending three hundred feet south of the pier, versus a $11.3 million plan for an

all concrete pier with no breakwater. The advantages of a concrete pier over a wooden pier were its strength against storms and its lower annual maintenance costs; $70,000 for concrete versus $200,000 for wood. Unlike a timber deck, a concrete lower deck, separate from the upper deck, would sink to the bottom if destroyed instead of battering the remaining pier pilings with its debris.

PRC felt that reconstruction of either pier design could begin in Spring 1986. An all concrete pier would take eight to ten months, while one of timber and concrete would take six to eight months after a five month task of reconstructing the breakwater.

While Gail Markens felt that the breakwater was "absolutely" necessary to protect the pier against heavy seas, and that the PRC was unlikely to recommend rebuilding the pier without the breakwater, some members of the board felt otherwise. Ernie Powell commented, "I'm of the theory that tells us a stronger pier is all we need. That's a less expensive way to go."

Public hearings for the two new pier designs were scheduled for Saturday May 18th, the weekend before the PRC made their final decision at their regular scheduled Monday meeting. The hearings drew forty-five people. While the public overwhelmingly favored a simpler reconstruction of the damaged pier, there was no clear consensus over the two lower cost restoration proposals. Only a slight majority favored a strong pier with low maintenance costs.

The Pier Restoration Corporation Board, to the surprise of many, concurred. They voted on March 20, 1985 for an all-concrete restoration of the damaged pier. They studied the risks over a fifty year period and found that a wooden pier protected by a breakwater had a 30% chance of destruction, while a concrete pier without one had only a 10% chance. The more affordable choice was definitely a safer bet.

The city estimated the project would cost $12.4 million by the time construction was expected to start in 1986. More than $7 million in state and federal funding was assured for that fiscal year. Work could begin in summer of 1986, or if an EIR was required, in the fall of 1986. The pier would open in either February or June 1987.

But in May 1985 the city ran into a potential legal problem with the reconstruction plan. The City Attorney revealed that the plan for demolishing 60,000 square feet of timber west of Sinbad's and replacing it with concrete violated the demolition restrictions in the "Save the Pier" ordinance. While they could ask the voters to change the ordinance, they couldn't risk delaying the start of construction because some funds like the $500,000 from the Wildlife Conservation Board required a contract by June 1986. A breakwater was now needed since the existing portions of the wooden pier could not withstand the brunt of a storm.

The City Council, with no recourse, unanimously approved the $12.7 million modified plan on May 21, 1985. It called for reconstructing the damaged portions of the pier with concrete deck and pilings, reinforcing the existing pier west of Sinbad's and rebuilding a nine hundred foot long, six foot high breakwater that would extend three hundred feet south of the pier. Since the city was short of funds they felt that it would be an acceptable risk to delay building the breakwater for five years and concentrate their efforts and $8 million in funds to rebuild the pier first.

The city had $4 million available from the Federal Emergency Management Agency and $1.5 million in other grant funds. It was only $3 million short. The FEMA also agreed to put an additional $675,000 towards the breakwater.

The winning bid in May for the proposed Carousel Park at the pier entrance was considerably higher than expected. FTR's low bid of $1,184,000 required obtaining an additional $350,000 interest free loan from the Coastal Conservancy. That increased the total loan from the Conservancy to $1 million. The City Council approved the contract on June 11, 1985, and construction began in late summer.

The Pier Restoration Corporation, in hopes of luring a more upscale crowd to the pier that summer, sponsored a series of free "Twilight Concerts" on Thursday evenings. They erected a huge blue and white tent on the approximate site of the old La Monica Ballroom and opened the series on June 20, 1985 with the Unlisted Jazz Band. It was followed by a chamber music concert by the New West Brass Quintet. The most popular nights were those that featured dancing with music furnished by jazz groups such as the Rhythm Kings. The concert series eventually became an annual summer event with the emphasis on a series of twilight dances; swing, country-western, reggae, roaring 20's, folk, and 50's rock n' roll.

During the fall the City Council voted 5-0 to begin engineering studies to strengthen the existing 60,000 square foot timber portion of the pier. They awarded a $47,800 contract to Daniel, Mann, Johnson and Mendenhall and expected a report by December. Work was scheduled to be completed by June 1986. A construction contract was awarded and the $800,000 project was completed in October 1986.

The Newcomb Pier portion during reconstruction; 1988

The pier nearing the end of construction. Rebar reinforcing connects the concrete piles with the cement pier deck

The Carousel Park opened on June 6, 1986. Ray Cammack Shows set up a small children's amusement zone adjacent to it behind the carousel. It featured a Eli 12 ferris wheel, a super slide, and three platform kiddie rides. The city selected Barbara McCoy to manage their carousel and Roland Crump, a former Disney designer, was hired to suggest colors for the exteriors of the pier's businesses. Signs were redone to reflect a lettering style of the 1920's.

The crowds that jammed Santa Monica's beaches for the annual Fourth of July fireworks display became larger and more unmanageable throughout the decade. The crowd of 500,000 that was drawn to the beach on Friday evening July 4, 1986 created an unsafe atmosphere that two hundred police and civilian badged employees couldn't control. Some fighting began as early as 3 PM in the beach parking lots, then escalated after the pier fireworks ended at 9:30 PM. Sgt. Barry Barcroft, the event watch commander, reported that most of the assaults seemed to be a result of gangs up to ten jumping, beating, and stabbing others. There were reports of several shootings, seven knifings, and a total of nearly two hundred fights. One victim was struck and killed by two motorcycles in a hit and run accident. The police, dealing with a whole army of attempted murders and assaults with deadly weapons, made fifty-nine arrests.

Santa Monica officials were aghast and vowed to stop holding their yearly fireworks extravaganza. Others felt that the firework's show shouldn't be directly blamed. It was obvious that any time you had that many people on the beach on a hot day, you were going to have trouble. The city eventually offered a compromise that would reduce the size of the crowds.

The gang problem near the pier remained a persistent problem, especially during the annual spring school vacation. While the college crowd preferred to go to Palm Springs, gang members from South-Central Los Angeles preferred to gather on the Santa Monica Pier during the day, and in the parking lot just north of the pier in the evening. Its exit immediately onto Pacific Coast Highway and the Santa Monica Freeway was convenient for quick getaways. Santa Monica responded in 1987 with beefed up police patrols at the pier and in the adjacent parking lots.

The Pier Corporation decided that the only way to repair the rotted supporting beams beneath the shooting gallery was to demolish the structure. On May 5, 1987 gave lessee John Brown sixty days notice to vacate and cancelled his month to month lease. Brown, who had been operating the shooting gallery for sixteen years and

A temporary 'trestle' pier was built by Kiewit-Pacific to aid in reconstruction of the Municipal fishing pier; 1989.

Bumper car ride; 1990

Train at the Fun Zone; 1990

Ferris wheel and other amusement rides in the temporary Fun Zone; 1990 (above)

who offered one hundred shots from an air-powered rifle for a dollar and a chance to win a stuffed animal, said that he was "itching for a court fight." He vowed that he would stay open for business and the city would have to file an unlawful detainer action to evict him.

Brown had his own civil engineer inspect the area under his building and he claimed it showed no major structural damage. He claimed the city wanted to evict him to bring in a more upscale business. The city on June 11, 1987 bypassed a jury trial by winning a court order against him in Santa Monica Municipal Court. Brown with no legal recourse, closed his shooting galley on Sunday June 21st.

The Pier Restoration Board met regularly throughout the spring and summer to study numerous proposals to renovate the pier. To meet their pier guidelines goal of reaching a financial break-even point, they considered recommending an additional 75,000 square feet of commercial space. Under one proposal 40% of the new space would be devoted to restaurants and fast food, 40% to amusement rides, and 20% for retail. The 250 parking spaces would be removed from the pier and a parking structure for 550 vehicles would be built on a lot across the Promenade from the pier. They felt that if the parking garage could be started during the winter of 1989-90 then the commercial structures could be built during the winter of 1990-91.

In June the City reached a tentative agreement with Questar Corporation of New Zealand to build a $15 million walk-through aquarium on the one acre old Deauville Club site immediately north of the pier. The 30,000 square foot facility would be modeled after Kelly Tarlton's Underwater Aquarium in Aukland, New Zealand. A dry 390 foot long looped tunnel made of transparent acrylic would allow visitors to view the sea creatures as if they were at the bottom of the ocean. The 1.5 million gallon tank would be filled with manta rays, eels, twelve foot long sharks, and other fish that live in the Santa Monica Bay. A moving walkway would transport visitors along the nine foot high tunnel, but there would be stationary platforms so that people could leave the walkway to observe or photograph the creatures.

Summer 1987 festivities began with a dawn Fourth of July fireworks show. Surprisingly over 50,000 spectators awoke several hours before dawn to attend the unusual event. The pier, beach, and Palisades Park were packed with spectators. The peaceful event grew in popularity over the years until more than 200,000 people would jammed Santa Monica to watch the fireworks each year.

The pier's third annual Thursday night Twilight Dance

A detailed view of the Santa Monica Pier's PTC #22 carousel; 1988.

series began on July 9th with a performance by the Rhythm Kings. Over 5000 people listened and danced to the music by the twelve piece 1920's jazz band.

Santa Monica finally solicited bids for the second phase of reconstruction of the pier in late July. Fourteen contractors were issued plans and specifications for rebuilding the western 45,000 square foot portion of the Newcomb Pier that was destroyed in the 1983 storms. Plans called for a concrete piles and framing, covered with a timber deck. The pier's added strength was capable of supporting a large amusement zone including a small steel roller coaster.

Three companies submitted bids on the project that was estimated to cost $2.9 million. When they were opened on September 2, 1987, Kiewit Pacific Company was the low bidder at $3,087,507. The John L. Meek Construction Company, that had worked on various pier projects for the city bid $3,996,415, and Mason Pacific bid $4,163,718. The City Council unanimously approved Kiewit Pacific's low bid at their September 8th Council meeting.

Financing for phase two was from a variety of sources. The Federal Emergency Management Agency, who agreed to pay for 75% of the cost of restoring the pier to its pre-storm condition but with no additional improvements or added strength, contributed $1,134,903. The Coastal Conservancy loaned the city $1 million, and the Santa Monica contributed the remaining $1,177,604. On August 21st State Lands Commission approved $3.8 million in tidelands trust money for all phases of the Santa Monica Pier's reconstruction.

Meanwhile design plans for the pier's new buildings and attractions, that had been approved during the summer by the Pier Restoration Corporation Board, were going through the arduous approval process by the City's Architectural Review and Landmark's committees, Planning Commission, and City Council. PRC's board, in making its design decisions, felt that the pier shouldn't lose its connection with its history or with the ocean, sky, and sand around it. They made sure that there would be plenty of views of the ocean from all points and that at every turn there would be architectural reminders of the grand old pier buildings of the past.

On November 1st Gail Markens gave notice that she would resign as PRC director and leave on January 1, 1988. She had become extremely frustrated and impatient with the slow progress in restoring the pier. There was much criticism focused on the Pier Restoration Corporation and much of it wasn't her fault. Its board was made up of diverse people of various political viewpoints

who combined with the city worked slowly to reach a consensus on various issues. Too much time and energy went into defining PRC's mission. Then they had trouble selling the pier to potential lessees who were concerned about dealing with both the PRC and the City Council.

City officials were also at fault. They were taking much longer than expected to develop plans to restore the pier and obtain funding. The funding shortage forced the project to be built in four separate stages. Further, a lack of funding and development plans hampered the PRC's ability to lure potential lessees. The pier lost $920,000 during the previous fiscal year if repair and reconstruction costs were taken into account.

Construction on the Newcomb Pier began in early November 1987. Kiewit Pacific fenced off the beach area immediately south of the pier between the surf and the bicycle path as a work and storage depot. The usual method of building a pier is to anchor a barge offshore to support the pile driver. However, surf conditions in Santa Monica Bay, especially during the winter were considered too hazardous for that method. Instead, Kiewit choose to work from a stable platform. Since Santa Monica's Pier couldn't support the weight of the pile driver or huge construction crane, they built a temporary metal framed trestle pier out from the beach directly beside it. The 100 ton crane, which rode on rails atop the pier, could easily transport the long heavy concrete piles and other construction materials to the work area.

On January 20, 1988 a brutal winter storm with ten foot high surf struck the Santa Monica Bay and damaged several piers to the south, notably the Redondo Pier. While there was little damage to Santa Monica's main pier, several buoys floated away and sand erosion caused damage to the foundation beneath the pier's staircase. Kiewit Pacific, however, suffered $16,000 damage when they lost building materials, fencing and auxiliary walkways.

The 138 foot wide by 357 foot long concrete pier section, which was designed by the firm Daniel, Mann, Johnson, and Mendenhall, used a cap and beam system to tie the 95 plumb piles and 76 batter piles together into a structural whole. The pier, which was only in six foot deep water at mean low tide, required twenty inch diameter piles 65-72 feet long. The longer batter piles, tilted at a 10 degree angle, provided additional support against potential winter storms.

Once the piles were driven, a series of twenty foot long, 16 x 24 inch transverse and longitudinal concrete beams were poured. These beams connected the piles' concrete caps and added rigidity to the structure. A

wooden deck and stringers covered the structure. The entire project was completed in August 1988.

City Council members, after carefully studying the Pier Restoration Board's $26.8 million dollar pier renovation plan, were about to approve it at their February 16, 1988 meeting. They had planned to vote on it in December, but the pier's merchants, who objected to the plans, persuaded them to postpone their decision. Finally, in February three key Council members stated that they would vote for the plan.

The pier's merchants, fearing that the new development's rents would price them off the pier, mounted an eleventh hour campaign against the amusement and commercial complex. They distributed fliers in Santa Monica and took out newspaper ads, charging that the plan would increase rents, create parking problems, and force out current merchants and their lower income patrons.

Despite the protests the City Council with one member absent, voted 6-0 for the renovation plan. The first phase of the project called for $13.6 million in private development funding for construction of a 40,000 square foot 'Central Plaza' commercial and restaurant complex, and to convert about 14,000 square foot of historic buildings into shops or restaurants. Construction was scheduled for 1990. In addition, a 46,500 square foot amusement zone would be built at the south-west corner of the pier in time for the 1989 summer season. The city agreed to spend $7 million to build a parking garage on the hillside adjacent to the pier, upgrade the pier's structural strength to support the new buildings, increase the sewer system, and install new lighting and railings on the pier.

Councilmen Herb Katz and David Finkel, in a gesture to the pier merchants, sought to give them preference in bidding for a future spot on the pier. However, they offered no guarantees.

The second phase of the project, which called for an additional 16,000 square feet of construction, would not be voted on until the first phase of construction was finished. Projected costs of the second phase were $6.2 million in city and private funds.

The third phase of the pier's reconstruction was approved by the City Council on April 5, 1988. They voted to spend between $3.5-$4.1 million to reconstruct the 420 foot fishing pier section of the Municipal Pier that had been destroyed in the 1983 storms. Up to $1.9 million would be funded by the Federal Emergency Agency, $500,000 from the state Wildlife Conservation Board and $1.9 million in city funds.

Several months later the Army Corps of Engineers

The Santa Monica Pier was completely reconstructed at a cost of nearly $10 million. It's dedication was on April 6, 1990.

Summer day at Santa Monica's beach near the pier.

Santa Monica Pier at dusk

reported to the Council that they couldn't start reconstruction of the breakwater until at least 1995 at the earliest. Although they were disappointed, they were pleased that the Corps had taken the first step with a $200,000 federally funded study. The study, which concluded in March 1989, was to determine if the two-thirds federally funded $4.2 million project would be worth protecting the pier businesses from storm damage. The Corp decided to continue its studies.

Santa Monica and the Pier Restoration Corporation's Board, after reviewing fifty applicants during a lengthy selection process, choose John Gilchrist to replace Gale Markens as director of the Pier Restoration Corporation. His salary was $75,000. The fifty-seven year old former Miami development official had worked on 'Interama' a permanent World's Fair that was planned for the 1976 bicentennial, but was never built. He was responsible for the $120 million 'Festive Marketplace', a successful development using both public and private funds, that was built on the waterfront in Miami. Gilchrist had previously lived in Los Angeles before moving to Miami in 1972. He had worked with the architectural firm, Victor Gruen Associates from 1955-1963, and was an Associate Professor of Architecture at USC from 1963-1971.

Developers began submitting proposals for the pier's new development beginning in June. Three developers submitted plans for the pier's 40,000 square foot 'Central Plaza' complex. One was Hal Griffith & Associates, another a team known as the Urban Centre Group and a third, KBL Associates, composed of Katell Properties, Babnew Corp, and Bob Little. One of four developers, Fun Photo, who submitted plans for the 4000 square feet of commercial space beneath the carousel wanted to install six "sensation chambers" that would recreate the sights and sounds of Santa Monica from prehistoric times to the turn of the century.

Other developers submitted plans for restoring the pier's historic buildings. Two developers proposed reviving Sinbad's as a restaurant and nightclub featuring live music. Surfside Theater proposed installing a "dynamic motion simulator" in the old Billiards Building. Patrons would watch action movies while strapped into chairs that would bob and tilt with the action. A firm called 'Pier Parlor' wanted to put a nightclub in the building.

By October 1988 the Pier Restoration Corporation Board had narrowed the choice down to three candidates to develop the pier. KBL Associates was picked to build the $12-14 million entertainment and shopping complex to be known as the 'Central Plaza'. Long Walk Ldt. was the board's choice to renovate Sinbad's into a nightclub restaurant. They also choose Surfside Theater, who planned to renovate the Billiards Building for $500,000 and spend another million dollars to install a dynamic motion simulator that would screen action films such as a ride on a roller coaster.

The PRC also reviewed three proposals for the amusement zone but frankly didn't like any of them. However, Fun Zone, Inc., a partnership between Irvine developer Donald Koll, Paul Hegness, and Syd Buck, and Ron Risch's New Pier Corporation already doing business on the pier, was amenable to changes that the PRC wanted in the plans. Besides, the firm had an impressive list of amusement park experts on their team and assured the PRC that they would be operating by late summer 1989. But shortly afterwards disagreements arose within the firm, the experts were replaced, and design shifted to a firm in Southern California. Naturally the company asked for an additional year.

Bids were opened for the third phase of the pier's reconstruction in October. Manson Pacific's bid of $9.1 million, Healy Tibbits bid of $8.2 million, and Kiewit Pacific's bid of $7.5 million were all beyond the city's budget by more than $2.7 million. The city rejected all three bids on October 25, 1988 and recommended that the contract be negotiated with the lowest bidder. Kiewit Pacific was persuaded to lower their bid to a more reasonable $6.7 million and the contract was signed.

Kiewit Pacific began construction of the Municipal Pier extension on January 4, 1989. Like their previous job, they began by constructing a temporary steel 'trestle' pier from the beach along the north side of the pier. First they built a welded steel platform eighty foot long, rising ten feet higher than the Municipal Pier. Using a small crane they hoisted tracks for the trestle, then began putting together an R-4000 travelling crane on top. The 150 ton crane with its 120 foot boom then hoisted a pile driver needed to build their 1100 foot long 'trestle' pier. When they were finished two smaller cranes, an R-3000 and an R-2000, were added to facilitate moving materials during construction.

The 128 plumb piles and 64 batter piles were precast in the Sacramento area. The twenty inch diameter piles had a hole down the center for jetting and were pre-stressed with six-one inch steel cables under tension and a wire cable that spiraled along the pile's length for added support. A dense concrete mix was used for minimal salt water penetration to protect the steel from eventual corrosion. The 110 foot long, 30 ton batter piles and the 90 foot long plumb piles were shipped, two at a time, to Santa Monica on flatbed trucks that required special per-

Municipal Fishing Pier; 1990

Fishermen on the lower deck of the Municipal Pier; 1990.

mits to travel during daylight hours only.

Piles were moved from the beach storage area to their final position via a supporting cradle that was used to lift and guide the pilings during jetting. Water was jetted down through the center of the plumb piles to drive sand out of the hole as the pile driver tapped them in deeper. It required five blows from a two ton drop hammer falling five feet to drive each pile one inch deeper.

Putting in batter piles required a different technique because pile driving a 110 foot long pile at a 10 degree angle would snap or crack it. Instead, as a first step, a 25 inch diameter hollow pipe of equal length was hammered into the sand. Then a smaller pipe was inserted to air-lift the sand out of the hollow pipe. When it was empty workers gently lowered the batter pile into it, attached a jet and gave it a few taps. The outer hollow pipe was then removed. This technique was repeated sixty-four times until the last pile was driven on December 1, 1989.

Plans called for a 42,500 square foot concrete waffle deck on the 434 foot long extension. A wooden framework known as 'stabath' was constructed atop the piles, and hollow boxes were added as voids to obtain the waffle pattern. Rebar connected to the piles was added for reinforcing. After the concrete was poured and left to cure, the 'stabath' and the boxes were removed. Twelve hundred cubic yards of concrete were used to construct the deck and another 1400 cubic yards of concrete were used to cast the 196 pier piles. A wooden plank deck was added to give it the look and feel of an antique pier.

The pier's thirteen foot wide fishing deck, set ten feet below the main deck on portions of the west and north end of the pier, was designed to break away from the main pier and sink to the bottom if destroyed during a huge storm. Two additional smaller fishing platforms were located further east towards shore. Access to the platforms which were fifteen feet above mean low tide was by either stairs or ramp.

Kiewit Pacific finished construction in adequate time for the pier's April 6, 1990 dedication ceremony. At precisely noon on a hazy Friday, workers opened the chain-link gates that lead to the city's new Municipal Pier extension. For most of the fishermen that fished that day, it had been a long wait since the 420 foot fishing end of the pier had toppled into the sea seven years earlier. Robert Khourney, an eighteen year old from Glendale, snagged a thirteen inch bass just ten minutes after the opening. The news spread rapidly among the anglers as photographers rushed to snap the young man's photo.

The dedication ceremony, held under a festive blue and white canopy at the end of the pier at 12:30 P.M.,

was attended by officials and more than two hundred enthusiastic residents. Mayor Dennis Zane said, "In Santa Monica, we like to say that the pier is the soul of Santa Monica and the further the pier stretches to the sea the more soul we have."

Judith Meister, the pier's manager and the official most involved with the pier's reconstruction stated, "I've been on the pier seven years and you really sense it has its own character, its own personality. It survives. It survived the elements, changes in the economy, and in people's tastes."

"They said it was worn out," declared a jubilant Councilwoman Christine Reed. "They said it was too old. They said it was a problem for the city. Well I was born in this city and I love the pier...The people of Santa Monica saved the pier. They saved it in 1973 and then ten years later, they saved it again when nature threatened to demolish it."

City officials then honored the woman who they felt was most instrumental in saving the pier. Joan Crowne, a former pier restaurant owner was presented with the first "Santa Monica Pier Prize" in commemoration of her "dedication and devotion" to the pier. She took out a second mortgage on her home to help finance the 1973 save-the-pier effort and was later forced to sell the house.

Pier attendance and pier revenue continued to increase throughout the spring and summer as more residents and visitors became aware of the rebuilt pier. Gross sales for the pier tenants increased 12.5% to $5,133,017 for the 1989-90 fiscal year that ended June 30, 1990.

The pier's revenue for the 1989-1990 fiscal year was $1,367,254. Amusements including Playland Arcade, a temporary Fun Zone, the bumper cars, and Fiesta's games contributed $368,113. Restaurants and food concessions yielded $291,605, sidewalk vendors $17,362, parking $410,457, and the carousel $199,174. Other revenue sources such as film company fees, interest, and miscellaneous earned $80.543.

Operation of the Santa Monica Pier requires a large staff to manage and operate the facilities. The Pier Restoration Corporation, which is responsible for developing the new facilities, operates as the pier's landlord for the tenants, and produces special events like the summer Twilight Dance series of concerts, has a budget of $497,924. Salaries for the Director, Assistant Director, PRC Pier Manager and one secretary are $274,000. Their budget for legal and design services costs $95,000. The cost of holding special events is $117,000 and the extra police foot patrols at night during the summer is $95,000.

The Pier Manager's office is responsible for the mainte-

nance of the pier and constructing city owned buildings. The office staff includes a part-time City Pier Manager and her secretary at a cost of $57,637. The pier's maintenance department consists of a supervisor, one carpenter, three full-time laborers. The budget for their department is $164,000. The pier also has three full-time custodians and six part-time custodians who work summers and holidays as needed. The custodial staff works on a twenty-four hour per day schedule at a budget of $120,000.

The City also owns and operates the carousel. They have a service agreement with a carousel operator. Debra Mandelkorn and her staff of ten, operate the carousel for the public during the day and host private parties during the evenings after the carousel is closed. Groups or individuals can rent the carousel for $100 per hour. The carousel's yearly budget is $197,554 and it earned $199,174 during the last fiscal year.

The Harbor Patrol, which actually operates under the auspices of the police department, has a sergeant and eleven officers. They have an office on the pier and operate a patrol boat called Rescue II. It is a 26 foot open deck boat with a 464 horsepower engine that propels the craft up to speeds of 30 knots. They also have a 15 foot skiff powered by an outboard motor that is stored on the pier. The Harbor Patrol's operating budget is $455,546.

The pier's budget also includes payment of $111,111 for a loan from the Coastal Conservancy to build the Carousel Park. The budget also includes $650,000 to construct a cluster of buildings at the end of the Municipal Pier that will house the Harbor Patrol offices, a restaurant, a bait and tackle store, and restrooms. Construction, which will begin in October 1990, will be completed by March 1991.

Two other pier projects have been authorized. The old Billiards Building next to the carousel will be renovated beginning Fall 1990 at a cost of $1.2 million. The Crown & Anchor restaurant, Seaview Seafood, and a third unknown tenant will be footing the bill. George Gordon is also rebuilding his Playland Arcade building. His new arcade on its present site will have slightly more space for games when it is built. Offices and repair facilities will be upstairs.

In September 1990 the City Council will fund an Environmental Impact Report for the future development of the pier. Construction will begin after Coastal Commission approval is obtained in 1991, hopefully in the fall so that the pier development will be completed for the summer 1992 season.

The key to the pier's future development plans is to provide adequate parking facilities with little parking on

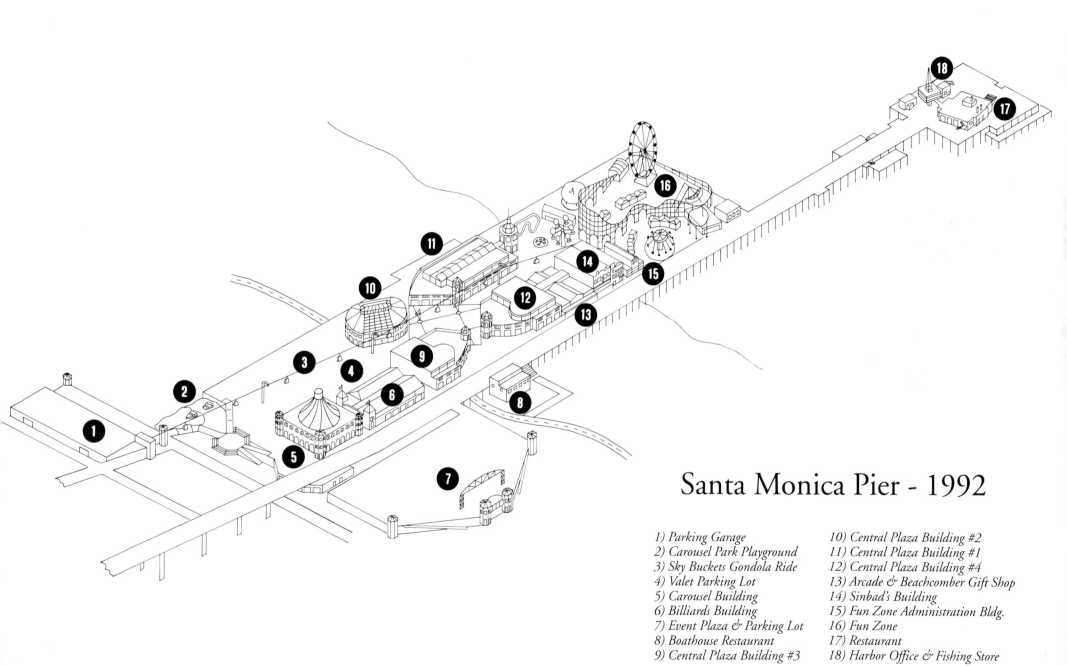

Santa Monica Pier - 1992

1) Parking Garage
2) Carousel Park Playground
3) Sky Buckets Gondola Ride
4) Valet Parking Lot
5) Carousel Building
6) Billiards Building
7) Event Plaza & Parking Lot
8) Boathouse Restaurant
9) Central Plaza Building #3

10) Central Plaza Building #2
11) Central Plaza Building #1
12) Central Plaza Building #4
13) Arcade & Beachcomber Gift Shop
14) Sinbad's Building
15) Fun Zone Administration Bldg.
16) Fun Zone
17) Restaurant
18) Harbor Office & Fishing Store

the pier. Originally a 660 car parking structure east of the Newcomb Pier was proposed. It would have displaced thirty apartment units that are currently on the site. Santa Monica's rather strict and inflexible Rent Control Board insisted that the units be replaced on site atop the parking garage despite the City's offer to rebuild them only blocks away on property they owned on the Ocean Front Promenade. The replacement housing on site raised the cost of the structure to $12.3 million.

The Pier Restoration Corporation in 1990 proposed a smaller parking garage that wouldn't displace the nearby apartments. Since this lowered the number of spaces in the parking garage to 244, they needed additional parking. They proposed double decking a small portion of the adjacent parking lot on the north side of the pier. This second story, reached from the pier's roadway, would have 152 parking spaces and would increase the beach lot's capacity to 974 spaces. With an additional 82 spaces of valet parking behind the carousel, the pier would have a total of 1452 parking spaces. The second story parking would be on an 'event deck' that would have a permanent stage on its north side. The cost of the parking garage on the hillside would be $3.2 million, and would increase to $4 million with the inclusion of the event deck.

The Central Plaza, which would be largely built on the pier's old parking area by KBL Associates, would consist of four buildings surrounding a diamond shaped plaza. The developer would spend $11 million for 53,300 square feet of commercial space. The two symmetrical structures with octagonal towers on the north side of the plaza would contain retail business' on the ground floor, and each a restaurant with an outdoor patio on the second floor. A third building of similar architectural style on the southwest corner of the plaza would feature a food pavilion with interior seating on the ground floor of a two story atrium. A terraced restaurant would be located on the second floor. An octagonal observation tower on the building's west end would overlook the amusement zone. The fourth building on the plaza's southeast side would be two story elliptical in shape and would house two restaurants.

Russ Barnard's Long Walk Ldt. has proposed to renovate and enlarge Sinbad's. His $3 million plans envisions a first-class restaurant similar to his Tavern on Main in Ocean Park. Since the building is structurally unsound and unsalvagable, it is likely that the building will be duplicated rather than renovated.

The pier's amusement area will be developed by the Fun Zone, Inc. partnership which includes Ronald Risch who operates the pier's games and bumper car ride. The design calls for a mix of adult rides, kiddie rides and a games area. The partners plan to invest a total of $6 million; $4.5 million for rides and $800,000 for games. Transport from the parking garage on the Promenade to the 'Fun Zone' will be by aerial 'Sky Buckets' but is not part of their operation.

The largest amusement ride will be a 65 feet tall steel and wooden roller coaster that will serpentine through the games area and make a tight 360 degree turn directly above the bumper car ride. Unfortunately the proposed $1.2 million ride has only one long drop and a second short drop after the 360 degree turn before it ends just thirty seconds after the top of the lift hill. Short sighted budget constraints has produced a coaster design that lacks any of the lower tiers of hills and dips that normally adds excitement and length to any coaster ride. It will likely prove to be an unpopular ride. Admittedly space is a constraint, but they could purchase any of a number of compact steel coasters like a Wildcat or Looping Star from European design firms Intamin or Schwarzkopf. The tallest and most visible ride will be a 110 foot tall Ferris wheel. Other adult rides will include a boat swing, a Caterpillar, bumper cars, and a Wave Swinger.

The proposed children's rides are in many cases smaller versions of their adult counterparts. There is a small Ferris wheel whose cars are hot-air balloon gondolas and a whirling swing. The area also includes a miniature railroad, a children's play area, and two platform rides; Red Baron and Turtle.

The games area, several fast food stands, and administration building will take up about one third of the Fun Zone's total area. Game booths form a central corridor in the center of the amusement zone and also form a semicircle around the perimeter of the Wave Swinger. The rationale is that skill games are not only popular but they are projected to bring in the most income to the 'Fun Zone'.

The big question is: will all of pier's proposed development be built? History has shown than when a developer who has lined up financing proceeds immediately, the project gets built. However, whenever there is a downturn in the economy, or a project is delayed through years of planning and permits, the initial developer drops out and a new developer begins with a completely different proposal. With the economy potentially heading into a recession during the Fall of 1990, and with banks tightening credit, it is possible that one or more of the projects could be postponed or redesigned by another developer. Nobody can predict the future.

Jeffrey Stanton, author of this book, sells his own photographic postcards on Ocean Front Walk near Windward on weekends. He is the author of Venice of America - Coney Island of the Pacific and eleven computer books including two textbooks on arcade game design. He has two engineering degrees from Rensselaer Polytechnic Institute.